Diary As Sin

Will Alexander

© Will Alexander 2011

First published in Great Britain in 2011 by Skylight Press,
210 Brooklyn Road, Cheltenham, Glos GL51 8EA

All rights reserved. Except for the quotation of short passages for the purposes of criticism and review, no part of this publication may be reproduced, stored in a retrieval system or transmitted, in any form or by any means, electronic, mechanical, photocopying, recording or otherwise, without the prior consent of the copyright holder and publisher.

Will Alexander has asserted his right to be identified as the author of this work.

Editing and transcription by Daniel Staniforth
Designed and typeset by Rebsie Fairholm
Cover artwork: *Emerging from the Mists of Treason* by Will Alexander

Printed and bound in Great Britain by Lightning Source, Milton Keynes

www.skylightpress.co.uk

ISBN 978-1-908011-13-8

… the dead woman who rebels against her death.
— *Suzanne Césaire*

… consumed by ecstatic mad inertia …
— *Joyce Mansour*

A Vitriolic Prognosis

The book which ignites before you is a galvanizing instigation. A sum which extends beyond itself and becomes invisible emanation. In the deepest sense one can say that it is tragically anonymous though an appellation has been secured as the sole generating agent responsible for its existence. As far as is known our protagonist, Rosanna, was never inscripted with an official surname. Although born and raised in the Galvez household she was never officially governed by its stamping.

We know of her mother Zomaya, according to confusing documentation. Zomaya Galvez was given three different datings for her birth. The first being December 29th, 1955, followed by November 14th, 1958, and finally, July 25th, 1962. Apparently three separate certificates were issued for her arising. There is a sustaining secrecy concerning the date of her appearance. Because none of these datings seems to have been secured until the middle part of the 1970s. What is surmised is that she was home delivered by an Apache midwife without note. We know she appeared in public with her parents, Edmundo and Catalina, sometime during the 1960s. There are no accurate accounts. As of yet no photographs have appeared, although we know that Edmundo and Catalina sporadically attended Mass, as well as some of the other Christian occasions, and enjoyed for a brief time a delimited local celebrity prior to, and during Zomaya's early years. I'm guessing the reason for such attention was that they always seemed to possess an unspoken means. Edmundo, although officially no more than a mining foreman, gained voracious financial security by covering up a series of mining catastrophes. According to him no human death appeared on his watch. Apparently he was rewarded by a copper company proto to Chino copper for his assiduous inversions of the facts. He kept all investigations occluded. But in addition to this financial intrigue, the secrets in what Rosanna calls the "hacienda" were of no mean significance. Three other births occurred during this period, and like Rosanna, were finalized in secrecy. Oraculos, Esteban, and Jesus were born on unknown dates, and like Rosanna were not officially recorded. Perhaps the dates wrought for Zomaya really stood for the births of her brothers, with the birth of Zomaya being a year or two prior to the 1955 assignation. As for the progenitors of the clan, Edmundo and Catalina, a fair guess of their births would tend to conclude upon the year 1929.

But all of the above are superfluous readings of a forgotten New Mexico and its ambit.

The main concern here is Rosanna, begotten by incest, born of Oraculos and Zomaya again, on an unspecified date. What's crucial to her character is her emotive eruption from the families' core of occulted dementia. Honed by callous privation, so much so that at an intolerable acme of her resistance to this privation, she is placed in a private Catholic home, St. Catherine's, located on the outskirts of Albuquerque. Sand blind since birth, we know that Rosanna threatened disclosure of the crimes inflicted upon her, unless she is provided with tapes onto which she can record the private vulcanisms of her angst. It amounted to internal blackmail. It worked.

We know the Sister Ornelas mentioned in the text preserved the tapes after Rosanna mysteriously collapsed from exhaustion one evening and disappeared from chronology. Prior to this we know that day after day Zomaya supplied Rosanna with tapes, and though blind, Rosanna was quite adept at placing them in a recorder. We know she lived alone in her room and spoke to herself night after night. It is unlike any diary I have ever come across. I think of Wölfli, or Artaud, or Tutuola, in terms of the energy expended. She uses English as if she were an inspired cadaver. As if she crossed back and forth between life and death. The pulsation of the text is unbelievable. She was an idiot savant erupting verbal fissures as if from another plane of existing. I can truly say that it is a consciousness that I've never had this close of contact with before. The way she says what she says is searing, multiple. It is like she's speaking from an emptiness escaping the gravity of compressed Suns. The history of the text is quite curious. Soon after Rosanna's collapse she is absented from our grasp. St. Catherine's closes, and re-opens years later as a hospice for travellers. A Mrs. Gonzales discovers four sealed boxes in a closet with each of them marked by the name Rosanna. When she opened them she found each tape numbered. Apparently Sister Ornelas would mark each tape by number, not by date.

Out of curiosity Mrs. Gonzales begins listening to a portion, and what she hears is so strange and fascinating that she contacts her friends, the poets Rusty and Esther Chavos, to see what sense they could make of them. They were overwhelmed with excitement, and attempted to transcribe them, but due to reasons of health let them lay dormant for years. Through mutual contacts, John Reeves, a Lecturer in English at the University of Texas at Austin, got wind of their existence. After an evening of listening to them at the behest of Rusty and Esther, he contacted me here in London, with what he called "his spectacular excavation." After several hours of listening I too was smitten. Her voice smoulders with an otherworldly rawness. Relentless, eruptive, unerring, she strikes dumb with her vitriolic prognosis. For her, humanity will either evolve or disappear. For her, there is no option. I immediately agreed to transcribe them. The tapes themselves were in remarkably good condition, nevertheless I had all of the contents transferred to disk. After thousands of hours of listening I feel I got as much of the essence as was possible. It is at once a naïve and sophisticated English full of spectacular repetitions. I found immediate comparison with Tutuola's Palm Wine Drinkard. Like Tutuola, the immediacy of her language scorches. There exists an unnerving dignity in her power of focus. She excoriates the Western identity of God, and his central representative on Earth, the Catholic Church. How she knows the things she knows is beyond my comprehension. I can only call her the uncanniest of savants. A lone figure in the firmament. Apparently she was never instructed in Spanish. Yet the flow of her language seems kindled by its rhythms in complete contra distinction to English as rooted in a Germanic base. In this tenor, I hear in Rosanna's voice elements akin to Paz's prose so electrically kindled in his Eagle or Sun, or perhaps the incessance one finds in Garcia Marquez, throughout his Autumn of the Patriarch. But ultimately, these are approximations. My sense is that authors such as Blanca Varela or Rosario Castellanos would be proud to writhe inside her symbols. In this book New Mexico springs unannounced from the invisible, sending us on a journey which the cosmologists provisionally term the "ad infinitum."

Oranzio Perez

A Poet in London
Early Spring

Diary As Sin

They tell me I'm Mexican and Seminole and carry the aura of a lean voluptuous beauty. That my face is tanned like fragments of rye, that my waist is a finely spun silver which vibrates. Of course, I have never seen my schema whole on, or witnessed my own profile, or visually tested my own emetics as shadow.

I am blind, my eyes tragically scorched in the womb. I was born as a vapour at the end of a frayed November Sun, untraceable, blown about like a seasonless dusk at rainfall. Of course, I've coagulated over time, by taking on the airs of the crucified, then giving vent to personified regality. Now, I'm merely considered as a strange fictitious humming, as an ancient tigress caught in shale. Perhaps I am a terminal bride from a negligible diaspora, culled from a wavering menagerie in nothingness.

They say that I hallucinate because I've announced the death of my living mother, although she trembles with every utterance of my name. Of course they never reveal to me the context of her whereabouts, or the present procedure of her wayward contrivance.

If I am contorted by the continuous onyx in my eyes one can never tell since my eyes don't blink, and I stare in space like a somnolent in-vector. Therefore I could never be accused of galactic infection, or causing by my motions stars to be sundered so that they rise and explode.

If I am complex, it is because I inhabit an eternal inferentiality, this being my own zone or plane where I attempt to unify the starkness which writhes in my mental gargantua. Because of this wrenching I've accrued a sense of my person so that I sense my enemies when they waver, when they collect themselves and combine themselves in the wake of duplicitous evils. They seek to ensnare me in their wiles as though they had ingested an array of suns fallen from a grave. And this is not based on a false mnemonic, or errata which has risen from my personal debasement. No. It is like an incisive lightning in the wisdom, an engenderment which comes from circling a heightened reptile's hissing. And this hissing is like the psyche of concussive toxins, or a primeval leather claimed from thwarted lynxes.

I am an individual whose movement is like the diabolics of wasps, abrogating, insisting, upon a wild inclement honing, yet with another range of apparitional neutering. In this sense I have surmounted the stasis and anti-stasis of physics, of the spark of its trans-location, even when the fire of evaporation transpires. I have fallen through a world transcribed as erasure, yet always forming in my voice the beauty of magnets which coalesce in screaming. These being the ruined integers, the broken entities in my speaking. And because my nerves burn and scatter so strongly, it is useless for me to depict my own jealousies as they seek to ascribe themselves to a baleful or in-luminous counting.

For me, life is a water of circuitous electrical trans-missives carrying in my wake an electrically studded bodice. Because of this I now understand bereftment and waste, knowing them to be the stunning nouns in wicked rural pictures. Given this realia I am inoculated against shivering reminiscence, against a worn genetics, against roving holocaust memorials.

With the aforesaid in mind you could say that I have sworn against my family, against its rotted murals, never once provoking sentiment as a private occultation. First of all, let me weigh my anger in terms of grammes, by existential leaning into torment, drinking down potions from chronic degeneration. Understanding that the blizzard of language is tourniquet, is force field, is armadillo warren, and is the signalling of molecules through a curious storm of diacritics. Because, what remains for me is the miraculous embodiment of bitterness, of in-fabulatory osmosis, filtering through my body as vacuum, like an immaculate serpent's light possessing the dementia of remorseless debacle.

This is my enigma, born under the sign of an implicate algetics, yet my body giving off the vapour of succulence and rainfall. I make no pathway to any outer specification, instinctively knowing that I cease to lend my kinetics to the explicit, to the momentary. It is because I have transmuted the sepulchre of panic, the frozen modicum as denial. I only want to express those blank and indivisible tourmaline enrichments, those fingers choosing the most creative and poisoned symmetries which decline and overtly minimize as quanta. As I masquerade by anaemia, yet refusing to take into account my graft by incelibate soaking, or the deprivation condensed in my pestilential wizardry.

Because of this I've been accused of psychically sprinkling cinders, maiming the very attributes of wheat. Ah, they say, she casts her burning spores upon the waters by making nature vibrate as though expressing an interior ulceration. It's like making an occult vibration in space creating powers imbued with electrical inharmony. This becomes for me a wiry millenarian weaving full of corruptible psychic debris. Having taken from my world a hysterical potion of stamens, then adding a glossary of tainted mineral oils, giving me the power to ransack an old Dutch crucifix with serpents. And I think of these serpents as being at the cusp of present possibility flying and reacting like mosses under a prior, yet convivial atomization, a 100 million years ago.

Therefore, any truth that I seem to capture can only be tested as a force across a stunning parallel dimension racked by duality as voltage. Thus, I admit to focused thirst, to Sunlight formed by gregarious erasure. Again, I am like a Sun powerfully quartered in mazes, speaking of a light weakened by bickering. And by bickering I mean the tropo-pause of bickering, strangely structured by a seeming anti-harassment. Thus I admit my rambling affliction born as Zomaya's deadly and infactorable secretive beast. Of course I am not speaking to myself as a scattered memorial, but attempting to square the dice in my forehead with dialectical gestures inside the circumstance of fire.

Every day the nuns seem to whisper that I am buffeted by scorn, governed less and less by the voice that rises from rational accommodation. To them, my voice explodes like short-circuited pyres. Perhaps this is the result of my struggle for existence, for my existing as a less monitored substance. And what I mean by less monitored is the inscrutable in life, those rays which escape the contagion of a death induced consensus. The nuns say that I am travelling along spoors which hallucinate, which describe themselves as biological remnants, as atomic cryptography. They whisper that I have surpassed restrained ideals, that my behaviour has been distorted by declivitous sensitivity. Yet I exist to myself as that hierarchical witness like a bird soaring off from anonymous blue shale. For instance, I call myself the blinded bird who maintains herself by the ingestion of photons. Or perhaps I am the kindling of flawed emotional emergence, my weight not unlike a mimed or feigned oracular furnace. Or perhaps, like an echo in plaintive crystal spinning in the stupor of old heraldic waters. Because I speak from this osmotic principia of sound I know by my hormonal whispers that the life I've known has been surrounded by feckless cretins, who raped me, who then proceeded to parade me around the chambers of their damaged villa. My mother, Zomaya, being the empress of damaged gardens, having me, then passing me off to the jackals, Oraculos, Esteban, and Jesus, my father, my uncles, who used me over time in their stunted outreach for the erotic. To them, I was an ashen tower, a bleeding wintering grub, who has remained for years self-scornful and disabled, writhing in the wake of villainous scorching amidst in-transcendent neurons deployed by self-critique.

This is the acid from which I've evolved, attempting through my voice to rectify disability. I being blizzard as model, as curiously rising anti-persona; as failed and unenviable harvest from Chaldea. Thus, I am a radical absence, exercising worlds far beyond the grasp of the human spectrum. For instance, the soured iguana that I am, as the holding stable that engulfs me, knowing in my blood the challenge by embodied enigmas. Not the cells amassed by observable decimation, but a chronicle of seeds rooted in a cloudless ochre prairie. Then sensing from these seeds a strange blaze of camels roving deracinated high ground, my challenged perception running as a link through curious barriers spurred by in-doctrinal persistence. Because my voice has never been tied to a plotted chemical foundation. It is no longer prescription for condensed glass, or splintered bread, or what the sighted would concur as a sea inflected wine. Therefore, my voice perceives that Suns meander, that poles split apart, that snows re-configure by splendiferous abandonment. Because of this I am not of the race of entropy, not of the race who dwells beneath the form of copious chastisement. This is what Zomaya senses, this being the spark of her interminable stealth. She understands that I am not of one persona, not of one mystery, but arrayed with intransigent neurons and timings. I remain offspring as quanta, daughter as calumny or adder. And because I persist according to genetic malfunction I have evolved no tolerance for acquittal. This is what Zomaya configures breath by breath, thought by thought, step by step. I persist in her thinking, always forming in her mind as welter that's evolved from three different Suns. Of course this remains most prominent in her nightly waking disorder. Her confusion forming from my articulate declaration, ringing in her sleep as a ringing clavicle ministry. Perhaps an assiduous but crippled dazzling, yet this is what the momentum of honour serves to enhance. Keeping my soils enriched by dislocated spasms in the Sun. Because with these spasms a portion of life ceases to conspire against me. I possess in my calling something outside the contortion of the era. It's as if I were brought to the equator in the year 4297 facing massive doses of rays, testing the limits of my form by means of ultraviolet transmogrification. An energy outside the human backdrop possessed by unknowable integers and spells. This being my present evolutionary cipher, this power to ingest and re-form rays. This is what Zomaya senses in my blindness. She seems to think that I'm carving a symposium as a core, holding a conference inside my own wisdom, bringing to her doorstep cacophony after cacophony as un-cleansed indictment. And she is right to riot inside her skin. To wander around her lakes of rancid ore, telling herself that the incest occurred as a random act of slippage. That Oraculos goaded her in her sleep, that each subsequent encounter took place in the midst of the hypnopompic, that she was the victim in this circumstantial blemish. But how explain the use of my body by Esteban and Jesus for a period which lasted over 27 months. This is why she remains riveted by my surviving. Therefore, the scope of her outlook, acidic, schizophrenic with constraint. Of course she fears the nomadic ether in my speaking. Yet she does not know how my whispers coalesce, how my disadvantaged scruples convene to open her by means of my stark interior emotion.

Because I respirate as the invisible I am no longer buried or siphoned off by depression, no longer a conch to be gutted according to the behavioural opiates of hypocrites. And I am speaking of Zomaya, and Oraculos, and Esteban, and Jesus, assiduous practitioners of the Catholic rituals, with their rapt and unalterable defence concerning its "hierarchic structure of bishops and priests" ... concerning the American dioceses with the constant allegations of rape and mishandling. And this is not a didactic or moribund persuasion seeking to cajole an unforeseen enmity from any future recipient of my voice. I consider myself an invader, someone who has evolved from insoluble hypothesis. I who have advanced through scars and serious danger, fallibly emerging from a thankless gravitas writhing in my system. Because my eyes were occluded at birth I've been given a curious alien sensibility. My remaining senses have developed a blank electrical toleration, a riverine and motionless interior verticality in which broad summations of vacuums singe my corpse with dangerous intuitions. At one moment singing as a debased cadaver, at another, conjoining the thread of a transmuted pessimist. Therefore, I go back to my claim that Zomaya enacts her designs through stunning irregularity and evil. For instance, she has never claimed the higher concepts of birds, always clinging to the raptors and owls. Never the warmth from a hidden jonquil furnace, but always the bizarre, always the spirit approaching disequilibria. Nothing outside of debacle, the zodiac for her, splintered grafts of disabled Sunlight. For her, a mapping of treasonous sutures. Again, Zomaya, composing her foundation upon calliope and plague. It is known at one time in her thinking she captured documents like food, she embraced the zone of the saints as if the fervour of their bleeding had collectively renewed her. She smelted language into deconstructive torrents, as if she could somehow construct a clarity from a sabotaged sub-species. Thus, she could recite from a multiple deafness. Say, one could create an eerie ventriloquy of the sonic motion from Saturn, this was Zomaya, reasoning that this power was the result from a punished yet consuming saviour, always confined to the epic of revenge. In this sense she was both Catholic and Heteroousian, knowing that "God the Father" and "God the Son" were separate and iconic, not unlike insatiable raptors. This was Zomaya's explanation for death, for torture and ill grounding which decides the common fate. This was and remains her definitive code knowing in her essence every lugubrious infidelity. Remember, I have always heard her speak. I have taken shards from her vocables and re-spoken them with a trans-migrational force that listeners can now feel. So every time that my voice has recorded her demons it has osmotically filtered their remnants so that their palpable flames re-extend back into sound. Now this sound enacts itself with a rage totally unlike the mendicant's honour. I do not beg, nor do I hope for future advancement in the heavenly realms. All I can say is that I've been sacredly stricken by an inevitable verbal invisibility, stumbling across the intuitive abductions of an occult conjuration. In fact,

I have grown thin by my efforts, revealing and de-revealing the strength that I've garnered and its natural tendency to vanish and go latent. You must understand that my intuitive genes have always sought to destroy me, to place me inside a warped incisor's nest so as to alter my ability to ingest the three revolts of consciousness. I'm thinking of the Indian scale of the mind which acknowledges the sattvic, the rajasic, and the tamasic; more simply put, the uranian, the quotidian, and the hellish. In spite of all the deflections I've encountered I've been able to float as avian quanta up and the down this psychic verticality so as to respirate at the level of transmuted inflammatory riddles, becoming in the process magically clairaudient and hidden by osmosis. Because of the latter I can now cast spells from an emptied flask of monomial brewing which has taken on the task of evincing superior purpose. What I can proclaim without flinching is my ability to dispel clannish pre-emption, no longer consumed by parochial discomfort, but feeling the human as concerned by its larger solar disposition. No, I do not splay stunned seeds into psychic soils of fictitious erosion as if my heart rate were measured by blindness. No, I have evolved through fructification having escaped the demons and their outmoded self-tangling.

First, I project a holograph through the infinity of Mayan numeric cartography, testing its momentum by means of cosmic patois, knowing in this leap that I have freed myself from Zomaya and her circle of suggestion. Secondly, I've conjured elliptical cures which burn in my thoughts by mean of repetitive injunction. And as a third remove I've entered a crystalline respiration which has casted itself beyond the wattage which infers the conflict embedded in human disjunction. Saying this, I can magically dispel Zomaya, which de-activates any leaning towards human blood rats and their desires. If anything I can count as heir Martinez Pasqualis, the alchemist capable of re-igniting selected microbes in schist. A capability I've been breathing which has the power to inveigle rays, by bringing forth a semantics which singes the skin with sudden auditory gold. I, the latter day conjuress emitting from my voice the blank equation of gain. Not gain in terms of a core or pontifical riot, but as sound inside the sea spinning as a powerful sodium tornado. And it is this tornado which enlivens me, which builds itself spell by trans-rational spell so that it now speaks to you as this riveting transitional diamond. And this diamond mixed with ink and uranian proto-botany, always keeps Zomaya unbalanced by means of its absorptive re-creation of adders and whims. Of course she does not know the specifics of what I say, held as she is by the hostage of my living presence. Because I advance such voraciousness of mind nothing in her calling can ever subsume me. I've arisen in her mind as a threatening germinal queen who parallels as a deity commanding flanks of bad weather.

Diary As Sin

This weather, involving atmospheric melancholia, *gives* me strength to *hiss*, to weave as form the realia of direness, thereby proclaiming my body as sand which spews through the flask of shifting electron currents. I suspect Zomaya considers my speaking as a surreptitious pageant, as a flayed and re-assembled verbalis. Yet at the same time I understand through the trellis of voice, the taste or thrill of smoked peaches or avocado. A savour reaching beyond mechanical definition, over and beyond a powerful weakness as authority.

One must understand, that at precise moments there is ritual incandescence which combines in its power a soaring multitude of anger, which is brandished and absorbed as if listening down a well to susurrating Nightjars. This culmination that I've reached is like a signal which burns me by invasion, which crowns me with debility making me moan in my sleep. Therefore, Zomaya has instructed the nuns to leave me alone in my moaning, assuring them that I would ascend from sleep armed with demonic panic. She tells them that I am constructing a perfectly formed heavenly enclosure, and that my struggle bears the mark of one whose praxis wrestles with demons. Zomaya has power to convince with a passion which seems momentarily disembodied, so that it tends to take on the tone of a *spirit* absorbed in tintinnabulation. Knowing her powers from my core I feel assured in knowing that I have risen above her plane of Euclidean medusae, that I have risen above her lower class of ravens so that my nightly chattering is never felt as a civic theurgist even as she harangues them concerning the dominant flowering of my goodness. I've heard her tell them "she is simply overcoming her blindness."

Because I can hear fields, within fields, within fields, I can plot the uncanny even as it seems to take advantage of my blindness. I listen to the thinking which surrounds me. It is no different than listening to the genes which travel inside a spore. Which brings me to the crucial understanding which underlies the paradigm of creation; the complication in the respiration of motion. When I say this I am not provoking some messageless roundelay, thus studding myself with a powerless grandiosity. No, this concerns the intrados of auricular intuition. Understand, that only the uranian can imply this, only the uranian can imply the workings of animation at the core of what I'll call explorational maturation. This is what I consider to be a hurtling linguistics, at cometary height over-spilling with auras. Words rise up by means of their own electrical ilk and they give me the sense of climates in distal advance of the human moraine. Of course I'm amaurotic, full of harried self-perfecting, moment by moment my being slowly evolving above the barrier of instants. This is the difference with Zomaya; she who clings to the perfection and the bartering of corpses. In this, I have no regard for her she being no more to me than an assiduous civic nuisance. She who seeks to hide me in this hovel, she who seeks to leave intact a perfect family chronicle.

Believe me, the weapons of my person have been tested. My womb, desecrated and resurrected from obliqueness. And because of this resurrection Zomaya always considers the infinity about me, never fully knowing my range, or the true power of my assessment. She knows there is harm in my advances, but she is always looking to the obvious, thinking that I will catalogue the rapes and confide in Sister Ornelas. Her only concern is the protection she's accrued from sustaining the secrecy of my existence. Knowing that what I'll say to any person or agency will condemn her in total to public excoriation. And believe me, Zomaya is more concerned with public excoriation than with imprisonment. Thus she sees in me webs and rotations of webs, whose ethos exists like a judgmental spider gone awry. To her I must remain this threatening helical monster who scratches nouns across mirrors. Of course she seeks to contain the slightest evocation of my presence. As for Oraculos, and Esteban, and Jesus, they are only important as regards her uncovering. If I accuse the brutish attempts of Jesus, it is the vampire's needle to her heart. But without the threat that she sees through them, she would no more take account of them than she would of spoiled loaves of bread. They are expendable, yet she keeps them hidden as if exposing them would blemish her neurotic sense of composure. Her vector to God, tubercular with damage. Yet this damage functions for her as a heavenly sense of focus, as an incalescent shaping tool. A fractional level of her psyche curiously senses that I know this, but as for her conscious awareness there exists no rational consensus concerning her thoughts and my recognition of these thoughts. This is why I've bonded with my own observations, testing them according to articulate discomfort, according to my ravenous co-existence with destiny.

Certainly war has been waged against me, but I, the sovereign dice player always carries in her seeming culpability sigils beatific with distraction. And this is not tautology, or a wayward or disposable botany posing as insight. Having come to such a level of toleration, I am able to raise moons from my lectern posting signals from dazzling aural sensibility. Certainly not an escalated error, or a trap conducted as a seduction of false signs. What I can say is that there are different motions that tend to form against God, different and substantial epics which send out their unlettered remnants as oppositional distrust. Perhaps, I am a portion of those remnants which has accrued from a generally invasive suffering. For me, I can only relate to cataclysmic soaring, to suggestive ethers which celebrate themselves as flameless ethers in the brain; finally coming to the point that it is only the bones which stagger with ideas. And these bones again I'll call Oraculos, Esteban, and the thrice-maligned Jesus. The latter who suffers as the protagonist of God who rapes, and then waits in line for erotic scraps from Zomaya. All this being compounded in his case when he listens to insults which demean him for his darkness.

Of course the trapped conclusively stammer, and so the family stammers, collectively haunted by I, Rosanna, I, who no longer bemoan my suffering according to conventional conquest or law. I am the curious shadow who multiplies in their hamlet. Because of this inner whirlwinds occur. Because of this curious calliope it creates a nettling sensitivity which forces them to listen to saffron break while turning around in discomforting psychic puddles. Therefore, they thirst according to unquenchable rebus. To me, they're more like demons who've acquired a taste for their own uncertainty. Like molecular compost in schism they exist in themselves as fumes from libellous Pentecost. And since I see them through my listening they are no more than egregious adventurers talking to themselves as egested owls. They then condone themselves by a power of faceless strategies, always attempting to claim my realia according to facts of subversive scrutiny.

As beasts they threaten to consume me, but on the other hand it is Zomaya who micro-tunes their impulse, so that her role exists as an intellectual agitprop who only reacts to the pressure of her own unhappiness, which day to day deprecates in her mind like a psychic form of gall. She will mimic Savonarola in her outcome, not so much tortured alive at the stake, but as a living oracle of the reversed, breathing her own depths inside an unimpeded chaos. Somewhere in her cells she will know that her language is done, that her former imposition has intrinsically contracted.

There exists no level of reasoning in my assessment, no scholarly criteria of my in-person genes. And I do not ascribe to implanted Kirlian photo-genetics seeking to erase my voice *according* to the fact of untraceable conditions. As if I had been summoned by laborious gargantua *in-condoning* my own capacity, my zodiac thus limited to a mourned and nullified ascendant. As if I were the cause of my own harriedness, minus the unfavourable criteria known as Zomaya and her Myrmidons. I have been captured by spiders in their invisible net of molecules never to perceive the higher root ingested with phonemes. For instance, letters with the sound of spackling oars, rowing inside the proclivity of magic. This is something Zomaya had never wished upon me, knowing that my lack of language would completely validate my lack of existence. In-articulation as blindness, as captive in her wooden stationary coffin. This is what Zomaya desired as my outcome, an uncomplicated beast lost prematurely to the void. This being the perfect criterion for my exile, someone who once existed without the living rights of a person. But through language I've ingested the great heretical fleece, I've ridden the continuity of chariots through unknown grammatical hills, crowned by particular blessedness that my blindness has brought to advanced refinement. Thus I do not condone the empirical as parable, girding my argument according to the stories garnered from accessible Judeas. As for me, I walk beyond the known on a gemstone scaffold, without the point-by-point chronicles, without idea by leprous idea, shifted into world according to the fact of superficial declaration.

I cannot declare my existence according to the rules conducted by jealous antecedents. What they have sought to do is to insult my realia, pulling me into contact with a stark accusatory pumice, so that I'd negate myself, and deny myself of orational mutagenics. That I'd deny myself of the afterlife no longer attempting to live from the flow from inscrutable cisterns. So that I'd never know history, the 10,000 years blazing in my system with its invigorated rubric, its spellbinding poise, never sullied by religious deception. In this sense I am Oriental, which by extension is Egyptian. According to the Western schisms I am mirage, I am the concubine bewitched by leper's concussives.

At the beginning of life I was not unlike Isis healing by respiration a dismembered Sun. In my instincts I threw from the most sumptuous balconies those most flawed, those most satanic in their tenets. I've known this from birth, and I continue to exist from such aforesaid interior, so that in the halls of my first possessive mind I grow from invisible willows as Queen of the falsely repelled, as seminal onyx witness, allaying fears by the compassion which dwells inside wrath. I've gained such dark clairaudience by means of the negative cataclysmics initially wrought by Oraculos and Zomaya. And I, their offspring smelling of deleterious pattern, have never reversed my arc, moving as I do as a climate, insuperable with hail.

Perhaps this is the result of a uranian pre-genetics, a Sun from symbolic ovens, brought to *despair*, then resurrected by volcano. You ask, how can I clarify such acid, such lightning transfigured by intensified singularity. Perhaps I am miming an occulted blood fragment, an anomalistic hydrogen, blurring the zones on a treated clinical table, my phantoms then explained by explosive retro-causality, by a-synchronic motion, by tales.

Say, a group of Suns collided, and from this niche of blank advancement a line of waves transpires, energetic, phantasmal, which causes self-conflagrated fragments, knowing each bird that flies to be hollow, knowing every word that's uttered as useless leper's omniscience. The latter, synonymous with my concussive biography, my family chronicle alive as these ill begotten Suns, like the Demi-urge lost and transgressive with stupor. An atmosphere where I was forced to eat snails for Zomaya's entertainment. Then the random insults directed at this aforementioned imbibing. I could ignite at this point a whole catalogue of maiming, but a realia which continues to gall was when Oraculos snatched me one day and spoke of his desire to create a living lair from my faeces. As he spoke to me this way, he also spoke of the beautiful rye of my skin, of the palpable milk in my breasts, then without warning pulled my womb to his mouth and in his sickened way attempted my impregnation by the force of his saliva. A detail, yes, but one that has marked me, and sent schisms down my spine, and forced panic to run about me.

I've been insidiously prone to suffering because they say that I am Catholic, that the saviour suffered, with me, Rosanna following in his wake. I am not culpable in this regard, I am simply chronicling this close-knit pyre of sociopath's misnomers. I've been the emaciated ghost inside a terrified vignette. Poised in this colourless ascension I've fought these mixed battles in order to survive, so I can speak at present with this eclectic, punctual mis-lettering. I've had no sister named Cordelia, to take me in her arms and comfort the child in me with Elysiums, with the mitigation of suffering by caresses. After the first assaults by Oraculos, I somehow knew I'd been siphoned from the zodiac, that I'd caused the angels to explode and descend into the nether fathoms, because they no longer gave me the powers of the transmundane, with its tuned electron sheaths, with its holographic crystals. As for implication by nunnery I could never take the vows of one who renounces her powers of body to the insomnia of heaven. I remain erotic, turpentine, explosive. And the latter are not denials, exhibitions, trapezoidal tasks, subservient to a society which inscribes its marks through hypocrisy and withdrawal.

So to plagiarize my own temperature, to embrace a cold and advancing ransom, would be the most debilitating, the most infectious attack on my body of nerves as it seeks to enunciate inside you. I, of the weightless ozone signals, of the graph dissolved by blank neutrino bells, am now awaiting in trance for delirious transference to other motions of dust, brewing unseen shapes by means of eclectic vertical seismologies. Because for years I've monitored the bleak implosive world of genetic martyrdom and flux imagining myself to study certain extremities comprised of cold and heat. Perhaps, I remain a sickened skua a fallen into depth, magnetized by wrath.

During recent times I've ascribed myself to the powers of dead authors. To Lorca, to Juan Larrea, to Cesar Vallejo. I've imagined that I've telepathically embraced them as allies in war in defence of an intuitive source of language. Language which roams inside a futuristic Sun where one can open one's ducts to heights, to roads which roam through poetic vertigo mountains, where one can pulsate, where one can give voice through creative grammatical hounding, in forfeit, in muzzles, in strange infinities, as tigers. This remains the thought inside my leakage, as I sit here, spinning in the sum of my sullen anti-persona, not from a terrible gift, but from the centre of linguistic monsoons. This remains my pineal, my blackened cerebellum, much the way that I sleep in the depths seemingly lifted by massive amounts of rainfall.

For instance, washing the brain of its brine, so that there transpires the feeling of cleansing, the empathy for riddles. This being the mind in the sense of old Egyptian reclamation, having arrived in Macedonio's Lion Country where none of the demons transpire, where seizures are negated. Not the realia of imposed choice, or the insufficiency of reason, but a populace of voids where rays are felt, where photons transgress. This is the mind which takes its clarity from powder, from a ruse of natural in-audia. I understand from imaginary Braille incantatory camels, these being all the edicts of horses and blood. The chronicles have shattered, and I've felt the blaze pouring from optimum obscurity. I'm convinced that this is the way that candles burn, empowered by the feeding of dust. Again, this is how the moon trespasses, bleeding like a lamp in virgin haciendas. This explores my teeming verbal craft, my sudden cellular actions, expressive of the mode of anticonfinement. Such is the mission of shattering, of breaking assignments and barriers. Light, for me, being the sound of Albanian castles at moonrise. For me, such hearing observes and breaks the fount of cruelty, breaks the absurd and mediaeval assignations designed to pointlessly modify the psychic decor of fear. The silence, the abrogation of bait, which negates the rhymeless seasoning of terror. The imagination provides at its minimum the breakage of flaws, the negation of rational simian grammatics. Of course this induces concussive personal strain, a poisonous non-recognition. Conversely this provokes a strange flotational ascent, a molecule of vapours wafting one upward into the mind of the phantasmic. Zomaya and her ilk having reached no higher than the status of lizards, they exist through the parables of darkened physical greed. This being, the essence of regressive minds, always subject to immolation and retreat. In Zomaya's case she prides herself on hoarding spoils from inconclusive mystical exposure. On the other hand, arriving at voiceless sums as if listening to glacial tremors, I understand the slightest nuance, brief inter-active interlopings, like nutational magnetics, so every whisper that Zomaya conducts I have already ingested and understood. As for Oraculos and both his graceless myrmidons, Esteban and Jesus, they simply whisper as derivatives, much like the sound from poorly extracted tin.

Because of the above I am a traveller of furious roads. A tornado of carrion, full of dangerous verbatim and ether. Of course, this is the emphasis extended from outer conditions as devastating principates, as deranged memorial concerns. This being the dicta of hypnotic scarring, of pointless particles in the mind. The latter remains a curious portrait of Zomaya speaking in defence of an antidimension, of clauses historically beckoning placing a devastating emphasis on objects. This is what she'll call her spiritual stewardship. A misleading rapport between human life and the land. How much fauna can be claimed?, under what specifics can expensive flora be possessed? These are what I'll call Zomaya's emphatics, her stealth, her admixture of in-sonorous conjunction. As sand blind I understand that her facial design is mixed with Andalusian Berber. That she walks by collapse. That her nerves are consumed by negative instigation. Her howls are quite the opposite of the momentum which instructs the Pleiades. Thus, she only points to elective absence, by immigration to the core as reversal.

She has placed herself as the Christian queen defending Olmec subjugation. She derides all knowledge of the Maya, the resurrections in Kemet being unthinkable. She pleads absence, she pleads the essence of germinal decay. Because of this I understand new focus through struggle, prompting renewal by the tempest of persecution. Knowing this, the Maya have become my aeronautical elders, with the burning codes of rotational hieroglyphics. Not simply a material jurisdiction, but infinity. Voluminous stampede which spins by basic number. As Rosanna I've arisen from limits, no longer the ingénue entrapped as rotational concubine. As of now, I persist by sporadic linkage. The latter for me being the freedom of indifference, attacking Zomaya, taking on Oraculos, pointing out the traits of Esteban and Jesus. I have lived through the pious rituals and know that they are despair. That they convulse and leave one panting, crawling to confession like a motionless arc as repetition. I've known the thoughts which cohere in decimated groves as if I could feel their anti-reflection as a saddened kind of unison. At this level of tension I was prey, I was subject to diabolical code, to feeling the trespasser's sting. Zomaya knows this and continues to know this. This is not a false assessment, or a stony or negligible source attempting to interpret the leanings of her mind. I understand her reptilian scrutiny, her issues with Gnostic symbols. She became a calculating conduit, attempting to disguise herself by verbally pointing to angles of strife. She sought to multiply tense warnings, she sought imperilled soil describing its meters of turbulence. She convinced Oraculos and the myrmidons that she was the heavenly refugee, returning to give them succour with her body. She would then enclose herself in nostalgia and warn them of the error of their hallucinated circumstance, then one could hear them scurrying like the homeless towards her scorching zone of favour. To this degree, I was listless and parallel, like an alphabet of meteors, fallen amidst an aggressive sea of badgers. After having me one hour Esteban suddenly blurted my name as Blind

Cortaenia Simplex and the others just laughed as if the nonsense replicated their poison. Because my eyes were erased at birth I became to them as a unifying sparrow, suffering from aurific weakness. Yet I was the body with the skin of smoked honey. I was the fugitive doll in embryo, the unbrightened bell, tolling in a plaza of proto-assault and fear. Again, they laughed, they wanted my feelings withered. In my estranged perception I felt the lightning of eternity, the muscular ache of a prone crepuscular body. It was my deranged, my hypnotic advantage. And I say advantage because I discovered the power of confoundment. I somehow understood the carnivorous roundelays of debasement. I seemed enriched by debility, wakened to angles of tragedy. It was like feeling the fire from lightning in straw. I became embodied voltage, as if I were a tiger floating in blinded indigo warrens. Mind you, I was not a balanced or decisive embryo open to rigorous social adjustment. But I understood the law as susurration by impending catastrophe. I knew results, I knew my bloodless extremities.

Not a staged, but a seminal complexity. Say one wakes up on the other side of dreaming finding oneself in an eerie parenthetical cathartic, with one's name depicted on an ashen marquee. I would suspect a global monster alive behind burning glass, I would suspect his faults leering from the roofs of trespasser's schisms. There would arise a brutish melancholia, a psychic mis-transplanting, feeling myself as some elliptical shrew, walking and speaking through declamatory stammer.

I maintain, there exists a conspiracy to throwaway bodies. And by throwing away bodies I mean the expression of subconscious negativity, where the destruction of bodies means the destruction of exception. And I know that I exist as this exception, as this erogenous integer, whose claws are inclined at times, towards a state of malicious drifting. And as result of this drifting I've come to know that my cortex has escaped an unreasonable imprisoning. I was constrained to accept the shattering diagnosis that my pre-birth had configured. Of having Zomaya drown my proto-body with a wilfully ingested rum. Thus I was born subsequent to my own ghost, of course she hated me from the start as I existed as a nauseous extract. She saw me as an unacceptable carking, as a nuisance derived from the central spectre of guilt. As if I had meddled in my own affairs discussing beneath my breath a rapacious eagle's zoology. I, being the architect as plaintiff, my body then reacting as disgusting axial chastisement. And as I was allowed to jive I could do nothing more than to isolate my wisdom, to listen by concentration, learning from my struggles to separate rain from the sea. Thus a cataclysmic want, a confinement in vicissitude.

At a certain point I would mentally remove myself even as Zomaya and Oraculos would argue over who was next in fondling me. I somehow knew of the largest asteroid Ceres, and at greatest humiliation I would absent myself and feel in my marrow explosions on Ceres. Not bombs of course, but quaking from natural events. The thought of something alien caused me freedom, caused me to sit up in myself and cherish the rewards I had gotten from blackened minimal spelling. Of course, this was a fragment I had garnered from Braille. One of many fragments. Because I am only capable of fragments, only capable of acquitting my curiosity by knowing the part as the whole. I know of Saturn and its ring system, I know of Mars with its hurricanes of darkness, with Jupiter and the outer giants as occupants of neural vacuums. These are the fangs I've trained by eerie compulsion. And they infect my prayers, they shatter and transmute rote. Therefore they challenge my lack of worth, my dysfunctional foundation, giving me a level which absconds my constant debasement. So for me, the uterine realm became a breathing of multiples, an invidious vacuum, a rainless irradiation.

Aren't microbes damaged? Isn't the Sun in its tribulation ensnared by expulsions and erasures?

Aren't the above not unlike my monthly cycle of blood, my monthly ratios and enigmas?

During these times I would speak in the language of fearful calliope concerning vertigo and pestilence, concerning my claustrophobic insecurity. I wandered, yet I was internally freed. Furtive hookworms would smoulder. I was tossed about by pestilence.

Here I was, mangled in early womanhood, caught between the family, and at a higher remove confined by the bickering particles of God. I was always numbed as if forced to imbibe a turgid cobra's fuel. Not only was I slandered by my journey, but condoned as a circumscribed mirage, as an intermittent angst. When I appeared at Mass I was always the visiting niece without context. Questions were never advanced. And when I got older I osmotically disappeared to the countryside. Zomaya maintained my appearance and disappearance without flaw. She simply nurtured me with irregular periodics. I was always a figment. A sporadic ambush doll scantly noticed by the assemblage of the faithful. The believers at the cathedral were without the power of a deepened critical weight. Appearances were always given without the smallest point of questioning. Thus I created no pattern, no sustained amount of interest, I remained the pious little believer.

As I physically developed I remained the captive of the brothers on Sunday. Oraculos would drink wine and then have me. Then Esteban would linger and relieve himself in me, then Jesus would assume the scraps and finish with his brutish laughter. When Zomaya would return to the dwelling she would ask the brothers to describe me, and then she would relentlessly sigh, giving the signal that all was in order. It was nothing less than the torture of draconian day war; of modelled infernality, Again, I was the scar that was always milked. Daily, explosive testaments would collapse and then just as quickly reappear. I was surrounded by treaties in constant annulment. There was always psychic fading, along with a tacit sense of fissure. Ensconced with beings who seemingly had no birthright, who were lost in the sound of their own onslaught. Zomaya was the leader as a curiously stained harlot.

I always felt subject to enigma or tirade, to in-solution by congestion. Maliciously consigned to the whims of a brutish cannibal's roundelay I always felt my body showered with sulphuric sugar. I was possessed of old derivative odours. Simple cleansing could not solve this. I was stained by my forced involvement. The circumstance had claimed me. I had devolved beyond the point of confession. It was the lower realms of Dante.

A prophet would have perused my condition as living at the juncture of devils. Of staring without succour into my endless and momentary personage as blankness. Shorn of the motive for law I was a transfixed and broken concision. A maniacal document, a blazeless adder always threatened with drowning. Can I place my morals within cohabitation as impulse? Or do I decide against my name bearing as it does immaculate elements which sicken?

I admit, I've been debased, I've been sullied by friction and danger. This is why my present verve must overcome the feral losses which I've suffered. Even now, my blood counts are jagged, my marrow remains transcended. Which exacerbates, which splinters. This is why I speak in tense amnesial rivulets, in desecrated circles. Yet the loss I've borne destroys and re-invigorates, and becomes a source of mathematical liquescence. The churches with their vocal manikins and believers, manifest sightlessness in their ability to crawl, in their ability to place at common disposal only the thought of thwarted ideals.

Why do I exist as this available beacon, as this primeval particular? Is it because I have grown on myself, and taken as sudden neurosis my ability to expand myself unit by dialectical unit? Is it because I spell my name in Persian? Is it because I have broached my need for the inversional food of vipers? I can only say that I am dust, that my need for remedial paradigms and barriers has quite monstrously ended.

Is it because I have deflected the seeds from an auroral Pentecost that I am able to defray my life of previous consequence?

Is it because I have challenged old bloodstains that I have sculpted my unbroken fortitude?

I can answer the above in the affirmative. In the quiet of night I verbally evince miraculous gales, which blow me in my blindness across imaginal horizons. Listening to the liberty in my dreams while feeling shale ignite. I listen to the way branches take on remnants, to the way my mentality transposes stars. These are traces which Zomaya can't follow. Of course I am driving her to distraction. She has lost track of my mind. Until I emerged at this level I was no more to her than the damaged looking glass girl, I who existed without crystallized identity, I, who carried no identity in the shrines. I, who existed without institutional priority. I, the hidden viper's cub. I, the un-resolvable possession. Now that I am gregarious with intent she flails, she gathers droplets from the nuns concerning any leanings that I enunciate one way or the other. She remains weakened by her own connivance. She wanders in her untenable pagoda. She is no less vicious, no less in-desirous, but the scale of her crime has been negated. She no longer has me. She's forced to satisfy the appetites of the wolves. And because she has to satisfy the appetites of the wolves she has embraced a sudden vulnerability. Esteban and Jesus are always dripping. She now depends on Oraculos to help in her present discourse. I sense all this because when she comes to visit her voice seems frayed. She seems caught in chasing her own manipulations. I remain the illusive prey of her delirious hunt. By day, I am remain the aphonic figurine, the taciturn periphery, the blinded gull in the window. Perhaps I am the pre-figuration of decay which quietly unnerves her. She is not the same.

Am I prone to gloating, to sketching the terrified steps to my enthronement?

What is my power as regards the macro geology of the ozone?

How will my circumstance gather in the voice after 3000 years? Concerning the first question I must honestly pause. I cannot say that I am indifferent, dispassionate, feeling quivers of delight when Zomaya suffers. As she suffers I know the animals will suffer with her. All three of them fear her. She feeds them; and since she feeds them she can play with types of arsenic. Because they are useless she could protract their deaths over time. Of course this remains one type of scenario, one type of combination.

As regards the second question I do not see my conscious form as a prevailing nutation, but according to my invisible motif I feel the zodiac shifting much the way migration feels when travelling by the stars. By overcoming Zomaya I feel poisons have reversed, certain gravities have let go. As for posterity I condone no personal feeling, only to say that perhaps I will exist as a long buried truth come to life.

In the present age one is taught to project one's prayers to an outer void, into an ellipsoidal premise, which recants, which damages, which wipes out human advantage. For me, it incorporates an inner death. The arousal it purports seems unequal to the tension that it carries. One then reaches the brink of distorted mutation. One then condones as scripture selected parables of carrion. This I call life by utter harassment, by codes of vernacular weeping. Because of blindness, because of the breakage and rising of my mind, I've been occulted, I've been socially shunned and eviscerated. These are my steps. The feeling of being a tapir, a victim in the revolving diabolics of execution.

Call me a dour Cambodian princess, call me an adder, swearing on a book of reference; I continue to tarry after nightfall, whispering by assault, clause after clause, rising from burdensome waters.

Perhaps I honour myself by belligerence, by foreswearing my compulsion by indigence, as if, in a former life, I swam through years of hounding, banishing my effects to roiling Siamese waters. And these are not abstract waters, but a precipice, a crack in the ray of the systems.

Therefore, conceptual posturing never travels within. I, who mask myself during diurnal acceleration, can never debase myself according to arrogance, but accept my poltergeist as an intuitive double, who confers by inflection, by stakes which configure according to solemn methodology. Such solemn methodology is warning against its own parallel methodology. So I never cherish or punish according to indefinite resolve. Take what I say as a thirst, as a premier dislodging, according to the sigil which protects the mind in its quest for singular integration.

I have broken the spell of corruption. I have torn through wasted facts. I infer by imaginal discipline. If I spell out the fact of Venusian plateaus, if I wander around the zone of the Earth as atomic fault line, I can conjure all the miracles of demons, of huertas transmixed with huertas. There seems no seminal connection, no measured bonfire road. There remains for me, the obscure challenge of suggestion, the feeling that transpires in disconnected parallels. This is why Zomaya remains suspended, attempting to isolate all suggestion, to decomplexify my unseen rhythm turning it to dross. It is chilling to her that I am no longer trough for her vile behaviour. The truth being that because of my age my presence became too threatening. I was no longer the pliant hijuela, the little daughter addicted to the tensions of spasmodic rape. In recent times, I would attack their approaching shadows with cups of scalding water. Jesus was burned near the groin, Oraculos contended that his hands were injured, yet I continued to suffer attacks. After a period of violent dismay Zomaya announced the removal of my presence. She once told Oraculos, "… she'll uncover us one day and somehow have us slaughtered." "She'll have me" she continued, "eat the linen from my loins." Oraculos responded by attempting to beat Jesus with an ironing cord. He responded with a knife, there was blood. So more and more Zomaya would satisfy the three of them, all in irregular order, with Oraculos consuming the density of the pleasure. Of course the depravity deepened. In the house there lingered the smell of unwashed utensils, of spilled urine in the corners. According to Zomaya the blinds were never raised. A listless panic prevailed. On the final morning before my absence a drunken Esteban prevailed upon me attempting to lick me in my sleep. Then Jesus began grunting and I also felt his darkened form upon me. The noise was not unlike a sickening jactitation. Zomaya panicked with enragement, awoke and pulled my body from them and threatened them with a vial of acid. Oraculos throughout the attack remained in alcoholic coma. It was then that Zomaya decided to absent me, to dispense me to the nun's yard. Here I am possessed by the secrecy of belligerence, by the base priority of an onerous badger. Of course I breathe by incalculable seething. What sustains me is my gift of punishing clarity. I feel. I am freed by repossessive excitement. So, Mother Mary and Ignatius of Antioch have left themselves in ghoulish dispossession being no more than spectres at the vociferous graves of lions. For me, they are king and queen of Sunken ersatz heavens.

Mother Mary: womb of he who never existed.

Ignatius of Antioch: creator of poisoned appellations.

Me, I'm blasphemous, much in league with the rice fish who perpetually caters to twilight, to swamps which glisten in black twilight. A wild and articulate twilight brought to refulgence by conformity to despair. This is how my optics transpires reduced to trance-like shapes, sensing pitch, coal, sable, and crow. The four figures in my life purposely Stygian in demeanour. Of course these are Zomaya and the human animals she directs. And extreme as my life has been I am not judging. I am simply recounting my awkward experience with evil. Thus, I have gained belief in traumatic suspicion. I am not asking of life for patterns to follow, for guttural hypnotics to lead me to a utopian port of the feelings. This is not the quest of my urges, not the summa which invigours my element. Some will say that I remain malnourished, that I've retained my previous nullifications in order to court a gregarious sympathy. Which means that I have engineered my fate according to a-priori design. I can emphatically say, there has never existed any untoward calibration, or any mystical act according to Divine entrapment. I have never created such sanction against myself. As for mystery, as for proof by intangible boiling none has occurred. The priest in his electrically rotted cassock has no power over fumes which consume me, who eat me by the anthems which sound inside their ethers. Having lived at the source such primal dementia I have sculpted a *tolerance* copious with commanding indifference. Not that I have relinquished my resentment, my wrath, my asperity, my gall. For me, there exists a weight of different angers, a whole zodiac of angers. There exists the chronic palpability of Zomaya. Then on certain nights I'll dream of Jesus, or listen in my heart to Oraculos ambling towards me. But what created Oraculos, what made the circumstance of Esteban so erroneous? Were Catalina and Edmundo so annihilated when they spawned them? Were they practicing the arts of hell when Zomaya appeared in the womb? Were they divining a form of hatred when Jesus appeared as genetically Seminole? Rationally I can reach to these parents of Zomaya, to their base concerns as effort. They, who lived from criminally inherited fortune for their comfort always conducted a barbarous sin in private, much like the Empress Faustina conceiving Commodus while wet with freshly spilled gladiator's blood. Edmundo with the plutonic ureathea. and Catalina, with reception of that ureathea. This remains the illness in my bloodline. This is why Esteban always lingers in a sonically felled bottle, always reaching for a ghost, always tangled in private emptiness.

Zomaya belittles transaction. She keeps the family funds in hidden portfolios. Because she is so effective in this regard none of the brothers has ever left the home. Of course they are stunted. When Catalina and Edmundo departed Zomaya was left in charge of the capital and so she provided the adolescents with copious shelter and raiment, with unmitigated indulgence. Then she began giving her body to them; they have never left the dwelling.

Since all births took place in the home, official records are missing. So it's as if none of us are living. Since Zomaya is the oldest she has claimed a basic documentation of when and where she was born. I surmise that she is no more than 39, but I only surmise this given the nubile tenor of her voice. She remains hidden, unsuspected. The family name, crystal. Albuquerque remains such a private base, that her unholy arts can only deepen and deepen. But I've destroyed her private base, I've stripped her blouses, I've thrown ointment on her fire. Young Rosanna, who she taught a type of Braille who continues to upend her process because she knows not what I say. Yet she knows. I could announce to Sister Ornelas that I've been raped, that I'm an inconvenient pawn, that Oraculos attempted me at 9. She knows that I know. So she gives me these tapes into which I now speak. This is why I unnerve her with my presence. I remain the uncalled for.

Every day I hear her hungering after the nuns looking for things that I have said in my sleep. When she comes to me she examines me, she carefully jabs me with her voice as to the structure of my feelings, as to my current mental impressions, always looking for a ray upon which she can begin to gravitate. But I remain evasive, neutral. It remains a strenuous repartee by which no one advances. It is like chess when a pawn has threatened a queen, no one can move. So at night I advance these verbal nutations as one who elaborates from the void of a second body.

Zomaya remains constrained by buying boxes of tapes. I start the recorder at the midpoint of night and whisper, and celebrate my whispering everyday before the dawn befalls me. I have Sister Ornelas label them by dating. For instance, it may say on the tape, 1-1-95, or 2-2-96. She remains precise in this regard. The instruction I've given is to never let Zomaya touch them, because it is Zomaya's private gift to my person.

Of course Ornelas suspects the awkwardness of my presence. But the monies that Zomaya has bestowed on the home have mitigated any crimes she may have ignited. I remain the cloistered enigma, the youngish virgin in transition. I stay alone with myself, with only Zomaya committed to my presence by dint of her totalitarian concern. As if I were an oracle to be monitored, to be checked according to the facts of her daily utterance.

I feel every night that I intone above the voice of God. That I reach a level of suspension where only the Sun can expire and re-live. It is a charisma not enmeshed in conquering, in crowning my contextual superiority, but of newly living in myself, with electric bolts of wisdom coursing through my system. This is my freestanding premise which Zomaya must deny. For her own sense of safety she continues to construct her own inner facades, allowing my presentation as the helpless niece with the phantom background. The home has been paid to conceal me so I remain this nubile phantom who conceals her momentum by the hushed explosion in her voice.

At the earliest stages of consciousness I was partially convinced that the Holy Ghost had nurtured my blinding, that God had moved his hand so that arc of my seeing was constrained to no more than densely riddled shapes. I was flawed, a sunken nautical figment whose initial growth amounted to no more than an unmourned memorabilia. One who was cursed by umbilical fermentation. I feel like hellish moaning by inference. Smouldering in her birthright, in her formless mystification. Thus I am the ambush bird amidst a tracery of blood plants. I have been forced to barter my essence for time, brooding upon my body as a strange conducting sheaf. As a phantom in my weirdly lit cortical hovel, hearing the eras of history as they flow back to the Sun. Perhaps a folkloric dread, or a criminal analogy pointing to the present time as a tamed and woven ochre rust. And for me this rust has remained at the root of the Mass. To celebrate a bleeding saviour, to take into account his biography of absence. It is a stoning of impulse, the body then condemned as a sign of guilt. I knew this as a girl. I felt the trap of its cosmos, its working on behalf of an orchestrated strangeness where I could do nothing more than rise through the status of the nunnery. Of course, these zones have persisted as givens, as influential vacuums, as purgatorial narcotics. Yet for me, belief is nothing more than a circumstantial weakness. It causes glare and internal abatement from the genres of life. A wasp in its essence, freed, its activity of research unscathed. Not that I am reaching for lowered insight, or flight through carnivorous meadows. No. For me I feel the seismic road, the longing for sporadic dimensions. These are waters within a brewing moon, suggestive, erasing pronouncements from Jericho and its concomitant autocracy.

Every night, this spate of alchemical nerve linguistics, against monarchical intent, against the grinding propaganda advanced by millenarian centipede. Me, an ambush bird in a formless mongoose cradle. A distorted leaf frightening in proportion, hearing ink inside my fingers, not unlike the fire that's felt in a blazing marsupial wand.

Me, under a pressured double fate, between blindness and revolt against the cosmos as given. The rancid micro-forces, the empire poised at carnivorous stasis. For the sighted it is not unlike a tragic glossary of murals in which the body appends an appointed kind of action, always imperilled by the diabology of dying. Thus, a hounded being in divisive equilibria. I know that I enact a brief hurtling through distance, through the confusions periodic with fetid joy and debasement. Because of this I feel numbers in my eyes, like the number 2, or the number 6, terse with secretive imbalance.

Again, I ask, by what deficit do I roam, by what statistical mean do I covet as implosion? To be freed from such deficit there must exist a stunning proto-assault, which remains in a state of enriched invisible potentia. In explosive predilection, in inferential volcano. All the hatred I've accrued, all the disciplines I've soldered and buried, so as to sustain my rhythm, my in-cauterized solemnity, which opens the feeling to multiple infinites. I can say this because I am hypnotized by spells, by inclement vectors, which inculcates my substance with the power of miraculous figments. Thus, I am capable at certain angles of tapping the hearing of the zodiac, of hearing it move to another species beyond any of its previous preponderance. It is like invading a treatise on theories so as to deepen and decipher levels of knowledge at the peak of what I'll call the knowledge of knowledge.

One entrances depths like Buddhist oracles at Lhasa. One advances molten codes with uneven strength. From the heat of pre-existence, I've haunted the Asuras, with their traps, their advances. I know the way that they cook the Sun and leave it cold with impersonated fracture, with pre-arisen statics, so that its light is staggered and voided in fragments. Because of this the era now stands as a fictitious cove, like trying to transfix a theorem in the darkness of Vesta. A theorem, aimless with magnification, jotting anti-relativity as conifer, as the sound of a pointless pelican in ash. Thus, flight in non-reverberant arrow, in subordinate bickering by isolation. It creates a tempo, disparate, neutered by escalation. What remains is the Roman disposable body, with its truncated windings, with its corruptible solstice through frontal personality as cult. Therefore, the being, turned against itself as derivative injustice. Parts of the soul then forced into negative compunction, so that they compete and simulate themselves as separate priority. For instance, the blood at war with the breathing thereby creating a chronic pellagra, with its nervous symptoms, with its violence. Thus, the totality is left seething from a bitter unregenerate conception. And any living that is less than suffering is considered by such conception as villainous trespassing.

Life is conceived as precluded assumption, with status maintained as consensus by scar. The result: Zomaya; the household. There is practice of caste registration. I know by inference that Zomaya is light complicted, aquiline; and Oraculos not unlike Zomaya in this regard. As regards Esteban, I am told, he is like a darker Arab from Mexico. As for Jesus, they speak to him as if he were refuse, as if he exuded unpardonable plutonics. His colouring completely unlike the heritage of the family. He was always raised with suspicion. Catalina despised him. I'm told she regarded him 'as my unbearable Seminole.' When she died the reality altered and intensified. "Clean my womb with your tongue," Zomaya would utter. "Erase saliva wherever you find it." Oraculos was particularly proud of her latter utterance. For him it contained malicious creativity. Then at times Esteban would beat him. If it pleased Zomaya Esteban would have her privately. The atmosphere was always fulminate, violent.

As for punishment, would the 4 of them be tried on kidnapping, or would they double their guilt by adding the chronic pestilence of rape? Would the sentencing mean death, life or 7 lifetimes in confinement? I know no law, no repartee between criminal and witness. As regards the English-speaking world I possess not the slightest specific. All that I know is that Zomaya shivers with fear when she sees me. I always feel it in her voice. Probing, always probing, sifting for any evidence that the nuns were tacitly privy to. After a few words with me, she always spends her remaining time with the nuns, searching for any leaning in the wrong direction. This keeps her stressfully balanced. This keeps her mind poring over strenuous waste. As a result, she slips Sister Ornelas extra sums to privately superintend me. Of course, she has never trusted Ornelas, always making sure that these tapes are stored in an iron container which she checks on a daily basis. But she has no proof that Ornelas does not listen, that we have not formed a bond of blackmail over and above the original blackmail that I've verbally in-scripted. Zomaya possesses no key to the strong box of the tapes. For the first time she hovers without power, she can no longer in-script her ruling. I now exist as the begetter of ruin. As someone who has survived and come to unlikely benefit. True, I've swallowed flesh, I've poured wine into my system, yet I've never been resigned to powerless in-solution. Even in the most perilous of moments I could somehow feel the flowing of persistence. When approaching the nadir of degradation I would always experience a sudden spinning in the Sun when there was seemingly nothing to acknowledge but pain. The old crude logistics I could only relate to the futile simile of Chronos or Saturn. The latter for me means the heritage of the Mass, with its peculiar melancholia, with its theatrics of discomfort, so that Roman deliberation takes on the syntax of disastrous hibernation paradoxically pointed to the rationally in-somnific. In contradistinction I am mirage reversing what I know of the solemn Corinthian visage becoming exo-neural, "neither included in nor dependent upon the nervous system." Not even the "jugulum of a bird", or the energy of the stones reeks of a judgemental stasis. I am somewhere outside the latter assessment, like an Andean iconography which expresses shadows which burn. This is a state incapable of purchasing lambs for slaughter, incapable of mimicking ravens with their excited cries when approaching a carcass. I've become osmotic, my respiration spins inside proportionate conundrum. Thus, I am simultaneously symbiotic absorbing surrounding voids breathing the carbon which engulfs cataclysmic mystery. The emphasis no longer on confinement, no longer keyed on the dissonant swaggering of Gods: So how can I be swayed by the calculable powers of the Demiurge, drinking powerful cups of mead, combining in his trumpet the sound which equals dictatorial dispensation.

Being blind, I continuously absorb the fractions of infinity which pour into sleep. This is my daily filtering. Taking on the deepening of listening in translucence, then entering an upward draft as an anti-neurological oasis. This is beyond the gross seduction of bodies, but with a charisma for the primal, for the mixture of lightning and carbon, knowing that I've parted a river of mirrors, that I've gotten to a realm where beasts cease to govern, where there ceases to exist the cathartic of the soul with its three cadaverous levels encoded with suppositional angst. For me, frustration is now blown about and buried, is now sundered and turned into grainless animals' fire. Its substance of significance has been transmuted beyond its inconclusive torrents, which, now irrigate, which now ceases the condition of ungainly resistance.

Resistance being the sentiment which precludes the pristine, the dazzling aural paradisics, where desiccations cease by entering utopian topology. This being to exist by precipitous mirage, awakening to blazing farming bells. Then studying sound according to poetic polar inscription thereby understanding a microbial dialogue with absence. I call this the dense progenitor of health, Akashic with the clarities of transmuted herons.

Nevertheless, I've constructed psychic battle tiaras, so that no one can haunt me, so that no one can claim the source of my trans-liminal neutrality. Thus, my range of probing condor metrics, always flying to my first instinctive homing instinct, into my first protracted dissonance of light. One can call my existence a blending by grafting, by spinning vacuums inside a high green solitude of darkness. So when I say green it is by the interior grace of sound, by quickened flow, by leper's mercury. This is post release beyond a claiming family trauma spun as it is poisoned by elixir and ferment. This is where the Catholics claim that the angels sing, in a parallel exotica. Thus, the anti-magnetic, the weightless banter plagued by a weightless liminal God who ignites through spurious gift human opposition and confusion. And the fumes from this confusion upwardly drift and infuse uranian palsy. So that the angels stammer in tongues that resemble poisoned psycho-geographies. What then descends as sound is a furtive insomnia, a groping for an instant in liberty, which hypothetically transcends adenoidal trans-fixture. Saying this, I am neither focused on nostalgia or extinction. I know that I have risen beyond solar chimeras, beyond skeletal idolatry. Because of this I am without the mundane which contaminates facets. As for me, I listen to the sound in skittish tourmaline omens, in tenacious baronial devastation. My mind, then struck by neural fricatives invigoured by ballistical sucrose. Zomaya resents my isolation, the new found wariness I now possess. Of course she suspects myself and Sister Ornelas in concert. She suspects that she is held as a double hostage by what I've told the Sister of my past, as well as by the history that my body has now stored. Add to this her own imaginings and the variations on these imaginings and you start to hear a nascent form of brittleness in her voice. There increases at each visit an uncertain parallax where I feel a stumbling within her own compounding. She is no longer mixed by impunity. Her adders have crested, she carries in her wake the aroma of fallen hill tops. Every time she sees me she feels the leakage of power. She feels an uncertain mercury. The fire has fallen from her tyrannical embellishment so that she is now conscious of the circuitous; conscious of the fact that sequential combination no longer has answers to bear. Day by day she is more and more the discomforted witness, more and more she feels in me the spectacular of the post-cadaverous. An energy not unlike the eerie as resurrection. I am trans-missive with staining, with an occulted synergy as if sprung from a soil tenuous with orchids. A demonical seamstress sowing my own momentum. My inclement posture, my pulsing viper's shawl, my rudimentary ordeals. This has created in me fundamental insight, a penetrant kinesis.

The question can be asked, why didn't Zomaya kill me? Why was my life not staunched in the womb? Why was I allowed to develop into a body? I know that she had to nurse me, to impart to me her milk. Perhaps the home was less devolved. She being the ingénue buffeted by fear and joy, had not reached the fetid source of debacle. The confusion of the circumstance must have harnessed her. Things were tantamount to order. Catalina and Edmundo, having recently passed, money accrued in the coffers. Oraculos had no rival for Zomaya. Esteban and Jesus were regressively nascent. Entanglement had not spun.

As I developed she paraded me in her mind as maid, as concubine, as use. As someone pragmatic, as underling justified by blemish. This is what she sought in me, a fragment to be culled from the formless. Now that I know this I know that suffering was entwined by her power. And now she is engulfed by her own delirious foundation. She advances in sickness, in cosmic deprivation, because she does not know the true north, the north not found in terms of measurable projection. Allopathic in her views, she can never test the rising fevers of the inward pole. She who walks in allegorical ambit, can never ascend above the accrual of trauma.

Me, I've come to know the Sun as primal spiritual elixir, as a draft of higher heavenly darkness. I feel its form in these dimensions, with its spectral kinetic igniting my limbs with wave after wave of furtive invisible salt. I have transcended the mocking parameters, condoned by old mercator's static. Thus I've reached a compound dialysis which replicates as a senseless palpable empiric. An empiric re-enforced by circular histrionics. Thus, I fail and reinvent a new genetic palpability, with its convivial want, with its hidden empowering disguises. Of course I am as remote as someone who enunciates the Yukon, of someone so removed not even nuance can scan her. Perhaps I am a sea with exploded fishes, with waves of poisoned molecules and hydras, breaking at a shore of pure rupestral damage. So as a person born without optical acuity I hear this rupestral damage, this thankless insistence, which enunciates its core through philosophical obsession. For the sighted, it would be like prayers sent up in crystal, or mirages invoked, or having lightning turned around into labour. So here I could invoke a proglomania of lists, a redundant feast of spectrums, squandered in the fragments of a furtive nightmare stitching. It's like psychically walking through explosive trapping mazes only to emerge without knowing of any visible existence. Because I hear through the power of error I become threatening, I become the angel who speaks on behalf of the libellous. But all I've done is spontaneously quote on behalf of interior telepathy, pledging my spores, my seething seminal crowning, attempting to quench my seasoned thirst with a draft of vertiginous lavender fumes. Of course, not a grating fiasco of morals, but a fluvial kindling, intuitively dispersed like a dreaming mental lava. This is the first feeling of hydrogen, the first incessant fleece woven by imploded lettering inside sand. Thus I am able to speak at a level well beyond the primeval, beyond the hatcheries with their birth spots, so that ferment looms inside my burning activity of justice. As to my frustrated gall there always looms mental seismic invention. Thus I reap little by little a zone which is rife with miraculous distension.

I have released a former world, a world no longer of climates, and dawns, and the realia of lands as we know them. This is the world which makes Zomaya shiver. To know that I have risen from her colony of fate must increase her trepidation. I, the passionatory oracle, I, the moneron who lives beyond consecutive salivations. I, prepared by the powers of calliope, speaks from one soul, from one blindness. A body given passage to the stars, to a level beyond ravaged utopias. She sees me, semi-iridescent with fatigue, yet always emitting in-felicitous spoilage. It is a weather where neutrons are riven with inconclusive equation. A carking liminal isle, a suspended electrical implodent. Not a hoped for reward, but a spasm. Stealth, neutered exhaustive invention, feigned rapiers, ironic claustrophobias channelled through a trinity of bison. A parody of great laws, of dialectical pallors, of tense trapeziums alive in the central liquids of the spine. This is the infinity of blizzards, of broken water arrows, of thirsting heavenly acids. Saying the above I appear to Zomaya as a being who subsists by neurological plague, as a mind tormented by disgraceful ingestion. And you ask how can someone the ilk of Zomaya complain about disgrace? How can she act as a functioning critic?

She has no grounds for complaint. She who has soaked her acts in the realms of rapacious lower waters. She, whose body emits a tangible disgruntlement. Being sand blind I carefully understand her offensive displeasure, of she who now to a great degree rejects her intangible self-poisoning. She cannot exhume the dissension that was Catalina and Edmundo. She cannot blame them for extending their diabolical leanings into the roots of her causes. She cannot say that she remains a trapped genetic drone. When she became the sole inheritor of the copper fortune she could have left portions with the siblings and let them fend for themselves. Instead she actively cohabited, she produced me, Rosanna, the plague, who remains a nettling inside her context. Catalina never acknowledged her own sons. All of home birth, all invisible by means of nonexistent documentation.

One could say that she was young, that Catalina and Edmundo passed prematurely. *One* could say that. That essential being was distorted, that the family trauma compelled her towards evil. These, of course, remain external as regards true solemnity or depth. She remains brazen with superficial equanimity. As regards society she remains the lone creature in the dwelling. She, the fully documented offspring, she, of pristine, of viriginic reserve. When she appears in public she is graced as the enfiched proto-widow, who at 39 years remains consummately immaculate. The four of us, myself, Rosanna, and Oraculos, and Esteban, and Jesus have never officially existed. Those who have assisted with home care and births have been compensated with largesse so that not a word has been uttered concerning the background of the family. To the community at large Zomaya remains crystal. And I suppose such secrecy has become commonplace in a society which exists on the brink of engulfment. I cannot know this in terms of specifics; but it is something I feel which extends beyond the clutches of my continuing misfortune.

I do not perceive the latter as oblivious comment; as personal bribery to any receptor of my feelings now, or at any time in the future. This is not a registration schizophrenic with conspiracy. Not a case which settles for argumentative splendour. No, I express the unseen vortically spinning at altitude. Which specifically includes the simple reach of nouns. This is why I so assiduously undertake the human debris which surrounds me.

At the level of a rhyming verbal glare I understand the simultaneity of burden with its pre-elliptical glow, with its rancourous symbologies. Any glyph that I utter is never pointlessly sounded as if all I could stomach was by its nature condensed into the nausea of vacuums. Believe me, I understand ruin, I understand the moat of disruptive vegetations. I do not orate by rigour the rote of assumptive creed. No. This is living animation, a force of record more phantom than the ancient springs and oceans on Venus. Leanings, certainly not on the order of egregious didactics, far beyond the plague of quantifiable opacity. This is what I call the higher mercury and its miraculous evocation. Not a wizened discourse and its boundaries, not the tone of a classical imprint, or a withdrawn schism Newtonian in demeanour. I am collapsible, I have merged with incense and spasms, with those frayed intuitive distillations.

The questions could be asked – what empowers my resilience? What condenses my staggered mental coffers?

There are certain things that can't be learned, that can't be known simply by touching or somehow weighing the known. That is why I am always empty, that is why I can do no more than weave my own noun by suggestion. For me, never the miscellaneous, by self-intoxication or retreat. This is not to say that I quantify a falsely held perfection based upon a self-engendered sterility. No, I have never besmirched myself with a wilful imbibing of rum, or thrown myself as victim at the owners of my body. I have never been wanton, I have never been developed into a calloused monster wandering inside her own acids. So I have never retreated, I have never self-consented to a warped or tautological neurology. As to rancorous symbology I am never exhausted. I have escaped the neutrality which once trapped me. I no longer have to suspend myself in psychic vapour in order to survive. Zomaya senses that the fumes have turned against her, that I no longer gain existence by the scars of visibility. I am the orchestra she once conducted. The nausea she once possessed has now turned around and claimed her. I, Rosanna, have shattered into glyphs which consume her, caught as she is between the secrets that I utter, and the rapacious hyenas who demand her very salt.

At times the most striking revenge is endurance. To live, to wait out the thunder, to endure the flames of the lightning strikes. Every time the brothers would bathe me in saliva I knew somewhere in my depths that new energy would appear, that Jesus with his brutish desires, with hellish disregard, would suffocate, would feel his moments decay by means of sovereign disrepute. My intuition informs me that he has sunken to new prostration, that Zomaya out of spite no longer loans him her body. As for Esteban she gives him intermittent foray, with Oraculos consuming the dominant bounty of her pleasure. The balance has been lost, the power of the clan has been siphoned.

She is always facing threats from Jesus. Esteban then combines with Jesus. Then Zomaya counter threatens to burn them in their sleep. I sense this from my own remoteness, from my sensitive internality which opens a kind of deafness. And this deafness engenders new hearing in which the feelings become taut with appearance. I feel these things from her pores, from her insistence on a porous control.

This level of hearing, never culled from assumptive creeds, from conjecture applied to burdensome misnomer. Things come to me as living animations, as phantom springs, as vegetations from Venus. Leanings, certainly not on the level of calliopes or drills, or on the plane of quantifiable armoury, but of course miraculous evocation keeping its discourse beyond boundary. Nothing to do with Newtonian persuasiveness, or having models constructed from the code of glaciation, something to touch, to be invaded by handling. Although I sit, I am not of the ilk of an unmoving thaw. I have re-stolen my living claim as a creature. Some of us are born obliquely, perhaps crippled, or cleft lipped, or sand blind. We have travelled a poisonous birth route. Because we are stained the ingenerous gains inside us. We are left to maunder in ourselves, broken as regards embrace by comradery. We remain unmerged, like a crop of tainted wheat at market. This has been Zomaya's power over me. In previous times she could always say to herself that she let me live, that she clothed me, that she taught me words in a basic kind of Braille. True, as an impressionable child she allowed me to feel a galaxy of language. As for her deepest reasoning I can only say that a kind of guilt made this response, or maybe it was because she knew that even a hidden draught horse had to articulate her motion. I don't know. All I know is that I have a feral understanding of basic style, of verbal expression. Perhaps I speak by solemn therapeutic, by barbaric definition. Perhaps I have merged into a fated trespasser's state. As to classical leaning I can only say that I feel absorbed by clarity, that I have passed beyond nullity. I've become a being practically impossible to configure, or to conceive as tolerable. It's like I've come from the zone of dishonour, only to replicate my ship sailing four or five levels of quanta. So when one breathes by a secretive methodic, breathing morphs, the spells one casts are infinite, degree by uncountable degree.

I speak into glyphs which burden, which shatter the pre-elliptical, so that I must rise to the level of titanic destination, sustaining myself by verbal adjudication. I say this because I'm attempting to keep balance in the vacuums, to keep as my compendium a therapeutic ballast, not in order to condemn myself, but to lend myself the power to simply wake everyday. What I can say is that I'm lending barbaric honour to my hearing, to the maimed Rosanna who inexhaustively circles in her dressing gown.

In my trespasser's struggles I have felt the power from a flood of post-mortem forces, so that I can sense the power of the thoughts that Catalina is now living. This does not come to a visitor at a tomb, but to one who approaches the great gulf of quanta with heightened auricular concern. It's like I am opening a tragic pint of flame listening to her ashes speak. There is openness, there exists the methodology of cosmic skeletal drift. And this is how I hear her, wallowing in mirages of salacious verbatim, her loins quivering like a haunted flock of geese. It's not that I'm laying in wait for her spirit, she comes to me through Zomaya. We are not a triumvirate, solely linked by bodily saturation, but by breath, by what the Egyptians would call the electricity of the BA. The electricity which permeates the universe, and its infinite parallels far too intense for the human mind to comprehend. Not that I am singling myself as somewhere beyond the human, but I know there exist realms where not even myths or galaxies commingle. Yet the electrical subsists, that breathing that I breathe, soaked with mists and spiders.

Thinking in this manner I remain a fugitive fraught by a pointless nautical anthropology. A plummeted urchin in a poisoned sea grass nursery. Here

I am poised at the tragic core of circumstance by means of buried verbal surges compounded by my voice as free volcanic labour. My voice as a pre-existent hounding, as curious trans-literal fountain. I relate this hounding to the way that invisible marking abounds, to the way that the weight of death is released through millenarian erasure. To me, a language is floating brine, coded in higher Caspian tenor. These are obscure paths through incommensurate utopias. Therefore the shifts, the burning scopics, the sudden fragmentary gall. So as I speak, an occult Sun overhead, the thoughts suspended as carking lunar hyphens.

These are thrice bitter zones which I inhabit, always dazed, tending to listen to myself through an arbitrary rust, the sound being a salvo conceived through agitated expenditure. As if I had verbally bleached the thorns inside my being, as if I had raised my agony through listening. No, I am not praising my agony as though it had reached the legendary realms, as though I had sparked the wrath of titans with my thinking. As to willed deracination, as to wild de-operative blinding, my in-ambulate state ceases to fit the part. It is night, I remain kinetically sterile, my body as described by Sister Ornelas is felt by her to be "a chaste theurgic model". Thus, I am someone who now exists beyond the frenzy of self-harming, someone who has advanced beyond the violence of self-deletion. I am not an Aryan import, I am not by nature as someone constrained in her effort by pessimistic tundra, walking on its brokenness. Zomaya is the city-state, Zomaya remains in her essence, a storehouse of doubt. She, the mistress who chews on splintered wheat, emitting sorceries by means of threat. I know she has attempted to breathe inside mirrors, to capture by her breathing sudden beams of light. And I continue to know that it's not possible, always struggling with her mind. Again I'll say, she has too much of the north within her, too much in-diaphaneity in her system.

Fated by blindness, I always see by my essences, by the utter hearing in my skin. It's like having in my aura a general glossary of moons, whispering, staging contiguous error, so as to musically scale assumptive perturbations. Because of this I always feel that I'm rising, that I'm scaling a harsh myopia of toxins. And so I can say to myself that I've tested mineralogy, that I've tasted a prodigious dampness, and come to the point where I can feel the land spinning as windmills and barley.

An unbalanced diptych? A pharmacology of atoms? I seem to solicit drift, listening to neurons escape beyond boundaries. So by listening to boiling flowers, to hearing minimums escape lead, I understand the centrality which accrues from wayward auscultation. Thus, I am convinced of fortuitous sums. Not sums the sighted would concur with, as if surrounding themselves with mirrors consumed by flames from Lithuanian glare.

Perhaps I've gathered this figment from arias of vertigo, No, I am not weaving my sources from radium, not weaving a foundry from acid. Yet, I could be construed as a mime who serially concocts poisons, who fuels a heat from old mazes. But these are mazes which occur from dendritic blazes, so one shakes from inner neural explosion. The grasp of the body becomes tentative, then the senses scatter like amorphous rural doves. Perhaps a fricative waste, or juggled saturnine orations. Thus I am able to swing my one free hand in order to overcome the principle grounding of the blinded. Therefore, I am not the precious voice consumed by a sound that matches antiquarian crystal. Not trapping myself, not hurtling between junctures on a circus trapezium, marking a caustic genesis. Because I cannot know the various fates of Aeschylus, I feel more combined within myself when listening to the fate of nebulas. Not a less incendiary contact, but the sense of feeling in my hands weights from various lunations. I call this the gift of handling phases, of surmounting random grafts of biology, transmuting the essence of vertigo. Not a motivated flaw, or a context formed by episodic abuse, I am now freed when I speak. Now I've dismantled starvation in my sleep. Not mind you in the typical fashion, but as result of carrying carnivorous bonfires in the mind. Thus I understand carnivorous prosthetics, and their falling away from random integers in the mind. These being integers which test themselves, and because they test themselves they disappear as obstruction, forming symbolisms which scorch, which transmute the spirit. What results from this are whispers in the blood, whispers which spin by means of a code of revelations and inklings.

So, to inter me, to entangle me with lists, would never disrupt my sense as regards the inward state of the future. Perhaps I sense my role as a charismatic creature, as one fated to undress the scornful on behalf of those who are truly afflicted. And I am certain that Zomaya has deduced this very element in my psyche, no longer replete with the powers to contest me. I have never acknowledged myself as a primal carrier of rays, as substantive matriculation, as blind calendrical ballerina. Instead, I now explore myself through basic tenets of removal. As to any marking by extrinsic qualification I have none. As to grasp by date of birth, nothing seems to have transpired. So from this life as basic absence I've come to be in these moments. I've come to escalate my own estrangement so as to eliminate any distraction I might carry. Because I've reached such understanding Zomaya has become a conduit for the voice which continues to issue from my remains. Not that I don't know her as sullied, as occupier, as pre-emptive suffocation. But because her presence is so exclusive she's given by my voice for want of a better term, alchemical magnification, in that I've understood my own exclamation as a lioness who leaps beyond her own inclement system. This must be conceived as the one true sinister distance beyond those pointless intellectual contusions. Thus, I've become a substance absorbing apogees, being a body congealed in a lightning basket. What concerns me is its uttermost voltage, is its primeval flames, is its energy which consumes. Of course this floods the field over and beyond the riveted body as the self. Perhaps Sister Ornelas can see the ohms retreat from my visage, perhaps she sees my profile in blank water. This can only be the result from a strange alchemical secret, always revolving in quiet like a secretive Jerusalem Adder. So I sit through asymmetrical bursts, through dialogical asymmetrics. Language being sound as dimensional paradox, is an emptied Hadean ray rising above its startling confusional mass. Some could say that the language I exhort is merciless, that it requires a stunning conflational peril, in that it expands inside the mind so much so that lasting imprecation is evolved and is transmuted. So this is why I speak to myself without breakage. During the time of the Sun my mind is sleeping, my stuttering goes blank. It's as if I go to a world where nothing exists. Sunless, without galaxies or any atomic possibility. So I sit in my sleep without access to any power or snare, coded as they are with cryptic possibility. In a certain sense I could name it a spinning proto-fire, partaking of a realm unknown to ailing genetic subsistence. Not gibbets, not gradational gendarmes, overextended in themselves giving lessons to the law. No. Further, I can never speak of its electrical roundelay as possessing the powers one finds in weather composed of adrenalin. There is poise, there exists a source of selflessness where the body seems absorbed in a rising compositional liquidity. Perhaps an elemental nitrogen, or an energy of refuted ganglia, because this daily blankness occurs I have refused to disinter old regicides, which have created in their wake delimited invictas. The latter being no more than intellectual rubric. A superficial rigour which can only attend a superficial leaning. Even if I was sighted I could never speak with deliberation concerning subjects I had chronicled. During the day the Sisters keep my blankness secret. During this time Ornelas is the one who mops my brow, who attempts to feed me at one sitting. Blank though I am in terms of formal communication, I know she is there, attending me, imparting to me her applicable vigilance. So when Zomaya arrives during what I consider to be an early afternoon, I feel her just staring at my perfectly stilled body she so insidiously engendered. It's as though I hear her and I feel her within the scope of a somnolent neutrality. Because I've retained this partial connective to waking I am always aware of extrinsics, of proximate palpable surroundings.

I have no model of myself, no former looking glass pinnacle by which to judge. I remain empty in this regard, seemingly lessened by my former disruptions. True, I've been soaked in harassment, taunted by reckless stupor, always feeling the pressure as if surrounded by a bonfire of corpses. As if each side of my apparition had doubled, according to what the sighted would describe as strabismus. So I am never the particle, never the drone in the rudimentary dressing apparatus. I am always compound, always twice the initial assessment of what one thinks *of* as Rosanna the blinded. I breathe through impalpable tangles subconsciously understood as filled with the mystery of phantoms. And these phantoms behave in me as unbalanced balletics, so that I can never configure the simple points of my utterance. This remains the central reason for Zomaya's current unease. She's seeking to find how my balance is wrought, how my temperature convenes through her calamitous apprehension. As of now I evince something far beyond the common curses of the profane. This is why Zomaya gropes without let up, always attempting to gather from my visage some shard, some prominent accumulation.

It can be asked, what of the topography which instils me? What of its grasp? What of its damaged stationary atoms?

This is strange, because this is where Zomaya has halted. She remains suspended between my physical annularity, and the dangerous silence I always convey. Therefore she is trapped between massacre and apprehension. On one hand she wants me dead, and on another, she remains decidedly fearful of my death. The result is that I represent fumes, like a queen of structureless combat. When will I strike? Will Ornelas offhandedly challenge her? Will the Sisters vocalize a ubiquitous hatred of her presence? This remains her quandary, she being the hieroglyph in her own magnetizing fiction. She approaches me during her visits as though I have become a vacated star. As though I've become a smouldering ambush chamber. Perhaps, an in-hygienic wattage. I have no other way to put it than as praxis outside of the zodiac, outside of its measurable boundaries, which convene in accessible shadows. I haven't spoken to her since the first day after my arrival, and it is then that I told her all would be lost unless I were given the privacy to voice my own feelings. And she knows this to be the case, so every day I am supplied with two tapes. And every day Sister Ornelas dates and labels my voice, and deposits the debris in a very large strongbox. In this sense I have both Ornelas and Zomaya in the grip of my powers. Without such prompt co-ordination Zomaya would risk destruction and Ornelas would void Zomaya's unending largesse. A victory for me, yes. Like an underdog in chess I seem crippled for pieces, yet I've held out against reality being tenaciously frayed by ongoing struggle. Does Zomaya respect me, does she secretly harbour my threat inside her veins? I would answer in the affirmative. I would answer that she sips the dye of my being every morning. So I can say to myself that I've become encompassing, that I've become this deeper technique of static.

Yet this is far from boasting. I have simply begotten an arrangement which now allows me to thrive. To speak night after night without exterior condemnation. Thus, I've formed this vaporous wrath seasoned by my own personal ammonias. I feel as if I'm now living anterior to history. Beyond its maiming, beyond its dialectical scratch marks. For instance, I can only picture Stalin through blood scattered Braille, as for the leaders of the Earth they are no more than scorpions in waiting attempting to siphon from themselves a post-mortem clarity. Of course such assessment meshes with Zomaya, with her constant matriculation in secret. This why I reverence no one. I am void of the need for intercession. The need for priests, and judges, and leaders does nothing but inspire my absolute contempt. And this is not mere didacticism. Even those who know the scrapings of astronomy will understand the absolute singularity of a self-heating system. They call us dwarfs, Brown Dwarfs. Therefore one populates the void with one's principles. One could call me in-cherubic, or say that I resemble a human strychnine furnace. But again, I remain a singularity, un-broached in terms of law, or finance, or any of the scruples which litter common thinking. At the same time I am not creating for myself hierarchical clauses. For instance, facing a mob as queen, or assuming various roles assumed by the structure of a prime minister's position. And I do not say this from spite, resenting my state according to the forces which conspire in keeping alive my continuing dis-recognition. I remain immaculate in this regard.

True, according to standard deduction I inhabit the impossible. To the sighted I am perched upon a cliff of monstrosities. First of all I am privy to a raw incipience, which always guides me to a brink. Because I have not yet fallen I take succour in the fact of my incombustibility. I continue to speak, to lash out at all corrupted priority, in one sense the priests, in another at God, in another at Zomaya. The above have no order. For me, they are privately connected. So if I monitored my larynx I could conclude that Zomaya is the linking presence ambling between God and the intercession of the priests. But I am not a sworn commander linked to deleterious campaigns. For me, there is only witness, only the channelling of un-dissolved uranian transmission. If someone could hear me speak I would be accused of untenable charisma. Of someone who has dwarfed her own person, who cannot subscribe to self imposition by limit. Therefore, I have no inkling for limit. That is why Zomaya is linked to God. And I mean God which derives from a stationary spectrum. This God of Zomaya is less than 2,000 years. He is vindictive, he hides himself in ether, only making noises when he kills. No, I am not speaking of the God which has fathered Saturn, which links the Sun to its invisible purpose. Not a parochial malevolence, but a voice which empowers natural forces at its root. I call this versification by drone, by compexification, by cosmic admixture. Therefore, my response to exasperation has vanished. I have risen above the central tenets of the Visagoths consumed as they were by the pessimistic body. This remains the tenet of Zomaya and her material understanding of the parochial as the Divine. To me she subscribes to a blank or unwarranted ghost. Thus, she is always subsumed by the art of malicious accusation, by the principles which gather from loathing and panic.

Of course I could never converge upon a simple caustic grammar. Even though I've swallowed misery and horror I can never devolve to the squalor at which my seeming fate has placed me. I do not pity myself, or delude myself concerning my present victim's status. As regards continuing cure I am seemingly engulfed by hunches, by curious verbal scents, which allows the movement of spirals in my body. And these spirals exist as movements of origin, as primeval motility. What's resulted is certain grasp of things, understanding the sound of the first mountains on Earth. When saying this I am reaching to some untold era before the Devonian or Mississippian. To some degree I must possess some of the feelings of the first sharks or bats. What I'm coming to terms with is inter-dimensional feeling. The feeling that connects beyond the boundaries of species and time. By surviving the feral as I've done I understand the way glass burns, I understand the way insects are decided.

Of course I've never been guided to what is social. What I know of the daily give and take has never congealed as action for me. Everything for me has been as brutalized direction. Rosanna eat this, Rosanna, satisfy Oraculos. I paraphrase Zomaya, but this remains the level that my body heat was privy to. Yet I was never addicted to the utter depths. I always loomed, as though listening to my body from great distance. And so I've absorbed the tenuous, the fraying which comes from danger. This is why I can only speak to myself, this is why consensus repartee utterly holds no value.

I will never be privy to the great riots, to the wars and the tensions which extend from roiling social waters. I will never see a flag. I will never salute the fact of a state run doctrine. None of this applies. Even if I were sighted all seminars on learning would be useless. Because I know in my heart that I am incapable of the linear, deducting facts, engendering sterility, capacities I will never possess. Because I have a hatred of stasis the current systems of learning exist for me with nothing but disregard.

I cannot say that I've mastered balance, that I sit here in perfect concurrence with myself. Nevertheless, I've felt neurological release from the plague which exists as a psychic fettering noose.

Duty to this region of history, public relation to the state, as I so recently stated I have no dealings with. It could be thought by some that I am a pointless copper heiress with only personal demons as her interest. I can only say that something exists outside me, that the punishing mental climate and in general is replete with demise of the material plane. I am only riding the momentum of copper so that I can speak this once before I'm dead. The cliché exists that money is only a means. True, it is only a means, but those who acquiesce to its psychology become lizards who exist without bread.

Not that I am engaging the didactic, or engaging my voice according to a paradigm fraught with terminal mephitics, I am only stating my intuition as it accrues as philosophical irruptive. Because I've not exported to anyone the root of my struggles. I cannot blame myself for Zomaya, for the legacy of Catalina and Edmundo. I was simply born as I was as a body in an incest garden. Perhaps karma, or was it strictly material chance? As of now I ascribe to no story. I exist. To Zomaya I remain detached, savage. I've become over time a nascent proto-demon. True, I've spawned no daughters who sell death, nor have I concluded upon a carefully wrought plan to promulgate ruse by ruse assassinations by ghost. Yet to Zomaya atrocities compound in my person. To her, I am the usurping queen who dispatches war across the mind. She walks about as if she carries no role. She comes to me by day attempting in the process to monitor my utterance, yet finds nothing but frenzied scenarios as her yield. Thus, this tense condition spins, stoked by her subjective altering ideals. Therefore, I remain resolute in my distance, my mental gait always alien and nomadic, always gifted with stunning imaginary omens, this has kept me from giving in to the struggles which assume the condition of anonymous fatigue. Never have I tested my talents by blowing on a cold reformer's bugle. Never have I scribbled in dirt official reply to the renunciator's forge. There are gaps, and interregnums in the mind where blizzards are condoned. So again, I am not hoisting myself into stasis as definition so as to confront the raptors who have maimed me. No, I am like those infinite subsets of the self that one feels in the throes when rising through meridians of sleep. It's like feeling zones of sound which issue from occulted germinal hornets, I'll call these sounds aural daggers from the Pleiades. So when Zomaya confronts me body to body I transmit those infinite subsets so that she vertiginously subsists in a zone curious with lapses. A space, perpetually confounded by impulse and seizure. Thus, she wanders through fissioning neutron selvas, which gives rise to nervous hesitation. She is thus less prone to aggression. I have by my blackmail created in her an occulted daylight. What I mean by this term is that the rays from my silence react like the solar force when impinging on a vampire. These are rays which pour as torrential sonar, so much so that I partially occlude her and she shakes, she remains annulled in her leanings. At some level she knows that I am more and more capable of destruction, poised with selective renewal of that destruction. Every night she knows her body is both renewed and destroyed. She knows by my own transformation Zomaya lives again as hellish icon who moans, being the night witch who always breathes her last flare. As I speak one can interpret her as the night witch who breathes through penultimates. As icon, her neutrality is active, her connivance transmuted. As icon, the hellish day star, as night witch she burns as imploded coriander.

This is not a nightmare edict, nor some re-arisen state where blazing lakes are recorded. Because I am sand blind I can imagine the shape and the colour of fire. I can feel the inferno. Because I know recorded words can live beyond the code of assaultives, understood within themselves as opium by brutality and fear. It is Pinochet, it is Stroessner, it is the futility of burned diamonds. There exists no power in their tortures. Not that I idealize a mantra according to the manner in which I extend personal meaning in the world. This, of course, is the only manner in which I can promulgate vibrations which alter the very code of heinousness, understanding that every microscopic cleansing results in building a bed of utopian coral. Again, this is not code as personal connivance, but I've seen the result in Zomaya, not because her basic substance has been emended, but because the objective through which she breathes is beginning to react within her system.

An idealized montage? Revenge by intellectual ether? Neither. I am not trying to develop in the main a primeval recipe so that other psychic amputees can replicate my standing. Can model their deficits upon Zomaya, claiming in the process that any autocrat is Zomaya. That the children who've seen their mothers slaughtered will be conversant with my amperage. That the children who've lost arms, or parts of their eyes, will be ablaze with hatred for Zomaya. But I can do nothing but speak, nothing but react to the stillness which consumes my atoms.

But it can be asked, are these atoms, germinal gryphons? Stormy neutron monsters?

And further, can the question be posed as to the simulacra concerning my capacity as a human? Can I be seen under the auspices of other than human scruples?

These are not tautologies. The first question can be understood as consciousness not quite having reached the sum of homo sapiens sapiens. The latter, having to do with the inter-dimensional as being. Of course, I do not ask such questions of myself, I do not propose to give to myself an importance which extrinsically extends my singularity as gravity. No. I consider myself as a philosophical felon, as someone whose ideas create no justification in the context of things. And when I say the context of things I'm thinking of the systems shutting down. The banking world, the family world, and all the sinister implications which issue from the military patrons.

Who am I, this blind reprehensible agate who bleeds? This persona who indulges her own verbal anaemia so as to sculpt her various instabilities? What I can say is that the millstone of the order is cracking, and I, this strange interior trilobite who escaped from the crevice as a non-existing person; as one who lives simply by the fact that she breathes, who trembles at times with tigers in her thorax. I, who always breathe beneath a canopy of principal, consumed by mesmerizing discharge, which encourages the spirit by means of a dazzling pitch-blended ocean. Because I know at times that I have circled the floors with a rootless damnation. Being a redoubtable scintilla I've taken on the power which opens the blooms in Mongolian blister gardens. In this regard I can be portrayed as the absence who speaks through devious angelology. A tense perimeter of fuels, being a ceaseless aporia in a poisoned mass of tropospheres. So *I* am not the concubine resigned to the harem, propped against pylons lisping her forgeries with an unseasoned rote. I can relate my sincerity, my specific critical implications, with all my sacrifice burning being sound which escapes an enraged mirage.

It is accepted procedure to ask for credentials, to seek out others who have approved you. In all these aspects I have failed. Thus, a general lack as to any worth that may be pondered. So again, on this level I don't exist, I don't register, I am to remain the incredulous specimen who exists without substance. So, according to consensus thinking I am less than an Indian starving on rupees, who can garner no favour, or post no credit to her numbing personality. I speak to them as if I were void, a hopeless grammatical fern blazeless in the soil. At best it could be said that I live within the acme of repetition, that I ruthlessly stutter, that my sums conclude as backward in rotation. Again, I do not despair, I do not enlist a pointless group to cry for me, so as to shift my burden allowing my grief to return to the fold. What exists for me is this suffering ad nauseam, always feeling a blurred leakage in my stomach. As if I whispered audacities to beasts and told them to sing according to sourceless instigation. And this latter condition was mine precisely. Attempting to avert the energy of someone like Jesus. Or discuss morality with the likes of someone like Esteban, wandering like he was across a pointless mental prairie. As for Oraculos I had no considerations, knowing that he had partially risen above the substance of brutes, so that he shielded himself with an intelligence not unlike a field hand risen to the bottom rung of authority. As for Zomaya, the articulate procuress, the conductor who sculpts damage.

It could be said that I drink a merciless cedar whisky, that I wear an omitted Hegelian tiara, never understanding the pole of dialectics, or the reasoning which issues from generic respiration. There exists for me this carnivorous battle juice by which I empty myself over and over so that I sink at times into stunning ataraxia. I know that psychic scars remain, I know that personal brooding exists through teeming parallel misnomer. The brazen motif of my rapes carry me, although I waver and carry myself through concussive counterparts of weight. I grapple with my audacity, with the strength I've been given moving in my body like an old Egyptian cortical plough. Thus, I understand other dimensions of the sky over and beyond the original study of the zodiac. I mean those dimensions which are blind to the eye and burn in other regions without ether or day. I imagine this is where certain pharaohs rowed, where the afterlife spun over and beyond any heat as suspension. Maybe this exists as a spur to my eclectic reasoning, to my temperature which engages the syllabus of night, with all its torrential silence which navigates the ash in my tenacious smouldering fingers. To Zomaya I constantly enact sorties. I constantly inveigle her with the mirage which always issues from my voice. This is the first time she's been stymied, the first time that the noise in her heart has been broken. She who's never considered confusion, she who's never willed the portent which comes from failure. In this sense I've become a mystery, a poltergeist, a being who's risen above the phantom code aligned with the winds which rush through certain Biblical explanations. In this regard all her stratagems have broken. Can she explain this to Jesus. Can she wake Esteban from his stupor so that he engages her with any meaningful repartee. As for Oraculos she can only imply her bewilderment, only imply her frustration as she seeks for brutish answers in her sleep. I've escaped this torment. This is why I've embraced silence, only breaking its symbolical portents giving me the substance to spin schisms. It is through this substance that I am able to sustain this secretive welter, this surge of ire which regales itself in mystery. I do not intend to enfetter myself in banality, thereby redeeming myself according to acceptable claustrophobia. I do not accept the role as the isolated mistress, as the dumbfounded monster strapped to the soils in a dungeon. This is not my methodology, to fulfil the dominant notion of an isolated temptress burning through her cells through pre-emptive pre-maturity.

One could say that I'm struggling with both blood and ethics, that I've surmounted myself only to stay rooted according to conscious patriotics proved by adherence to some particular cause. If the cause be war and my advancement against it, so be it. If it is against molesters and their ilk one can attest to my fanatically empowered enmity. If it is against those individuals who engage their own significance by acts of personal cruelty, my opposition remains complete. But things are over and above these concerns. I work through these zones of obsession so as to procure for myself life, and by procuring this life, understanding its motion as an unspoiled anti-stasis.

I in-script my voice by means of its haunted physiology, thereby eschewing any commitment to terror, to sullen shifts through imposition of discomfort. So I am seeking for something other than human rotation.

Am I seeking some dazed simulacra according to my body as model?

Am I delirious with strain and combustion?

Am I a drunken ether hamlet sired by genetic imbalance?

The latter questions can be considered in relation to the fact of my optical confounding. I have not been given a single iota, not even the barest quantity to live with. Not that I'm complaining from the perch of a sheltered commoner; all I can say is that I've been allowed to persist across the time of a double decade, which has allowed me at present to verbally enter my own condition. Since my balance has been destroyed I've come to penetrate on my behalf the depths of my seeming destruction. Yet I can now concur with myself, I can now empathize with the original lack instilled within me, which allows the raising of storms from despair. Because despair has done nothing but deepened me, has done nothing except extend in me a stark intuitive yield. And this intuitive yield can be felt according to hurricane, according to boats that row through fire. There exist symbolical partings, and further, there exist those partings from which one never returns. I call this the sensorium of surcease. In my mind, I have left the living and returned to the not yet dead. So I am liminal, no longer partaking in palpable calliopes. I can say that this separation has provided me power in that it causes wavering in those who approach me. Wavering according to that which can't be grasped and turned into integers which concretize the mind. So I am this ghost, this remnant, this broken idea which utters. This voice, which sunders empirical twilight. This is not the twilight which the sighted inspire, but that mode of the mind no longer subsumed by those who command conquest over bodies. Again, I fail to exist, so Zomaya can no longer surmount me with her former definitives. Of course this fact is known, but the rootings go much deeper. When one knows in one's depths that the self has been so shaken that it floats into zones outside of this life, the angels vanish, the stone of God collapses through sullied misnomer. Strength becomes divided, the air from the Sun no longer rises in the hearing. This is the realm Zomaya now senses. She's now bereft of the core of trans-functional leaven. Now she faces sets and subsets of nothingness. And what do I mean by nothingness? Is it the amplitude of fathoms? Does it spiral? Does it wander and subsume itself in parts and parts of parts? Perhaps all of the above, perhaps partially magnetized as figments? As it is, I've slowly increased the atmosphere. I've slowly become the central magnetizing core. Thus, I've become to Zomaya the blank interior Sun. I've cast a surreptitious holding power that Zomaya can't deny. So in this sense I've become her fuel, I've become the lava which absorbs her cunning fragmentary ire. And because I've so occluded her feral habituation, it now must have had an effect on someone like Jesus, who I now intuit as spontaneously starved by Zomaya. I can feel that he is eating himself alive, knowing in his depths his blazeless status. And since he's understood his instinctual in-succession he knows power over me has vanished, so the fumes from his heart must be staggering, must now have become a telepathic inferno.

A circumstance condensed by periodic monstrosity. So Zomaya knowing full well this monstrosity is more and more yielding to a shift in her circumstantial palace. Of course, my acreage has quickened. Not that I've condemned myself to ownership, but there now exists a protracted sufficiency. Everyday Zomaya deposits two tapes to Sister Ornelas, and whispers to me, and then consults the nuns concerning any nuance in my utterance. Of course she fails in her detection, day after unfulfilled day. She has not forgotten the terms by which I can destroy her. So she is prompt, she complies throughout this torment without seeming vacillation. In this regard she remains the rational sow, the inclamourous eaglet foregoing the kill. This is Zomaya, the neutralized insomniac, the cargo of worms spun around in stillness.

Not that she is the equal of a sourceless tabloid persona whispered as the keeper of consensus charisma. Even in her acts of forcing me to learn language I knew that she had explored a certain depth of pneuma. As a child I was forced to listen to the restlessness of Beckett, the peregrinations of Melville, the murderous kinships of Dostoyevsky. Of course I was drowned. Language ran from my pores. She had recordings of the Unnameable. Moby Dick and Myshkin she read in spurts from the texts. I would listen over and over again until my body would slump from exhaustion. I could have been no more than 7. Of course this was peculiar, extremely peculiar. She tested my limits to see how much I could take. Sometimes I would faint, at other times, I'd succumb to vertigo and vomit. What made it so perverse was that these hours long sessions were random. A week would go by then parts of Ahab or Myshkin would bracket me. Then for days on end silence. I was always unprepared, I was always the wretched little elf, mortified, skilless, always burning with palpable material panic. Retention was always subaltern, I was filled with prescient maniacality. But this gave me the ability to speak without let up. This served me well years after, when

I could entertain the brutes and somehow avoid their advances for days. I would always speak of what it meant to be a flying chiropteran. Of how its seeming arthritics could tumble through darkness. Of how the spell of a flying monster could inveigle their thinking. Of how the monster could listen to different filaments of surcease. I told them that each particular chiropteran knew increment by increment each particle of thought in the sound that each of them would make at their deaths. Through me Zomaya would enhance her control letting them know she was the linchpin of my learning. She would shower my skills thereby evoking utter ascendance on her behalf. I could sense this evocation as being particularly pronounced in its mental angling towards Oraculos, knowing that he and he alone was part property of my body.

By the time I was twelve I was able to verbally rivet. The walls would tremble with nuance. Jesus on occasion would moan. Esteban also would make sounds when I would discuss the mixture of chromosomal clouds in the blood. I would speak until the lot was drunk with insidious anguish. The pressure was astounding. It's as if continents were broken, as if the sound of moons were scattered across the confines of an iguana. At one point Jesus screamed and attempted to prove that he was deaf and couldn't hear the power flare inside his nostrils. Esteban, strained, would rattle bottles in order to attempt distraction. During these sessions no one came near me. At times, even Zomaya was eclipsed in her confined ascendancy. This remained the fare on random Thursday afternoons. I could choreograph darkness. I exhibited no limits when imparting the effect of sound upon the body. As a quasi-Scheherazade I always remained exhausted. Zomaya was the Caliph preparing me for the kill. She surreptitiously told them that this is what you'll eat when she evolves to womanly bleeding. She being no more to me than a blood thirsty matron, or a conniving virago. This is Zomaya in her element working her every nuance from a variety of angles. Going back to these terrors I know now that Zomaya was consumed by copious cruelty. I was always under pain of constant ridicule and attack if I ever evinced any displeasure at the treatment rendered. To listen to recordings, then have Zomaya irregularly hound me with fragments of the masters that she'd read, provoked in me a shunted neurology. I'd go blank in order to secure a modicum of survival. She'd mention names like Picabia, or Blake, or De Sade. She'd show off her skills in order to further confuse me. She'd demand that I know the similarities between them even though I had no skill at comprehending. So the issue from me was an unequal silence. I was always drowned. She knew that her questions could compress, terrify. And as I'd remain mute Zomaya would mock me with a laughter which implied my ineptness. Yet somehow this terror became reversed when I'd create from myself curious tales which exalted the chiropteran.

This was always a ghoulish matter. I knew at each moment that I could be consumed by the circumstance, that I could be devoured and my remains be disposed of with lime. But now I understand, this was Zomaya's power to mete out the discomfort, bit by abominable bit. So there was never any respite for play, for any other level than that of the pessimistic. Now I can see that she is biologically Roman, that her energy is not unlike the frenzied populace of the arena. I was always the plague, always the prisoner who suffered the slings from her unerring baseness.

Of course I am recalling threat and living merger with threat. Because of this all my liminal capacities have been startled, which has allowed me access to portents, knowing sounds to be alive in their deflective disparities. So this invasion by palpable mystery remains far removed from doting Biblical destiny. I am a destiny no conqueror has legalized. I have evinced to this moment a living capacity to struggle, to somehow go beyond theorems imbibing thought as aerial incessance. It is like a bell transmuted from perpendicular granite. A granite which I feel soaring not unlike a spiralling liquefaction. Saying this, I have gotten beyond material compounding. Perhaps I am the performer on a waking trapeze, spinning by means of tragic confoundment. My body at present time being a curious component of mystical calligraphy, because of this I felt I've transmuted the clinging, the wrathful pauses, the nostalgic insistence, according to inherence as posed by broken carrion.

The questions again can be asked, what am worth to the multitudes? How strong is the tide from my stormy interior sea?

To the opening part of the question I am nothing more to the masses than a primeval hazard. To the latter part I have no other power than a voice which issues from a root quasi-delimited by incest. A voice, which explodes from puzzling Braille. This is the damage in which my energies presently dwell. Perhaps to objective persons I am an organic ruse, I am a nightmare garishly projected. So if my soul is examined by any ordained brother, he will find demons in suspension, who attest to the probable mean I have struck between forecast and prophecy as regards an angelic mean. Yet I am convinced of their terrible ruling casting me into the bottomless domains where infinite torment through fire occurs.

I am forced to balance aural mirages, by distance, by the power of endemic annulment. I call them my seismic cosmographies composed of spores which spin inside seeming stationary rays. Even when blank I batten on hot diurnal grasses. But these are not the grasses that one smells in a garden, or growth that's splayed across torrential ambits. No, I'm speaking of an absence of weight, of ceaseless inner turning, fed by the convolution sprung from the irony of deafness. To be blank is to not see, is to renege on one's ability to hear. And it must be understood that I cannot proclaim innocence, nor absolution from a heritage sprung from the fangs of a galling folly. I am human, understanding the solstice of the history that that entails. At the same time I understand myself as the circumstantial echo, as the interstice perceived through stunning electrical blizzards. Of course, I am not positing the above according to the senses contained within accessible fraction. If anything I am a restless helical noun, an implicated wave which appears and disappears as if I could announce myself in this manner to those who condone themselves strictly on the notions of sight. As of now I experience myself as a wild impersonal summation who has evolved to immaculate parallel incarnation. As if I were magnetically born unbeknownst of myself. Therefore, living as parenthetical, both as a pre-existent kindling, and a consciousness which exists post obitum. Yet I remain the umbilical void floating through a mean. Again, it is from this mean that I've conducted balance, that I've survived the waking torture surrounded by concussives. To the ordained brethren I connive in sacred filth, I remain the unwitting hetaera conceived from the cholera of whims. I am not considered one of sacred potions, of one neither full grown or infant. All I can say is that my urges were exploited, and I became the wench who commanded a rotted dowsing wand. Thus, I am not considered to be human. Perhaps a doused rat, or a crumbling bird in the desert. Add to this my blindness, and the hours that pass in simulated deafness and you have one not even the scientists can conjure as alien. I am one who lives beyond the border of breathing neither living nor dead. Thus, I remain the enigma, the true challenge to living as evinced according to the statistical dictates which seeks by its efforts to clone the bizarre. I am not a bird created to fly and attack men. I am not speaking at the behest of a hovering craft with sudden beings who have merged from torture and experiment. I am not a grafted portion of the Anglo-Saxon thought experimentation. I am not a terrifying clone created for crowd control at the end of the world. Not the magnified invasion suddenly crystallized as menace. No, I am more the original Seminole who lives and can't be trusted. Who instils great disadvantage in what the Saxons know as systems of order. This is something that I sense. And Zomaya reveals herself as part of this order. As for the brutes, they remain the colonized branches strictly at the behest of her overriding rationality.

And so it is asked how could Zomaya be considered as one scrupulous in dispensation, with her toleration of Melville, and chiropteran, with her conduct at orgies, with her debilitating response to any sense of benevolence. I say that she remains that energy which seeks control, which seeks the optimum power for her own debilitating spasms. This is why I staunch her, this is why she trails me. Power has shifted, but not in the manner that the stationary realm depicts. I am not of the stationary, I am not of the ilk who seeks schism for the sake of schism, creating seeming confusion which then basks in the wake of an annihilating order.

So when I speak of my daylight deafness, it remains to me as simulation by camouflage. Because when Zomaya confronts me by day I am always quelling her invasion. Her attrition seems stopped by my deafness. As I have instructed Ornelas to define my deafness according to the stress I've incurred. Zomaya, being the cunning beast that she is, always suspects of something over and beyond what she is told. Yet she can never reach me, she can never rout me from hiding. So I am never exposed, I am never within the claws of her tenacious crawling. I, who am fuelled by a tenacious lemur's blinking. I, the caveat of tenacious cobra's fatigue. I, who strike in revenge at the impostors in life. One can say that I've become an empowered pariah.

The assumption exists that I am no more than reptilian, that I've been bred as a form by means of classic fornication. The belief has risen that I've risen from galvanic soil, that my atomic claim is less than the radical invertebrates. That I've been caught in a maze of instincts as a 2 brained being. An anonymous human topology at the acme of ghostly expression. At best I am a tangled solar charisma, a body which quavers like a heat which issues from blank congenital fuses. Yet, according to Oraculos, my skin is a ferociously coloured maple. To him, I am a finely blended ash point. Or perhaps an oil expelled from the mouth of the Sun. Being his daughter he understands that my colouring cannot state as its substance remnants from the Euro-Aegean. My genes have nothing in common with a Peloponnesian colony. I am condensed from the grammar of other psychic means. Because for me the invisible occurs, I never implant it with the rhetoric of doubt. Squalor for me remains the strict acknowledgement of the senses; the force of the 5 senses. I am not a European. I am someone not plagued by intellectual admonishment. I simply exist with experience that my own patterns have discovered. Therefore, I have not condensed in my blood the metrics of measurement. As to superfluous cohesion none of its boundaries exists for me. I do not partake of the powers which consent to remorseless salutations. I am done with such damage. So the salt, the carbon, the elements, thrive for me beyond endless stretches of dread.

So if the soils collectively meander I feel I am not condemned to such limit, sense something that condenses in my body even if the ozone has failed. By saying this I am not saying that I've arrived from one of the proximate planets. Perhaps an ether from Saturn, or a water bearing chemical from Mars. No, I am neither of the above. That is why I so distrust the notions of delineated beings from other objective physical criteria. They are nothing more than the European mind within the limits of demonish projection. And at some inter-dimensional threshold Zomaya hears me in this regard. This is why she ambles at times as though seepage has occurred. And by seepage I mean her power which formerly roamed in the sensate, which made demonstrable demands on the world that the senses denote as realia. I am no longer subject to her senses. I've become as strange to her as octopi in a curious ocean zone. So this is a shock to even someone as strange as Zomaya. Why? Because even she remains swayed by the pull of metropolitan osmotics. The keeping of name and reputation, the protection of illusion which is linked to her considerable monetary kingdom. With me, she's lost the ability to function inside the synapse. The interstice exhausts her. She can only condone the skeletal and the mind which evinces the skeletal. When she can no longer exhaust this condition her mind invisibly wavers, thus, the lessening of her powers.

When she comes to me she seeks to keep my metals burning, to keep my exhaustion within the scope of her routine. The era has shifted. I now respirate on the plane of an ectoplasmic absence. A skiagram, a shadow, a non-bodied body. All this configures as an eclectic essence. She knows that I have left her and become supernal and amorphous. I who have reached into blinding arcana. Of course I have left the confines which stand by superficial standard. This Zomaya can reach, this is the level she has voided by her instinct. But to reach this zone of the uncanny makes her quaver, makes her doubt the fire of her old destructive graces.

In this regard my time is scattered, my image no longer bickers within what Zomaya continues to know as the known. I am the plebeian's candelabra announcing the joltless message of a hyper-extended faith. Not the titles of paintings concerning THE EXPULSION FROM PARADISE, DONATION OF THE KEYS TO SAINT PETER, or SAINT ANTHONY ABBOT AND SAINT PAUL THE HERMIT. From what I know of the titles I sense that they are finely wrought visual propaganda. That they imply a single sanctuary in hell. A monodimensional survey totally unequal to a mongoose or a panther. I mean by the latter a stormy natural kingdom totally unlike the beliefs from old abstracted models of God.

For me, I've become the free gestation of wattage, the bell which evinces from its sound explosive flowering as model. This becomes the eyeless blaze of universal balance. So scope for me is not a claustrophobic figment, or a traitorous riddle, or allopathic waste. Thus, I am traitor to generalized belief as it exists as material audacity. To those who subtend the Renaissance I am a being who is blasphemous as figment. I, who sing my precious canticles in Hades. I, who both withdraw and am visible like a bane across the night.

So as bane, as being with conflagration as her adage, can no longer aspire to any reverence even amongst the potentially clear minded. Because this latter group can be swayed even in terms of their nascence. It will be said that her thought causes harm, that her mind remains unbleached. So I am not speaking in order to convince, to amalgamate following. As to quantity, its adjectives have run their course. I am not seeking to organize a clan of victims so as to storm the barricades on behalf of blindness. I am not stirring up those rent with basic maladjustment. I have issued desires to the Sisters to help me in weaving a one woman flag. Nothing of this sort has basis. So I remain steeped in the depths of oracular suggestion.

What remains baffling is how I've come to term without issue. No one in the lot was sterile. So this was always Zomaya's Achilles heel. The brutes couldn't be controlled by use of protection, it was like confronting a volley of arrows unscathed. Zomaya knew this so she maintained a susurrant kind of panic. Always concerned with the hiding and disposal of offspring. Such a condition wears and wears so one is subject to breakage by means of the slightest amount of pressure. And because of this threat I feel this is the reason why I remain alive today. For Zomaya, it was as if she were moving figures across a sulphurous board of chess. She understood diagonals, and the movement which issues from the absence of movement. Even at her most laborious baseness I always felt her understanding of calculation. Yet she could never control the energy of sexual denouement. Of course reason would evaporate in the fray. This is why I now exist the way I exist. Over time, I've ironically gained the power of a phantom isolationist. Now, I more fully understand my circumstantial diagnosis and the energy which snakes through my exhaustive critique. It can be asked what if this were different, and I laboured in untenable motherhood. Perhaps Zomaya would breast feed my daughter. Or perhaps Zomaya would leave her as human bullion on the impersonal steps of the fire house. Or perhaps she would starve us, or let us crawl through waste. But these are phantom angles. Suffice it to say such conditions have not occurred. All that I can say is that I've been claimed by damage, by heinous ordination. Of course, my neurology wavers, my throat parches, I struggle to keep my fingers from quaking. These are the remains of my partial physical system. I feel as if my body is scrawled, as if my blood condenses according to roughened perception. Yet something has arisen beyond physical congruence, so that I'm inkling another condition over and beyond that which craves its motion through breathing. Perhaps an invisible Sun Angel, or an ascended solar hawk, perhaps a shadow which flies from an incantated language. These are the blizzards I embody. These higher shafts, these deserted coffins and nouns. This is why the nuns have decreased contact. Even Sister Ornelas has withdrawn. I've created around me storms that not even a chronic sensitive can endure. True, I feed on halibut once a day. There is a salad and glasses of water. I always eat at the time of day that the sighted now name as dusk. I relieve myself daily. I neither chant nor pray. To Sister Avila I can be no more than an enduring object. For her, I am curious principle which I'm told she sometimes discusses. And I'm sure this is the case with the lot of them, Sister David and Sister Cisneros carrying an absence of difference in their treatment of me. So, at St. Catherine's I remain the untrammelled candle, the blank unlit throne. So I exist as potentia, as one kinetically untapped. Ornelas tells me that Sister Devota dreams of me as the in-lay of dragons, that something about me is askew. She's told Ornelas that my respiration constantly starves for holy renewal. But beyond all these different confusions it remains Zomaya's continuing largesse which ultimately leaves my presence unquestioned. Because of me St. Catherine's creates profit. Thus, my strangeness creates a favourable reading of the coffers. The Sisters are secure, the coterie is allowed to breathe.

Since I now live according to enforced continence Zomaya no longer checks me for spotting. Every month she would start to check me for blood. It was always near the 12th when I could feel her hands groping for evidence of fluid. In later years when the stains were confirmed one could feel relief issuing from her form. Of course I am dense and embittered. Of course I am always questioning the very notions of existing. Even Zomaya knows that I have reached over and above the zone of God in the mind. That I crave no human example. Again, me, the self-heated star, the flawed ambrosial gryphon. So perhaps Sister Devota has properly composed me as the in-lay of dragons. If I could apologize for God I perhaps would condone St. Francis in dialogue with the serpents. As Franciscan, I would pour out my fortune to strangers. I would, as the cliché goes, leave no stone unturned. Someone like Zomaya would be singled out according to my definitives of wrath. I would re-blend the world. Not as someone naïve with stricture, but as the spectre who evolves beyond spectres. As a neo-Franciscan I would point out her debility according to the state of her penurious reputation.

But again, I am not neo-Franciscan, I am simply Rosanna in struggle with alchemical saturation, knowing at some level that I'm obliterating damage. That I feel myself inside the ocean's mazes rising to new sensations inside the self. Someone like Devota cannot grasp me. She can only attest to understanding that which goes no further than hierarchical proportion. For her, popes, and cardinals, and kings represent for her the power which immures itself in linear order. She has no capacity to witness emergence. All she's known is the care of human cripples. Her capacity to know is confined to the solemn nature of intrinsic fright. And it remains the obedience of the body formed as debilitated witness. Thus, like Zomaya, like the mindset of billions, she is ultimately governed by the shadow of numbers according to addition and subtraction. Again, she is governed by figments, she can only embody a flank of separations. Because my fingers have quaked when she's witnessed me on occasion, I remain according to her inference replete with forces which roam the unclean. To her, I am expelled from God's approval. But because my energy announces itself without linear progression I baffle, I seem to someone like her to exist without prior sufficience. So I seem energized by a sun which burns outside submission. I create by turns confusion and antipathy. Confusion seems to reign in the sense that I seem immune to any inner stasis, and empowered by antipathy, because through this prior immunity I've negated terminus which is the commanding power of the Christian commandments. Not an inventive bribery, or to the inventively sighted, not a star inscrutably pulled from flaming polar waters. Perhaps this curious polar star is the topmost carat in a lessened solar door, perhaps it is an animated jewel carelessly splayed across agglutinated rum. As if I planted my powers in cholera or plague. On the other hand one could say that I am blessed with blameless quickening, that my body exists as a courier of nitrate. Not of course to lay atoms in the soil, but to acknowledge the entrails, the stained gladioli which flutter in my blood.

Knowing my body, I understand all conventional scent, all the tones which dwell in sensate purpose. This is no mean declaration. To have my genitalia erotically consumed in my own father's mouth, such ruthless aggravation has provoked in me a tenor which always concludes as spontaneous rage. The glamour of self conduct cannot always befit me. At some anonymous time perhaps Zomaya or Ornelas may be attacked. Perhaps I'll hiss and leap upon Sister Devota or Sister Charlotte. Perhaps I'll reduce myself to untranslatable vileness. Or perhaps one day I'll whisper to Ornelas my desire to have Zomaya tried by confessing her crimes to objective jurisdiction. But beyond these tenors it is the blackmail that empowers me. The power to transgress the extrinsic, the power to contradict the complex code of civil assignations.

As the immoral persona I am considered the instigator whose energy is rife with tapping into ruin. I, whose body lives by the codes of moral insult, who wraps in silk remnants from oneiric hunting splinters. This creates in those conventionally addled diacritical confusion. In my particular case this translates to a tenor far removed from material acquisition and survival. As regards the current level of the human epoch I feel no more included in its satanic operations. And by satanic, I mean that which thrives on hostility as limit. This I've come to by both immediate and general understanding. Of course, Zomaya, and her immediate hostilities, and on the generic plane the human mind now prone to the Northern murdering model. When neo-Stalinists live as tacticians of security, when Adolf Hitler inspires groupings in crumbling Aryan parlours, this is the symbolic litmus that lets me know that the species works daily at exhaustion and remains compulsively spent. They've regressed to the manoeuvres of insects and bears. The common experience being a series of depressive academies in which the vast majority psychically wither. Mental heightening is reversed. Billions are left to survey despair. Not that I'm speaking as some mythical chimera with my blood transposed into wings. But it is true, that I've come to decisive agreement with myself. I've come to fact that I am leaving the human colony, that what's been done is what's been done. I do not want to repeat the gift of birth, to go back to Zomaya, or roam in the welter of political misgiving. This does not befit the level of intrinsic dignity. And this is not uttered in the spirit of philosophical cliché. One needs live in the depths and the heights. One needs embrace the spark beyond phantasmal wreckage. This precedes all mechanical glyphs, all actions which maintain the adventitious as authority.

In the old church fathers the soul is divided by argument into creation, into that which precedes itself as origin, and the outcome of these levels as rotted traducian umbilicals. The latter being the perpetually slandered body. I think of Origin, and Tertullian, and the galling and contradictory Augustine. This remains the Church at its highest achievement. This remains its boundary, its cursed disembodied palindromes. So they are trapped, always relying on figments, on dispelling self-created errata, in order to advance a criterion which has evolved in a psychic hostility akin to the Eurasian steppes.

Daunting pronouncements, Basilicas of oxide, astringency in the service of a spiritually defective confinement, attempting to mimic a falsely created saviour. To such consent I am a furious powder urchin, I am the utterer of lack, I've condemned foetal resignation in the wake of these crematorial Christian theologies. Their wrath, their weight which accrues as disguised thinking. Of course I am not a Myrmidon, not a curious porcelain fractal, vertiginous within the ruins of a sweltering codeine plantation. What I can say for believers is that they are ensconced on a plane unwieldy with misfortune. Because the soul is divided by the body being banished. This remains a ruthless designation, an antiunification, much like a rock being smitten from flames from the void. The body being then consumed by the heat of linear famine, demeaned in diagonal lassitude, its powers then held in erratic reserve.

Being unspoiled by continuous attrition I am Seminole by the very fire in my resistance. The soil that I utter is mixed with abrasive conquest, with letters which perspire and float as ballistical danger. So listening to my voice is akin to having a response to a compound diacoustics arising from helical pressure. Not a naïve appraisal, but absorption of ebullience as psychic diaphaneity. I've heard Zomaya on occasion comment on the fact of the lack of my exhaustion, of my ability to confound her expectation of the hellish. To her, I am like a holdout in the Everglades. Someone from whom all has been taken, yet I continue to persist, to embrangle expectation. I am not a petitioner at conventional heavenly gates. One who seeks the habits of energies which hail from consensus prerogative. She knows Rosanna does not seek divinity. Rosanna does not seek the open help of God's practitioners on Earth. I simply sit here and I convey. In myself I feel as if I were the founder of Dodona. I who have hailed from Thebes, who has sailed with Phoenicians, who has known the cartographic realms as spiritualized adventure.

As for the New World, my mind is set and constantly Seminole in demeanour. As to origins I telepathically understand the Nubian power at La Venta, understanding in my mind its animated rocks and ciphers. Saying this, does my body participate in palpable archaeology? Does my form persist as someone from La Venta? No, I'm speaking as the eruptive inner body as alive as one with the universal instant. I am not simply Ute or Comanche. I am ambling on a land bridge to silence. Because of this I understand the root of sound as an alphabetic treatise. The sound which empowers delivery. Perhaps I am the ghost who burns as inspirational Wolof. Perhaps this accounts for the music which suddenly fills me with aptness, which makes my tongue ignite with instigation. Certainly I have nothing in common with Germanic truncation, with its contiguous locations which work to my understanding as coarsened bulletins or graphs. So do I speak in code through isolate paraffin mirrors?

Am I the one who sifts her voice through rabid neurologies? Is this why I so relate to various chiropteran? True, I gather light from constant echolocation.

In the case of someone like Zomaya I now posses a transpersonal depth over and beyond her individual wrath so that I understand the language of forces. For instance, my dossier on Esteban seems less deep but no less complex. My dealings with him have carried a standard threatening, but his depth has gone no farther than the arousal of my body. As for Oraculos the realia is more consuming. He lurks, to him I exist as the double image of the wife. So for Zomaya there exists for her an extra sum of bitterness in that she competes with me for the powers of Oraculos. Of course this is no secret. As for Jesus he poses no condition or worry. Yet I know in my heart that the situation is never left to itself. There is always tension, there is always the current of struggle. This is the source of my deafness during daylight. To indicate the furtive, to escape from preconception. Thus, I take on a voided exegetics. This is why I can extract from seeming lassitude, the powers of silt, and fire, and danger. Natural occurrences. This being qualitatively different from slavish uneven abrasion. In the latter instance I am speaking of a limited physical buttress, in the former I'm speaking of fumes. Because I echolocate with alacrity and depth I am able to work with the subconscious ethers letting me know the pervasive element which convenes in both objects and persons. Is Rosanna a vampire? Is Rosanna the pervasive simulacra of evil? To me, these are questions which arise from a standard mental conception. A mental conception which treasures breakage and isolation, which treasures dissonance and combinations of dissonance, because there always is fear. For instance, Zomaya always sought reduction of the universe in terms of her own human model. She always sought the conscious perspective in even her most irrational of deeds. This is why she's now breaking. To her, I pre-figure the level of alien constellations, those constellations where beings occur, but unimaginable to present sense location. A contrived alien in a space craft creates for her more familiarity than me. I am leaning more to the unimaginable, leaning more to the light year, to the inter-dimensional body. For instance, during daylight I spontaneously roam the heavens. I know that extra-dimensional proclivity exists. I am not looking for beings with a certain type of body, for eyes, for fins, for familiarized minutia. No, I'm understanding the fumes from all the elements, understanding at root the bizarre as trans-adjustment. So on one level when I go deaf to Zomaya I am deaf to Zomaya, but on the superior plane I roam, I go to a plane which no longer embodies kindling. I say this because my body temperature floats, the senses seep into transmigration, and then I suddenly feel the presence of a plane with two suns, sensing sounds, which are octaves over and beyond the sistrum.

This is the reason that I eat at dusk. I fall back into this dimension not as some type of wiring keyed to precise moments, but as is said in history, say, as circa 1255 B.C., or circa 171 A.D. I always return to the physical as organic seepage, always returning to these surroundings before the Sun's last rays have depleted. In this regard Ornelas remains my clock with my halibut and lentils always ready for consumption. She knows from observation that I re-populate my body never beyond the cusp of darkness. Thus, she understands my total awareness. That is why she always protected me from accusations of coma, that I was sick, and was disposable due to illness. She continues not to defer to Sister Charlotte, and any other of the whisperers who chatter concerning my blankness during day. And because the situation remains so oblique Zomaya has been forced to contend with the situation as is. So when Devota or any of the other nuns seeks specifics Ornelas defuses the damage by implying possibilities which erase the initial interest. Which allows me to migrate day after day as if a daunting light year distance has no power to impede me. As to contact, perhaps a moon or two in the Sombrero Galaxy, perhaps a Sun with an emptied spiral which spins in Eridanus. Thus, I'm always appraised by darkness, with its diaphanous boundaries as my subconscious lair. This lair which contains, Octans, Hydrus, and Circinus, being for me, an axial state on a trans-physical plane. Because I echolocate without schism I speak at times as though I were sighted. Let me say, it is the grasp beyond the sighted, it is the smell of moons which blazes inside my mane, So that I am a zebra with an owl hovering inside my fingers. This is how I see, this is how I weave deformity into echoes. Not an interval of retrogression, but a leakage of fever from a raped blind girl with the dissonance seething from her seedless amputee's delivery. For now, all I can do is to speak into this corpse of tape and murmur with each of my fabulous verbal claws, milking from the flow of thought unending germination. I've learned from sea quakes, from phonemes, from roving heliograms. Therefore, to justify oblivion, to haunt myself with justifiable arabesque, is no longer delivery, is no longer a beacon by which the cells are transmitted through the mind as a pointless transitory vacuum.

What I say is organic. I sit here. I hone my synoptic diphthongs on an insular cooking grate. And this cooking, burns away, microbe by microbe, all conscious voluntary movement, thereby looking with amaurotic eyes, understanding the sound from wingless saffron herrings. I call water and blindness flow from the primeval ozone. It is a flow which is taciturn, which counters the practical grasp with eclectic nightmare pillage. Of course such flow can neither be counted nor measured. For the profane, they can go no farther that what they perceive as a riddle. For the profane, the riddle is no more than the transposition of the known. They are incapable of understanding the monstrous energies of stupefaction. So, for them, I am no longer of the quantified, I am the ghost who embodies the nebulous, much like trying to describe to those immured in professions what the feeling would be when describing to themselves an avalanche of suns. First of all, the detail can no longer dominate the feeling of the general view. Of course there must be current in the thinking, there must be alive in the person a nascence of lava. In contra-distinction the professions are dishonour, they are distractions, they exist as psychic ganglia in the breathing. In this regard, Zomaya and Ornelas exist as critical sub-groups. Sub-groups in the sense that they've taken on tones of the exotic. For Ornelas, it is the gift of life which burns in heaven. And for Zomaya, the darker forces give her strength, which has allowed her passage to myself as the kindling which consumes her contorted dross. For either party there exists no assumption of normalcy. No, none of the conventional demeanours which condense themselves in rhetoric understood through every nuance as being through and through pro forma. I must admit that they are odd. Both bound to vigilance, one contained in attempts at the upper kingdom, the other, swimming in a fire, far below the soils. Of course Ornelas as the former, and Zomaya, as queen of the igneous. Thus, I live between them as curious report, as instantaneous construct subject to both assault and protection. Yes, I am buffeted, not by their direct involvement, but by the residue which stirs amongst them. It is like feeling my form condensed in a hatchery of smoke. To me, I exist to them as a misreading of proteins. And this is good to the degree that I escape the both of them, I escape the tendencies they exude concerning goodness and error. At bottom, both exist for a carnivorous simplicity, for an overall realia evenly divided concerning the apartheid of eternity. For them, the body remains the pressure of the one snapped needle, of the singular apastron charted to exhaustion. Yet for me, there is always the complexity of rising, with its insurrectional force, with its indeterminate apperception, and you have more than the apathetic, you have life which exudes while self-determining new fever. Of course, this is the thrill of the intervallic, the leap beyond the garment of the bell throwers' wool. Which means I am problematic, estranged, unassembled as to gravity as it occurs in typical aging. Not that I seek to remain Rosanna at this acme of living; at this cusp of catharsis. To the sighted none can say that my bones are always green, or that my eye-light is velvet. I am not speaking to attend the minor substance contained in miracles. The latter are merely the concerns of those deluded by the psychic colony of the profane. This is why I do not conclude upon Zomaya or Ornelas as being the elect of the profane. They exist for me at another leaning, at another remove, a step outside conformity. This is why I soar from a plinth. This is why I learn from lessons that inspire me, which seep from zones proto to tremendums. These are my animal tracings which wander, which take leave of the ordinary background. I am no longer heiress to chronic anaemia, and I mean by chronic anaemia the path which condones malaise, which sunders the steps of my enigmatic zeal. Thus, I am now beholden to no one. My path shifts, and dives, and anomalates, I am the chronicle that can't be known. I remain Rosanna, the sensibility who cannot be read. I say this not because I am the voice in the special hamlet, clarified by moaning bibliographies, or by special sorceries condensed inside a hand wrought Braille. This can be said because I am no longer intrigued by European desolation. Their canons of dearth, their reportage of pain, have long ago ceased to invent me. This is what removes me from Zomaya and Ornelas. They are consumed by historic prevarication. And what I mean by historic prevarication is that the idol that they cry to has never turned his face, nor walked upon Earth. The saviour, as I'll state on other occasions, has never existed, and remains always an inflammation of absence. So to clarify this boldness I'll only venture the name of Flavius Josephus, whose account of the saviour is minimally broached in his Testimonium Flavianum, yet his testament has never been appended by any other authority which has examined the ancient psyche. No other historicity of Jesus abounds. His life is never listed, no direct account ever tinctures his appellation. No other accounts of Jesus abounds. I know this as savant; and because I know this as savant I hold it like heat in my athanor, private, enthralling, insubordinate, obliquitous. And as I hold this notion I rise, not through the intake of demons, but as she, who fully resonates with living.

What seems to persist is the irony of the deluded. Of all the supplicants who have fallen inside mirrors. They are consumed with a saviour who thrives on ruination.

Who demands from believers belief in a history which has never transpired. But again, a saviour who has emitted the proposition that he is a mystic singularity. That he ignites the living figure according to the current, evolved from his central attrition. Yet, what seems of most interest to me are remnants of this attrition such as Ornelas and Zomaya. They are electrocuted, yes, but electrocutions who ambulate, who transmit signals, who are prone to random designs. I feel their curious paralysis in my inner canals of hearing due to elements which open my cells to arcane audition. They do not suffer so much as ignominious embodiments, but as Myrmidons, as obstructed eaglets condemned to carking strides across soil. In contrast, I feel Nepalese and winged, siphoned from a magic interior soil. I am that tenor of being who leaps beyond a nervous encyclical of wind. As if I have been summoned by invisible mongoose scribes allowing me life beyond the wretched assignation known by Zomaya as Rosanna.

To Zomaya I seem as wrecked cartography. So on one level she takes this understanding to be a totally convinced realia. But on a subsequent level she breathes as someone lessened. She understands that my living haunts her, and more than just my living, it is the way I linger, the way that my silence performs, the way the ghosts come forth from my pores. I am not thinking of mechanical powers funnelled through this world, or as some imprint of Christ conducting the affairs of heaven in a conservationist's enclave, holding up ironic infernos, promulgating the carpenter of Galilee as the one true mean. Even if I could issue particulars from the Ambrosian Rite, or speak from the point of view of the Carthusians or Carmelites, Zomaya could never acknowledge the implications of my listening. Because I am capable of listening at a more exact rapidity than nascent wind storms on Neptune. Yet, it is not the physicality of my eeriness, but that which seeps through hesitation. So to her, I am that irregular Sun, that solar metamorphic which rises from cells which condense in the inspecific.

If I were merely a biography filled with grotesqueries, with acts suffused with perfectly chronicled ammonias, it would be a world which exists for her within attempted grasp. But my chemistry remains of some other order, of some other stripe, where curious forms are formed. According to consensus visible authority it is known that I am known, yet I exist in some degree only by Zomaya's word, that I am her code at St. Catherine's. So in terms of this fact, I am presence, I am she who inculcates witness, who hovers as a victim, who suffers from the weight of her dishonoured truth.

According to lawful writ I have not surfaced as a being, so I know for a fact that Zomaya extends weekly defrayment for my stay. There is never any written transaction, basic cash is always in play. So not only does St. Catherine's benefit, but the nuns closest to me receive a private financial staple. Yet within this arrangement Sister Ornelas refuses any breach or revelation of anything I privately proclaim. After I've spoken she simply stores the tapes a moment or two beyond dawn. She removes the tape from the recorder making certain that I hear the strong box click. I understand that nothing is certain, that without effort she could conspire with Sister Devota to enunciate my ramblings to Zomaya. But inside the intuitive of my intuitive I feel absolved of any betrayal, so that night after night I remain this curious witness of pleromas. Saying such, I am not proclaiming myself as consummate, as singeing the flesh around me with lightning. I am not a stabilized proclamation, a concretized adumbration from which laws and encyclicals appear. This is what keeps Sister Ornelas off balance. She hesitates, her voice at times wavers about with vertigo, knowing somehow that a force has been encountered over and beyond her conscious thoughts about judgement. And it is this force which continues to ransack Zomaya, which throws her into to an occulted breech. Not an occult as described by someone the ilk of Pope Honorius, with his criminal conjurations, but an occult which rises above a lapidary being skilled at conjuring voices from old lanterns. Such, is none of my concerns. I possess no crendentia via sorcery, no proof which extends from its umbilical designation. I am not a life which accrues its accretion from chaotic loam. Again, I am not the blind sister of death who digs up elements and imbues them with suggestion. Here I speak with no malice aforethought, or to the blithesomeness I've seemingly lost. Yet I do not superficially seek revenge by becoming a psychic chiropteran, or in another key becoming a blood thirsty eaglet suddenly kept aloft by semaphores of ruin. No, I've become chiropteran because I've evolved to the level of echolocation. I hear a response from random worlds and suddenly map them according to sounds which respire at the cusp between the possible and the impossible. Do I divvy up insouciance simply to give to my rivals a comatose impediment?

Do I divulge to someone like Sister Devota duplicitous rudiments of despair?

The answer to both of the above would lean certainly towards infection. And what do I mean by infection? A current which burns inside the ears of my receptors so that it leans towards exported decimation. And this export does not pertain to an exact physical configuration, but only to the way my mind is leaning which generates a momentary fate on he or she who receives my intentions. So, yes, someone like Devota would yield to the fibre of my energy, which then confronts her latent schisms causing her to feel an unequal pressure which threatens the very core of her belief. As to Zomaya and her axis I know she is riddled and now carries in her carcass a stunning instability. I understand myself as this carking, de-energizing oscillation which takes into account the previously discussed off-centeredness and balance.

So I am at that cusp which trans-emulates absence. Which understands as its realm acts no longer replete with gravitational pallor. Which exists over and beyond the dialectics of law. Because law for me is a riven culpability. It is an arbitrary confrontment in one era condoning one behaviour, in another era, in staunch support of its opposite. Law as I understand it is the ultimate conformity. It is a region I never implicate in my spirit. I do not say this as a self serving rudiment, or as a culpable psychological ornament.

Because I understand starkness knowing origination as I do, filled as it is with pre-Cambrian meteoritics.

Therefore I know how the central nervous system speaks. I know its ventriloquial range, its simulacra as cunning. I, who could be formally ensconced in its treacherous scruples, in its impossible culpability, am not signalling triumph, nor lording my energy over the human vicinity. No, but there is a refinement which partakes of issues higher than the fate of bodies, prone in frozen juniper graves. It is communion with energies which seem to eat my very livingness away. On a gross level one can mentally point to Zomaya, to the stasis which enthrals the Beatitudes. But let me burrow a bit deeper. Why does one roam inside the body like a dishevelled beast inside skin? Why is thought a baffling cortical war? These remain as curious self-interrogations, pointless properties or edicts.

True, on this night I have lost all contact with the human domain. In this instance the human domain being the nervous system and its relics, contained as it is by stunted mental conservations. So, of all the species that have ever respired, am I, Rosanna, holding myself up as model, holding myself above all the prior millennia of being? So it can be asked if I am secretly modelling myself on Zomaya, thereby speaking to myself so as to further my circumstantial prowess and conquer the invisible?

According to certain thinkers I could be taken for a magician who has cunningly left the tribe so as to venture no farther than a glyph of new instruction. It could be said that I carry entangled codes mingled by various pronations of magic. But it is something beyond this. The Sun roars, and I hear its watery transpositions, feeding me a necessitous type of blankness allowing access to other levels of fluidity. In the midst of transition I'm beginning to understand its principle oscillations concerning the vapours which govern at the human barrier. These are vapours simultaneous with devolution, with keeping me placed as Zomaya's winsome wretch, condemned to a zone of Catholic disregard.

In contradistinction to hindering consensus, my body has ceased to be habitual, has ceased to lean on old impulse as a means for its survival. But it can be asked, what of my penchant for intercourse, what of my habitual seasoning by sperm? Is it something which is now latent, in seed, ready to spring into being as a jeopardous Messalina? I can say, not only am I drained but I have left such summations in the wake of my prior era. Not as some saint, or some ghostly declamatory gryphon, but as an energy, liminal, somewhere known, but beyond itself as known. I cannot call this a feverish beginning of God, or a new heptapic medium or gesture. All I know is that I feed like a Sun from mysteriums. My body always instigating a proto-locale. This may be the reason why not a droplet of sperm was able to entrap me. Why no bond was made, why none of the powers coalesced according to human pre-engenderment. If even the brutish Jesus could never impregnate, it is because of my advancement over and beyond the biology as dictation.

So am I saying that I'll never die, that Rosanna is the figment that over-extends and outlives the void? There exists no answer that I can give given the principle terminologies that the Northern races invoke, concerning death with its attendant fragmentations. There exists in this latter state the severity of doubt, the disenchanted in-flux always with lack, and the limits of biography in the margins of lack. This remains the re-enforced tenor, with its eclectic ions primed by cruel incessant hallucinatory motifs. Yet always for me, the sense of psychic hatchlings, the infinite lightnings which rove inside the cells. I mean by this that I provoke the energy which roams between beast and gulf. The latter being Zomaya and the Church, and the energy which I extend as gulf. Not analogy delimited to the eeriness of the Oort dimension, but those planes of life where dialectics remains suspended. Thus I live by telepathic scruple, by the disentangled vapours derived from burning hellebore cuisines.

True, I've not been protected by damage in the sense that the damage done to me no longer bears approximation to consensus understanding as physical registration. And what I mean by consensus is measurable suffering through physicality. As if only the psychophysiology were the sole concussive referent. So in no way can I be gleaned as figment moving through the ad-infinitum. Because I am of incremental burnings, simultaneously basking in the intolerable, with my aurum spinning as the beauty of dismay. Again, it is asked how have I not merged with the in-substantial, how have I not been lost in the fire of my own centrioles? Maybe this is why I give off the sensation of hovering. Maybe this is why I emit a viral spinning from my eyes.

Sister Ornelas has acknowledged that my countenance turns feral when I whisper in the dark. That my eyes glow, that the shadows from the blinds cast stripes across my torso.

Perhaps she is witness to a post-mortem banquet of doubles. Perhaps my body is this vehicular dialectic, this brooding dyslexia, this disfigured muscatel. That I give off this double transparency it is because I am a seldom seen spore from a nursery of disruptive comets. My breathing then being clandestine as sigil, humming in key as pointless plastique and tornado.

As for now, I possess no ophthalmic jealousy, no feelings of betrayal from my poisoned tundra of eggs. One can never accuse me of anaemia, or withered on a plain as a disintegrated dwarf oak. Because of this I am more anomalous than any rarity of beast, be it the Dales Pony in Britain, or the Sicilian Girgentana goat.

Further, I have listened to myself and taken each aural figment and multiplied its heresies allowing me to trace an emotional archaeology. Not a prone and didactic mysticism, but an eglantine charisma no longer ensconced in dysfunctional worry. As to the quantity of what my doubt will be it will contract around the essence of guilt and how its sums can be explored. But none of this besets me. This is why Zomaya cannot condone herself about me, lingering with complacency. She knows my psychic property has vanished and nothing now of me exists as in those former moments where she purposely planned and decided.

I've fed myself on human withdrawal. I've worked on ghostly battlefield motives through curious or unexplained synergies. This communes to Zomaya my arcane resurrection. This, of course is not quotidian resurrection. It is something round about, circuitous, which lives without title. Being bereft of monarchical induction I now exist to Zomaya as something condensed from scriptless witches bane. I say something because now I appear to her as energy almost interstellar in remoteness. For it is a remoteness which condemns her, which rushes in on her like compounded sonar. I'm now sending out inverse energies and rhythms so much so that light is altered and the recipients become unmoored from their parent personalities so that everything differs and circles in the mind. No, I've not rooted my powers in henbane and skulls, and circled a basket of serpents in my sleep. This is not a list from my inferno, or minerals akin to occult divination. I am no longer concerned with seeming limits of the body and its stark electrical reduction.

Not concerned with belief, in old vapour, yet I'm surrounded by belief in old vapour. The tendencies and the motives of old tendencies keeping the psycho-biology replete with repression. Yet I now exist on this plane as a powerful combinatory infant. I feel the cells shedding themselves of the lightning of death. I feel newly evolved dictation which stammers in my body of thinking. Which utters like a radius of excitement. Not the talons bewitched by enforced discovery, but the voice which empowers dense originatory rooms. And these rooms are not palpably embodied, but exist as structure accrued from eclectic humming. And this source of humming ensues from some unknown point vertically engendered, being a spark of light travelling groundward.

This groundward conduction I call Rosanna, no longer sought by myself as the subject of Rosanna. What consciously obtrudes Zomaya is residue from Rosanna who no longer lives within the old human borders. What intensifies itself to her is Rosanna as law and branches of law, as accusatory specimen, capable at one briefing of condemning her to long incarceration, or to characterilogical execution. When I withdraw during hours of the day, I am not only transcending Zomaya and the modes of St. Catherine's, but I am broaching an interregnum where living extends the biology to more than a fleeting example.

Am I saying that I'll exist as this Rosanna beyond countable time, consciously knowing that the Sun will expand with the weather on Titan being akin to the present waves off the Comoro Islands? Again, I'll stress the gulf of the interregnum, with its blinded insubstantials, with its transmutative geometrical evolutics.

Breathing at a stark recuperative angle I prevail on new zodiacs, joined as I am to a life beyond emptiness.

A typical believer would say that I've fallen into treason, that I'm chronic with puzzling, that I pose to them a bewildering agonistic. This is why Zomaya and Ornelas are odd. They swear by the Christos but by other means. We know that Zomaya can circumvent one's mental traces, witness the spellbound dementias of the brutes. Jesus, who continues to mimic stunting, Esteban, with his middling paranoia, Oraculos, with his enciphered saliva. On the other hand, Ornelas, perhaps taking her tact from bereavement, having to adjust like St. Rita to loss, after loss, after loss.

The death of two sons to addiction, combined with threatening spousal activity, has unleashed into longing for private ascent. Like St. Rita, she has withstood galling misfortune. So she has turned the brutality of chance into startling methodologies of prayer. This is why she understands the dynamic which exists between Zomaya and my person. She understands the circuitous insurrection which blazes in the morning of lives. She understands the contradictions that linger, the bitterness which discomforts the very soil in one's schisms.

In this sense Ornelas understands me, in this sense we breathe and confirm ourselves by telepathy. I do speak at times and I've spoken to her on random occasion and learned about her implicates, about her intuitive traceries. Her former spouse, imprisoned due to use of criminal substances, and two sons dead because of use of these substances. Yet we are not co-equals only in the sense that we are not co-equals. She delivers up her sorrows to unilateral authority. She subscribes to the singular mission of the Christos even in the light of divergent description in the Gospels. Christ for her is a plinth from which she attempts to soar in heavenly triumph. As for me, she somehow knows that we differ, me, having garnered no relief from unimpeded prayer. Me, knowing that Zomaya remains empowered to habitually engender her poison. Even Christ admits that God has failed him on the cross.

This is something I intuited even as Zomaya's little hijuela. I've heard pageantry, I've smelled incense burning, I'm reminded in Mass of commandments and behaviour. Yet I know and continue to know that the latter remains of no value, is powerless, and only emits a provisional magnetics so as to control a contingent of adherents. So if I remain a ghost to myself, if I am a power that even Rosanna does not know, how can the Christos contend with private persona? How can he feel the gargantuan misnomer of one's failed and personal riddles? As though I were static and strategised as sinner. As though I were a consumed and consuming anecdote; condemned as a gulf of dazed believers longing after the stunning blood loss on Golgotha. This is where I'm non co-equal with Ornelas. She in this sense remains the suffocated matron, the unexplored census struggling with the issue which equates with curious bodily salvation. Yet she intuits the damage which glows from my root, she understands the broken elements which sometimes taints my aura. But I understand somehow the meaning of the cells and the soma which pour forth from their cleansing. I am not filled with stories, with ultra-resurrections, with foments which instil a penchant for inner behavioural limit. Because of this I cannot be controlled. I cannot be summoned by words which signal transcendental mausoleums. Instead I speak of the beauty of intrinsic amalgams. But even so I remain haunted, and this is where I convene with

Ornelas at this level of tactical haunting. We tacitly understand suffusion by abandonment. Always knowing that a menacing registration is always circling about one. It's like smelling fumes of cholera from a hallway. But I can truly say that I am no longer an animal aligned with signals which feast upon relapse. Because by condoning belief I am condoning in myself stasis, after stasis, after stasis, in someone reckless with potentia. Even as a frail girl baby Zomaya understood that I was a being fraught with listening. To her, blindness condoned my sense of election. This awareness threatened her and she responded with equational cruelty. Thus, she was stamped by circumstantial jealousy. She created a behavioural mean by instilling suffocation. Because I now contend that my pre-existing was tainted by her stark emotional poison creating the blurred geometry in my eyes. And for this taint I must go back and telepathically consult the ashes of Catalina. Because I understand in my way how flawed genetic transmission equates with chaos in the morals. From what I understand, Edmundo and Catalina were conclusive with greed. Not as spend thrifts, not as new immigrants looking for status, but as beings pathological with method. True, I say this as would a proto-medium, flawed as regards certain particulars. As for Catalina, she was born in San Fidel, and Edmundo arose in New Laguna. They came to light in Santa Fe. To escape his Acoma laden enclave my voice tells me that Edmundo, at the beginning of manhood adapted the surname Galvez. That he aligned himself with the feral heritage of conquistadors. This became the core of his centripetal foundation.

Guess work on my part?

Aural mirage?

From what I gather Edmundo began as a lowly copper miner, somehow rising to the position of an unsparing foreman in the Santa Rosa region. Through ironical events he gained enough largesse to advance to premature retirement. As the offspring evolved it was felt by Catalina that no one would profit from the appearance of the males. The social body as it stood would prevent them from appearing. Thus, the myth began of Zomaya as the only offspring. Zomaya at Spanish social events, Zomaya at the Festival of Our Lady of the Rosary. I know that Edmundo was part of Los Caballeros de Vargas that would travel to Santa Fe to take part in the "Proclamacion y ordinanza Civico Religiosa" always with Zomaya in tow.

Because of their rising status they re-orchestrated their roles as Spaniards, as old inhabitants of New Spain. I suspect that they convinced themselves of being the latter hoping to quell the sums of Indian in their blood. And Zomaya, knowing that lies abounded in her make up began sprouting shoots of treason from her heart. She observed in this Spanish milieu, plays by Juan de Onate, such as Adam and Eve, or the Allegory of the Magi, events and spectacles which did nothing but twist her. Having consulted the ashes of Catalina, I know that at points in the process Zomaya was more than a daughter to Catalina. Add to this the nefarious desires of Edmundo, which inflamed the aberration.

But to the world they always carried a sense of moral worth. Catalina was always extended invitation to spotless meriendas, where afternoons were consumed over discreet cups of tea. And I know that Catalina wore shawls and mantillas in the spirit of Alicia Romero, or Josefina Ortega. This was the La Sociodad Folkloristica, of which later on Zomaya became a part. And never during the midst of these times were the names of the brothers broached. Their existence always dissolved when the three of them stepped into the Sun. In this sense they were typical, always hiding themselves, trenchantly portraying themselves as taintless, as being perfect as La Conquistadora.

So when Edmundo and Catalina passed away within weeks of one another, Zomaya carefully plotted separate cremations, and somehow held a brief memorial for the both of them somehow keeping the community neutralized concerning the deeper state of things. In the midst of this turmoil she was riotous with secrecy. Thus, she held volcanoes in her boundaries. Stating in both cases an unknown cause of death. Because the public only saw the family in sketches, there was never any probing as to the type of death which befell them. As far as my intuitives tell me, their deaths were alcoholic. As far as I can tell Zomaya imbibed brandy while both the mother and the father possessed her. And yes, the secrecy must have scorched Edmundo and Catalina, given that they were triplicate in befoulment, not only hiding their incest, but also the births of Oraculos, and Esteban, and Jesus, as well as the source of their old Acoma roots. By keeping their appearances oblique they moved as porcelain through the atmosphere. Catalina has responded to me about these facts, as she has sent hieroglyphic shivers across my skin. Of course, as I've stated, I am proto-mediumistic, understanding Edmundo through the ghostly promptings of Catalina. And because I understand him, I feel the fumes of their onslaught through the curious desires and deletions of Zomaya. I hear in their feelings a rhapsodized spasmodics.

This is what I'll call the biography of debris. Or, in a more tumultuous key, philosophical arson. Do I say this from the safety of distance seemingly absolved of territorial decay? Or have I secretly prayed to St. Dominic concerning the turns and balances which rivet my fate. No, I cling to no buffer, I claim no collaboration with belief in intercessors, with no thoughts or series of thoughts which subverts my own powers, which carries me into those technical machinations which void any suggestion of imminence.

Diary As Sin

I am thus condemned to playing with the repartee of shadows. Let me mention a whole trove of intercessors. St. Felicitas for barren women, St. Odilia for the blind, Our Lady of Lourdes for bodily ills. I could speak of Saints for butchers, for coopers, for layers of brick; for those who harvest milk. I could invoke St. Gregory of Neocaesarea concerning desperate circumstance.

The list could be interminable, but I, as Rosanna, have made migration beyond the zodiac. I am no longer trapped by the four originating signs as they originate in time. I have risen outside of circumstance living as I am beyond convulsive crises.

Listening to myself through my mental smouldering lens, I no longer threaten myself, I no longer give myself failure to demoralize my essence, stumbling over afterthoughts, so as to announce to some associate my allegiance to mediocrity.

What would I be conforming to, someone whose spirit is mimicked in Esteban, who seeks to please by over indulgence so as to staunch the conundrum at the core of existing. I do not say this from thought, as expressive hubris. I have no need for hubris, always alerted to the condition of my lulls and distempers. That I sometimes animate ruses I know this to be something over and beyond simple suggestion. Because there is no such thing as abstract perfection, no perfect integer of goodness which someone can quantify and weigh in one's hands. So knowing what I know all the Saints seem quantified by pressure. It seems they bless the rigours of servitude so as to condone all power which erupts from upper authority. This amounts to nothing more than theological abstraction, nothing more than strategies which enact formulaic salvation.

But who is saved and what enacts salvation? Can I call this samsara, or dialectic as samsara? Let me synthesize these notions. There exists subordinates and control of these subordinates with the stabilizing notion being fear. For instance, if I reach through my body to probe relentless motions on Neptune how do the narratives from Judea equate? How do tangential commandments apply to someone so far removed from the Sun?

So am I bluntly stating the impossible? Do I imply the body as a structure of neutrinos?

Maybe I'm structuring flames through the unknowable. Maybe I'm over-claiming the body creating in my mind a reality which lives through carking simulation.

By saying such, am I committing papal technocracy to other planets where life cannot conform to heresy, or belief in localized confinement?

I would have to reply in the affirmative. It claims that its power is overarching and I am holding it to its claim. This being the nuncio which presides over gamma radiation. And this is not said in concert with limits surrounding my continuing agitation. There can be no literal victory concerning the self through human transience, and I mean by this transience declared from a regional point of view. There can be no regional infinity.

What I'm saying is that the impossible is vociferously claimed. The governance of the entire cosmos is claimed from a holding grate in Judea. From this I gather that the nuncio strategises stone on Eumonia. Or orchestrates the systemic winds stretching across Saturn. And these are locales local in dimension. What of the biocosmology in stars a billion light years removed, north-northeast of the equinox?

I am not speaking of sealed portions of the cosmos where a single mass operates as belief. I am not suggesting that every hyper-extended nuance of breathing take its lead from any fixation I may seek to imply. Yet I'm not seeking a stabilized mechanics which shifts perfection to perfection removed from different levels of exhaustion, which results in glorified abstention from the circumstantial panic which abounds in the human enclave.

What then is error, what power poses threats to the tenacious quality of the species?

According to papal policy the uppermost remains carnal exercise of the body, remains fallacious adherence to the body as virginic identity. Of course this is a frequency which opens itself to dogma, to lines of thought which equate with constant displeasure. This does not constitute rigour as vivification, as rhythm which eats through self-disgust.

Instead, the body glances against itself, monitors itself as offending carnal function. This is what I'll announce as intensive carnivorisation, being the function of self-fate by that which cloaks its own power in the ruse of sterility. A nativity which consumes its own abstraction. A nativity which lisps, which has no ability to scorch or transform, which advances on believers the reasoning for self-withdrawal.

Despite excess and sorrow, all that I have known has been culled from withdrawal. And all those about me have been smitten with intangible dismay. I am not saying that I, Rosanna, have become guide to the human species, that I have taken on successive mentation so that the species has settled upon my birth date as upon some altitudinous fever, giving me deference which fuels a daunting celebration. Rosanna, fused by Cyprian metals at birth, arisen from a turbulent thesis of waters, then crucified on defunctive summits, so as to rise and haunt the populace with annulments.

This is not to wallow in destructive ambrosia. I have never increased my name as savage or idolater, or turned to higher origin only to decrease its vigour, according to the stamp of my geography or my manger. Instead, I am a circumstantial noun, a Bedouin who lives southward in her mind. I am not secular in disserve, I am not a gramme to be weighed, to be cradled as dogmatic map so as to suddenly soar as the source of celestial governance.

This is not the pressure or substance of God. Nor is it the pressure of the common mean, tantamount as it is to amount as raw finality. Not as boundary, or tumultuous coping with boundary. True, I've suffered from this double stricture of chaos, and coping with the energy of chaos. So at such clamorous juncture the nerves inflame, sounds seem to beckon with terms not unlike human suicide as a mean. This is how a leper constructs a psychic background, this is how the Sun declines inside one's system. Energy drops, and methodologies build and become a brazen kind of compost. One then ambles around as a carking non-persona. As someone speaking according to the unsustained as slippage. It is like adding up sums from an inconsequent mongrel language. When the lettering in one's mind concludes in schism, then the mind conclusively ciphers, and logistics concludes as devastating breakage. And when the meta-dimension commingles with this breakage one can only be factored by what the mathematicians call X, the ingredient which can never know its substance even as it concludes within its own combining. It remains proof by elusive integer, by carapace which excludes by unordered emphatics. Because motion remains trapped the identity that one feels is haunted by a nettling kind of gravitas. Thus, all the implicates vanish at the mouth of the unstratified. The mind then rattles in one position. It becomes the brutality of one affair. What follows is a neurology which commands by deficit. The mind becomes symbolic as homunculus, deafening its own range so as to attempt a pointless replication of itself. Nothing of this sort carries creative octaves. There exists nothing but various tenors of baseness. And because I understand these challenged levels, I am always buffeted by what I consider to be their saturnian criminality, provoking constant thirst in the heart, by plaguing my spirit with repetitive infernos.

But this is how I reveal myself to myself, knowing that I've blindly broken through the old saturnian window of sand, that I've taken away its powers, its seepage being diminished to such a degree, that I am able to feel those instantaneous settlements which have escaped entrapment of quotidian mental derangement. Because these instantaneous settlements are like beings inside my person who have escaped limitations which have sought to work inside the spirit of that aforementioned baseness. Such beings to me are signals, are motions which reveal themselves beyond gravitas, which ignite inch by sub-dominate inch, no matter my locale, be it Mauritius, or Papua New Guinea; what I can say is that I know that these spirits exist, I know that they channel flames from afflatus, from divine inspiration, far above the ravenous majority.

Again, I call this the baleful majority, those who burn with in-lit cholera by inference. For them, fractious gain by lucre, by general demonizing tactic. This being Zomaya, always cornered by stipends, always seeking to deceive and create monsters. She called us the Myrmidons, those whose condition amounted to no more than asps who bowed before royalty. As if she erupted from some underground inferno divvying up gains from exotic llamas and goats, bribing Gods by means of deceptive exchange. But in terms of the quotidian, Edmundo's lucrative windfall from copper created momentous advantage for Zomaya to play Empress with not the slightest bit of struggle. There was never any fear concerning raiment or shelter. In fact, there was always a copious amount of shelter. The hacienda, from what I've been told, hidden behind a glossolalia of greenery, providing the necessitous secrecy for the family to roam in and out of its ill-begotten deeds. She ruled this delimited vacuum with a dissonant fuel which now has began to subtend her powers. What I can say is that the hacienda remains gnawed by the potentia of my utterance, somehow spilling fire in the gardens, always threatening Zomaya with complaints from authorities.

True, I've gained power from the threats that I hold in my heart, yet what enkindles me most is the zone of interregnums; darkness, blind outcome, wavering, panic, psychic shifts from the future. Because, as invisible chiropteran I navigate my own stillness. It remains this difficult decrescendo, this curious flight away from burning. For me, it remains a stunning complexification, a pulling, a simultaneous spinning where no nostalgia exists, where the gravitas of damage is subsumed in this perilous psychic crossing, turbulent with concrete threat from assault, or a gossip which engenders susurrant low grade assault. Believe me, Zomaya is capable of this double harassment, perhaps physically attacking me in the dark, or whispering morsels of poison in the ear of Sister Ornelas, or fostering a general doubt in the mind of Sister Devota.

The question arises, when does one know when the Divine obscures its own lessons and becomes fully natural in the body? I say, it is like having sound flit through the cells like intangible violas. Yet being in the gulf of interregnums the void is mixed with its power, with any higher culmination seeming brief. If I am dazed it is because the interregnum has been a life long substrate. The body then becomes a hallucinatory substrate. So I can never be certain whether my moments will advance or retreat. It seems as if I'm soaked by failure as vocable by uncertainty. My physicality then gasps and restores its uncertainty through doubt. And what I mean by restoration is consensus solidity through basic touch and breathing. Such reality conforms to body type or size, or likes or dislikes, according to type of diet, or pattern of diet. Then there exists the photography of the skin, be it melanin based or xanthochroid, male or female according to chromosomes. Then after this the great lists appear according to principles of exclusion. Of what pigment casts the greatest social damnation. This was the reasoning of Vargas, to cast a spell so that a Spanish name casts a psychic registration, which in turn creates a xanthochroid registration. Thus the name Galvez, Edmundo Galvez, Catalina Galvez. Catalina always approved of this method which allowed her to move through the ranks of La Sociedad Folkloristica. As for me, I am more in keeping with Jesus when he called me Mexican and Seminole. Which means to me that I lean on the side of rebellion, that the moons in my chart can never be tested for being Christian, or claiming ethos with the Spanish conquest. I do not have hunger for land, nor do I thrive on territorial consumption. Yet my energy is consumed by remonstrance against those who have drawn out poison from badly stained wheat. And I mean those of the ilk of Diego Vargas, who have haunted the landscape with general damage to both crops and to bodies. Thus I remain as a singular resistance to Europe and its rancid colonial vector uttering out spells from my spleen and my kidneys, which has taken on an assumptive sonority, replete with carnivorous hauntings, always willing to invisibly assassinate abundance, contriving against their nature, by means of curious amounts of brokenness. I come from this acculturation of brokenness. What I intuit from Catalina and Edmundo is a heritage which strickens, which casts aspersion upon forces which align themselves with renewal. I am not typecasting, or conscripting Edmundo and Catalina to fumes which issue from the ossuarium. I am not speaking in this manner because they've lost the power to physically extend themselves, it is because of what I sense in the ethers which seeks to dim their kinetics, and somehow cast the past according to delimited infernos. For me, their witting deception has failed and come to an end in my voice. Not that I am the alien wraith bent upon what an old Shakespearian would call revenge. No, I am simply holding myself in primal suspension so as to inflame my judgement with an objectification of scruples which scorch. La Sociedad Folkloristica exists. Los Caballeros de Vargas exists. Add to this the Festival of Our Lady of the Rosary, and you have a staunchness which seeks at all costs to preserve the pressures of the unreal. For me, these are lives consisting of inferior calculation, consisting of the zenith of infamy.

Being blind I cannot consist of photometric observation, or to an exquisite colourimetry consisting of what I consider to be celestial timbre. Because I am so far removed from daily compost every whisper that I utter seems accentuated by illusive aural diamonds, which I hear in the depths being analogous to what I understand to be the cryptics of unquenchable exploration. This being concomitant with roaming aural luminescence. I depose in my forces pejorative conundrums, shifts of acid, ascent by ethical chaos. I have no need to commit inferential devastation. Deeds have been done, salt has accrued in my flanks. What I can say is that discomfort dwells, discomfort casts forces. Not that I'm weighing discomfort according to percentages of pain. For instance, remembering the date when I was first attempted by Esteban, or on another peculiar solstice remembering when Zomaya and Oraculos first consumed me. Then again, the galling dawn after the prior consumption when Jesus attempted his first physical authority.

The vertigo, the disgust, the exhaustion, exploding from my fingers. After such general demonology the brutes would consent to let me sleep, all the time knowing that they could have me whenever Zomaya consented. Because Zomaya was the key. If one of the brutes overran any of her strictures he was subject to hunger and loss of sexual requitement. So all of us were dazed as if we slept in a stupor of ink. The bizarre and in turn became the bizarre. All of this over and beyond the concussive as limit. I must concur that Zomaya is frightening.

It feels as if I were listening to a large unblinking lizard. Yet now I sense that the lizard is stumbling. Now I sense that its savagery is neutered. How else to account for Zomaya's hesitation? How else to describe her hesitant neural flames, how else to describe her scrupulous deference to Ornelas and St. Catherine's?

I play at conundrums making pawns from lizards and dice. For instance, I, Rosanna, once the frail, once the barely standing, am now ruthless and am now secretively heteronymic. I've come right up to the breath of the Queen without her knowing that I secretly spin about her. I've bypassed all the entrapments of knights and bishops, and have become elegant and numerous not unlike the world of someone like the Cuban Capablanca. It must be understand that I'm skilful with my silence, that I've been able to survive retaliatory hamlets. Skills, angles in the thinking, intuitive habitat without a single source acting as accessible referent. It is equivalent to multiple sigils burning.

Phantoms, masquerading as deficits, as a psychic plinth emptied of cosmic powers. Then there exist vacuums and sub-vacuums, and other tortuous and inscrutable phantomas that the quantum sources can only blankly imply. As chiropteran I can only be mimicked in terms of an after response, because I appear on other planes absent of ozone. Is this to say that one can chart my ambivalence on Eumonia or Ceres, or increase my substance vis-à-vis the implicate ice fields on Saturn.

All of the above configures without the dazed vote of the body. Therefore I cannot claim myself as Rosanna, as someone imbued by shaken electrical balance. Not that I have not suffered as Rosanna, the abandoned hijuela brazen with anguish, but I've advanced over and beyond the sums which singularise myself as the one incriminating habitat. It seems I am now the one who imbibes delimited fraxinella casting fire from simultaneous shadows.

What is of interest in interregnums remains the implicate, the intaglio of its substrates. Being a realia which baffles, it creates a sullen index which baffles, which undermines its own mesmerics. So there is never certainty in the sense that one can trace a mammal in a habitat for 1 million years. It is not this type example. So as I exist as this psychic chiropteran then meaningful index can concur. No numbers can ever accrue concerning quantity and the absence of quantity merging in a nameless meta-condition. So if I attempt to balance a numberless meta-equation, it still follows misnomer by misnomer so that universal germination responds according to the body condensed as a teeming participatory formation.

It must be understood that I am the voice which signals and re-signals interregnums so that I now advance as compound interregnum. Within this compound interregnum pressure builds which ignites the incalculable. This is not something science can describe as a bio-organic enzyme. It relates to the neo-inclement as vacuum.

Because at the marrow of its chartless condensation it is much like a star at the acme of its after-life. I am this star bursting across this chartless acme with seething alchemical dialectics. So, to someone the ilk of Torquemada I pose nothing but danger. This is not a complex assessment in the sense that my energy would have been singled out as a power conversant with the zone of fever. As is known, Torquemada had no ability to access complexity, he being nothing more than a moneron of evil. So what I've come to understand as complexification is nowhere understood in terms of the Northern technocracies.

Never is the Sun felt according to subjective magnetics, or the moon weighed according to its scent as blackened animal probity. Thus, the skills of being are never woven by the affective.

As chiropteran I know and feel that the compound exists over and beyond history and its recorded oblivions.

So on one level the interregnum may be seen as exhausted complexification, yet as chiropteran I understand it to be the proto-magnification of the Divine. Of course, this has nothing to do with visual instigation, but in terms of transmuted cellular transmigration where the cells flow back to the body out of death giving to the human the living condition of what once was described as the interior power of riddles. So if I fly, if I feel in my coming arc, the lands, the Suns, Rosanna in perfect profile, it can only transpire as a startling addendum to being over and beyond the body which now vehiculates new auras in the course of clandestine discovery.

So what is clandestine discovery? It exists as reality which knows the zones of all regions. I mean the fractal of the universe in the cells of the body. It is a level I know that Einstein inferred, knowing that each region of the universe constantly relates to the supercessional. Therefore, the beginning of something, the middle of something, and the end of something exists as an oblivious subset of order. Which means, to classically train, to de-limit by seeking to exclude the psychic power of aura, has become in my mind a technocratic kindling which in turn accrues within the human as fleeting degradation. Therefore the classicists are de-informed, and cannot possibly sustain what they condone as an exclusive right to be. As for Ornelas and the sisters, they understand the subsets of the delimited as portion, as model which holds in place the root of their story as believers in Christ. This is why I know my presence will eventually drown them with being.

Exoterically, I've had congress with seven beings, and I mean this psycho-emotionally. Zomaya, Jesus, Ornelas, Oraculos, Catalina, Esteban, and Edmundo. Not in that order mind you, but what I'll admit is the perfect orchestration of chaos. Catalina and Edmundo I know by intermittent telepathy. The others by immediate echolocation.

Seven beings. Micro-figmentations, always analogous with ruin. So how can I create a compendium of the human family from such an extreme? Numerically, the sample is taut, the psychologies at hand, infested with strife. How can they rivet as a summation of factors, how can they exhibit the vast originating ray which is China, or give sustaining example concerning life in Mozambique? There are limits, true, but I've gained enough of their specific regions to know that from the aforementioned ilk other conditions can transpire. I know, for instance, that in Nepal my life can be summoned by a thought practitioner, that spells can be lifted, or partial curses applied. And I am not speaking of an old French priest in Languedoc contriving to bring rain or heal wounds. I am not speaking of anecdotal fermentation which we consider in our upkeep as miracles. So in this sense, the 7 beings announced seem condemned as an enclave, yet somehow imply fumes which waft to other possibilities. For instance, Jesus was considered as a darkened animal, but even he in his throes was inspired enough to call me Seminole. Even he, sunken in his depths, had understood my telepathic rebellion. There was something in him which pursued a clarifying tonic, there was something in his substance which understood the Lupercalian as torch, which no longer possessed itself as fear.

This energy has now passed to me, so in one utterance I can suddenly clarify a rapist. In one utterance, I give to myself judgement over the outer forces of beasts, feeling in their ruin redemptive forms and implications. This is not to say that they are ironically redeemed as guruvas or shamans. No, Oraculos like Jesus under another power of causation may suddenly burst into an unconditional spectrum where none of the present spectres are applied.

What has become a hallucinatory spectre has been the codification of the Gospels. That a random human being is God, that he has walked on the land, that he illuminates deserts. We owe these assumptions to the Synod of Rome which codified the Gospels in 382 A.D. We owe this to St. Damascus and his conduction of the Synod. Given this context Luke is not a bolt from the uranian, Matthew, Mark, and John, are not cometary soil shot from the Sun. They remain political and budgetary anthems. For instance, during the fray of this period, writings like the Book of Nicodemus was cast aside because of its vigorous demonstration of Christ's transparency in hell. This has remained the rule for over eighteen centuries, yet a rule, which to my understanding is exponential with leakage. This being the doctrine from which St. Catherine's is wrought, sprung from the rancid thought of cadavers. For me, the scriptures are not rendered according to Divine insemination but lean more toward personal assemblage. Because of this they remain for me as nothing more than exoteric beacons. There is nothing that I have known which has been authored by virgins, or promoted by their wiles as an energy, which seeks to break limits. So following this schema St. Catherine's takes in its borders only a certain quality of human refuse. Those of us who have organisable damage. Damage which is considered to be within reason. Thus, I qualify as that damaged ornamentation, capable of ambit and basic vocalization, seemingly quiescent, imbued with a manageable form of blindness. More importantly to them I am replete with funds which trenchantly authors my seclusion. I sit and spawn no outward force of confusion. These tapes on which I speak are numbered by Ornelas and placed in one of several strong boxes in which no contamination can concur. Little do they know that these are sorceries which contain hurricanian transfunction. What little I know of authorship kindles no analogy in my thinking.

All that I know is that I always feel otherness burning in my driftings. I call them storms which the sighted would describe as rufescent, would term them lake-coloured, rubiginous, carnelian, lateritious. True, there exists in me anger, there exists in me bits of poison. As for anger there exists this on-going dalliance with tarantulas, with stunted crosses surrounded by hissing. It must be understood that I as chiropteran am surrounded by spiders, taking their scrolls of blood in my nostrils. So I know that their energy lurks, that their phantom expression furtively links with the origin of my past.

So am I that sub-conscious proto-matriarch fundamentally exhausted from rebellious habituation? Or am I a subterranean Catholic bridled in her depths by self-conflicted emotion? Neither. What I do is simply to compose my fractions as if taking dictation from locusts. Not something akin to Slovakian or Hebrew, but a treasonous account which extends beyond territorial embrasure. True, I have never worked, or been deracinated by objective time constraint because I have never known the world through the facts of work as they issue from the cries of bureaucratic owls concerning length of hours, or time constrained within assignment. Given the arrangement of my hours this was the farthest reality from Zomaya's extent. I was always subject to the brutality of the unexpected, to raucous clandestine summation. If I pose in my verbs the outer zonal it is because I have never been subjected to time, scorched as I am by illiterate marksmanship.

This is the one reason I've created no pursuit of the scholarly locale of the footnote as confirmation or status. Therefore I've accepted thought as a wall-less martyring gall. Because everything that I say is always at the cusp of the savagery of riot. As chiropteran I am always surveying coded scorpion reports unleashed by trepidation. Under a more shrouded context I am the sigil who fishes from a hovering female pontoon always sensing things which dart. In this sense I feel condemned by optimum sensitivity. So the agitations, the cunning world resistance, the general retrogression, I sense without puzzlement knowing that I am rife with in-terminal proliferation. Never one to issue sterile apologetics I've always procured interior ballast when embroiled in what it now seems in retrospect as a zone fully mystical with abuse. Yet I do not argue from the right of an empress simply to impose vanity and condone in my person misfigured risk. No, if anything, I summarize Osceola in excluding Christianity with its dearth, with its disfigured canonization as property. Certainly this is not a superficial assessment akin to grading seismographic husks. I can never address this level of the seismographic knowing the conscious mind can only pontificate at this level by use of a-priori dice. It can only seek out barren pines, poisonous here afters, baleful cryptologies. As I hatch these inner windings these husks will remain within themselves and be considered by the general populace tangential to their provincialised notions of infinity.

To them, I will never appear as the manifest conundrum. Because so much negativity abounds about me on simple inspection it cannot be understood how the sound of my voice can escape the oven of the pores. Everything seems against me, the psycho-social, the electrical. This remains the utterance which reeks from closed doors. A storm from burning after-breaths. Because during day my breathing takes on a dominate posture giving me the blankness needed, to roam the heavens and return to mystery during the time of the moon. Which allows me to explore beyond the poverty of analysis. I call this latter state corrosive carrion vapour. Because I am aware of galactic vapour, the carrion portion floats beneath me condensed with all its echoes postulating ruin.

So do I take on hubris when listening to the pores of Zomaya?

Am I claiming private hostility as power?

What I'm attempting to do is to raise the human instrument over and beyond the poverty of facts so that I become more and more capable of purity as it arrives from the ozone being what I understand as the original declaration of the infinite. So zodiacal gravitas cannot possibly infuse me with narration. Cannot leave me grounded with the rabid story of Zomaya dazed at the source of habituation. I cannot be chronically stilled by one to one events. Say, Oraculos enraptures me with the poison of subaltern sexual thirst begging for release. I cannot date such a moment of thirst and chart its degree vis-à-vis Esteban, or Zomaya's inverted desires. No circumstance can rule me in the sense that I breathe in rhythm with in-coming powers of purity. So as this purity increases increment by increment new stamina builds as origination within origin. So new directives appear as constant conduction which has no possibility of parochial acknowledgement. Because I'm always daring myself through isolation. I'm always imbibing resource from the zone where atoms disappear into themselves and vanish. This is where intensity can no longer model itself so as to replicate human fatigue.

This is why when a God is applied to a static symbol it can no longer investigate its own summations. And because it cannot investigate its own summations, it creates in itself authoritative a-rhythmia where surcease is its highest emblem or conclusive. So its believers become feral with engagement. Always God acts by acting as the experience of death, letting death occur by means of superior in-action.

Am I saying that God is the source of a trenchant criminality? Does he figure as a criminal mantra? Does he keep cadavers in motion over and above his wilfully stunted intentionality?

Anarchist?

Atheistic rhetorician?

I remain neither, having transmuted the very source of fixation, overcoming in my cells the very ghost which roams through their anxieties. Ah, God has been transfixed by human contamination. The human practitioner remains unskilled. Purification of the involuntary is the key, for instance, purification of breathing, purification of common sexual consent. Not that I seek to follow in the footsteps of St. Anne, or St. Elizabeth of Hungary. In a certain sense the rapes have procured for me purity. I no longer cast secret desires from my feelings. I am no longer haunted by what might have been, by those phantom branchings which trigger endless reticularity through comment. I now accrue no turbulence from such habitual fascination. Again, I'm wafting into the electrics of the body thereby evincing the purest elocution of the elements which compose me, Rosanna, blinded, wafting through the beauty of the aerial as confoundment. So by my experience of the aerial I feel by turns etheric, intuitive, elevated by misnomer.

Here I invoke no outmoded hypnotics, no retaliatory scrawling simply to digress inside fever entangled by intestinal ideology. I think of those old brazen imperialists dating back to the agony which ensued from the Third Punic War. I feel that Zomaya and Oraculos are old Roman incest bodies, attempting to pursue a non-existent order. To invest a scenario, Oraculos could lead the way in state sponsored killings. As rapacious underling he would merely confirm Zomaya's power as far as it confirmed itself in being a racial elite. With her supremacy ending Oraculos would seek exile in some parallel enclave where former killers could convene and swear allegiance to their crimes, and pore over memories, this being the prime colonial ground where joy is gained by means of supernal pain. In the deepest sense, such status seems to have run its course. Because human activity is circa, it seems that prior conflict no longer invigours, nor no longer creates a foreseeable agenda. The concept of battle has failed. It has lost its national consensus, and prevails for a while longer while human dendritics begins to re-self-structure itself. This will emerge when general torpor has been expelled. So it is from this incalculable tendency that my vertiginous rotation develops.

Again, I receive one tape per day. Zomaya uses the ration of this tape to see me daily. She places the tape within my reach. I have no problem speaking to myself for its 90 minute duration. It takes away pressure, and to paraphrase Zomaya's statement it helps me lighten my unsettled state flecked as it is with various nuclei of decay. To her, my mind can do no more than stumble in an unknown sewage. She has said "… your tent is dark water and I'm to see that you drown in its bedding." For her I deserve no more than a maimed bouquet, to her, I remain panicked, listless, suckled by an army of rapes. To her I am sulphur, that I was born through malicious herbology. To her, I should be hunted as an in-gracious condor, made to perish over and over as transmitted to my person by way of the scent from perished mandalas. Therefore I become through this nothingness a populous enigma, a living scroll of darkness. Therefore, all love is missing, she even seeks to disorder my own sacrifice.

When these words are revealed according to higher properties of causality the Demi-urge will have been wounded, becoming a mauled and infernal ruler, caught and dismembered by powers sprung from his immortal depravity. Because I am privy to all the higher and lower qualities which breathe I understand the punctual solemnity which elicits craving for higher forces. So in this songless pagoda I note words and ideas which are imprinted with poisonous tundra seals. It is like I am always executing sigils, always understanding forces beyond forensic confinement.

For this is a diary sown into the skirt of deafened medusae. Which remains analogous to Zomaya as pervasive medusae, circular with doubt and envy. When I say this I am not abstracting a glossary of evil to peripherally condemn Zomaya, and by extension the human kingdom. True, I've been isolate, true, I suffer from staggered result, that New Mexico has very sparse holding as regards the populations of the Earth. Yet I stand by my auto-ordination, knowing that Jesus Christ is the Demi-Urge and subsequent as Cosmocrater, surviving in the hearts and minds of an uprooted spell. Of course, I'm saying this at St. Catherine's. If Ornelas wanted to betray me she could fully expose my opprobrium.

She could have me symbolically hung. Yet because of the funds Zomaya bestows upon St. Catherine's I am never approached, my status remains illusive. To the outside world Zomaya still prevails as the only heir, immaculate, comfortably merged with the most regressive of elements. I could revolt at that level and at that level alone. But I've brokered a much deeper condition. I've floated through each conversational precipice in the cells, in this regard Zomaya has little advantage. I've gained power through inverted commotion. I've left the coteries of grasp. In this sense Zomaya is listed by ironic blessings through cruelty. From this seeming defeat I've gained multitudinous aspiration, being spurred to beauty by that which probes the inferential.

This does not absolve me from torment. This does not make me indifferent to the perilous connivance which has always convulsed me. There remains in me an evolved sense of damage. Poisoned by the over spills of incest, my experience has been replete with dangerous invasions, with the constant sack of the body. Always threats ruinous to my oxygen, the result of this being a harried metabolics forcing the body to experience alien sensitivity. Thus, I am able to summon energies which revel rather than tortuously recur. As chiropteran I advance secrets over and beyond categorized repetition. I have come to understand the Sun as inner sanction, understanding its depths as true implosional characteristic, as altered form casting sound from unscalable schism. One seems surrounded by jeopardous pressure. There is suffusional claustrophobia. The hands begin aching as if they had ingested a curious kind of heat. A haunted pairing subjected to libidinous residue. And within this residue there exists Zomaya and Oraculos, and Esteban, and Jesus, notorious with combined hostility. So it can be concluded that my body is nervous with war, that I've sprung from a savage happenstance in the cosmos. If one contends with the exoteric as power the anomalous is that which is erased, becomes that which is dissolved on contact with the pressures which deny the abstruse. In this vein I could contend that Zomaya is the blame and auditioned me for evil. Because I have no pressure as regards my reputation I've created no lateral compost. The greater community will never lessen me, or spread a general dissonance in my wake. So I do not involve myself with movement in minutiae.

I do not announce in myself a gregarious plan to regain an acceptance which has never existed. Certainly not an improvident leap, but crucial understanding of things as they've been, and continue to form at each hour. Never having had presence in the social agenda I cannot be accused of affecting it with rabies. I do not exist. The post Conquistadores have heard not a whisper when I enunciate the treasonous, when I slander their efforts to create post colonial prosperity. Even the telepathic can never unsource me, can never locate my atomics as they issue from dendritic inspiration. Even as I regale Zomaya with absence, how can those whose electrical priority is maintenance possibly conceive the whereabouts of my venom. Even if my presence were posed to the Virgin, to her power which convenes at La Conquistadora, she could never awaken my presence in her powers. So how can a ghost prevail? How can a creature without resource or document configure a struggle, or mount an opposition from seeming nonsubsistence? Within the current social context I am human site which reeks, which throws a kind of acid from her struggles. Even at conditional unction the human scenario remains convinced by the ilk which forms behavioural Zomayas. But I feel that what I say is more than a private or unsustainable tsunami. A level exists in me which reaches those aspects one would consider as being the general global field as though existing in Cypress, or Lahore, or Toronto, or Timbuktu. When I say this am I expressing a terminal rhetoric? Or am I opening up rapacious insufficiency on which human yield cannot dwell?

I cannot deny that I have no feelings in this regard. So can I love God and the progeny of God? Can I advance an optimistic assessment of a plane which boils with unfavourable registration?

For instance, the snow fields are more and more missing, with the remnants of bears now offered for more and more unseasonable display.

Certainly one in my position can never be accused of inflicting Imperial distortion, of haunting the human enclave with vile or prophetic jaundice, preparing for a time which will be shaken by punishments.

And what do I mean, shaken by punishments?

Apocalypse indicates motion through proto-phases of itself, with the rapidity and severity of events becoming more and more as inevitable sub-bait.

Perhaps certain winds are approaching which resemble storms more akin to Neptune or Saturn. Perhaps storms the equal of Eridanus, the equal of Cassiopeia. I am not saying that I wish for these dimensions to occur, but I am understanding the present state of the planet's exhaustion. And again, not a fanaticism, or an idiosyncratic thought stream fed by trenchant hysteria.

Or based upon the principle of unwarranted accusation. I can only conclude by saying that this is as much about timing as anything else. Maybe it's the way that storms are now concurring, putting worlds at risk disparate as Sao Paulo or Paris. Yet I've never studied with assiduous intensity the priorities of Daniel, or Ezekiel, or Jeremiah, or even graced in a wayward manner the visions of John and his dialogue with Great forces. Yet I know the undergirdings of their centralised projections, that the current portion of matter is ending, that the human family is condemned from having improper congress with itself. Yet I feel these remain predilections from the xanthochroids, concerning fear, concerning marginalized neurosis. They think like wary killers held in the province of historical isolation. For instance, I as Indian, and Zomaya as European. It is synecdoche. It is the part which substantiates the whole. So what follows from this is a break with forensic pattern. It is a break with old viral draughts. As chiropteran I explode through theoretical trees. This is why I am chiropteran, suddenly collapsed at one juncture then rising from another. Because I always smell stasis. And because I smell stasis I know where blood has withdrawn, I know how old deployments falter with painstaking regression. This remains the current system of life which engenders great repression. There exist none of the energies which take flight beyond themselves. Instead, there are senescent records which occlude amazement with the energies of withdrawal. In this sense Zomaya and the Folkloristica are withdrawn, St. Catherine's and the hamlets that it conveys are withdrawn.

Paralysis?

Entropy?

A combinatory code which threads through common meaning, and since it possesses no greater energy than itself it can no longer be mistaken for evolving from a heritage of voltage.

Broken fate?

Phenomena of wreckage?

I understand these designations. Yet I am not a circumstance mountainous with devastation. True, I've faced probes, I've had contact with hostility, I've felt darkening in the loins. Always blazing with risk I've experienced consecration by test. So I am living as array which casts fuel. Even though I'm stilled without seeming movement my conundrum articulates itself through seeming non-motion as error. Because movement is typically understood under the auspices of torrential measurement, of how quickly and demonstratively quantity occurs. One then speaks of an exclusive externality, of grasp between one locale and another. Motion across forward tending parts. This is the criterion I have never possessed. In fact, measure has never occurred to me, measuring the size of a sea cove, or marking the boundaries of an island. Mind you, this is not because I am living as blinded, but because my temperature conducts itself through chronic lessening. I cannot fathom personal accretion, because I breathe through error and can provide no status for the living character of quantity. Although seething with outward immobility, I am a repetitious persona who persists, who now begins to thrive through mythological accursedness.

I have not sought disintegration. I have not contrived to break patterns in order to summon an abstracted wrath or tenacity. What I do is live inside intuitive teeming. Which means every nuance, every dazed and inviolate event. So I have reached this hyper-inscrutability, this spinning illumination by flaw. At many times during my odyssey one could almost smell the hurt as it wafted from my pores. And this hurt would always seem to invigorate theological validation of the wounded who inscrutably rise to holy regeneration. As victim I was always posed as scandalous glossalalia, as a feral animal component not unlike unnerving ciphers roaming the Serengeti at nightfall.

Having been singular and consummate as prey I understand that plane which I have sought to explain by what I'll enunciate as linear elevation. That which only the eyes can see and extend. And because I have no eyes which see and extend I cannot coalesce with the code which condenses according to optic interpenetration. Zomaya now knows that I do not aspire to the aforesaid regression.

I have never cancelled myself with sorrow, or sought to plan a supportive coterie sparked by alphabetic declaration. Because I am blind I have never sought fundaments which subscribe to specific delimitation Not that I'm saying that I remain the sole and absorptive chiropteran etched according to singular circumference. Nevertheless I am chiropteran, existing as uneven strength cataclysmic with nuance. I, who in human form am exhausted with vertigo, being simultaneously seasoned by migrational combat. The labour by which I speak has nothing in common with seasonal work, or laborious combinations which pointlessly issue from the scratch plough. Nor is this labour from a mind who composes Circassian memoir, or exhausts her cellular intensity according to the telling of Aramaic migration. Not the Orontes, not Damascus or Aleppo. But here I am with post-colonial Nortenos, in Bernalillo County, near the Sandia Mountains, possessing knowledge of the cathedral of San Felipe de Neri. I, Rosanna, Albuquerquean, always configured by my trespasser's flaws. A trespasser's incensement at the specific condition of living moral negation. Since I am Seminole in spirit I would have attacked the settlers hold up at early San Felipe de Neri, opposed as I would have been to the so called civilizing compost, to the linear remonstrance which upheld the Christian doctrine of living. They, who sought to command those of us subdued by weaponry and iron.

Being Seminole in spirit I am that rebellious paralytic consumed by her inheritance of vertiginous primevals. These are the dust of zones, the interior ferment plains, the forming nether dimensions. So definitives are non-inherent, are inchoate with combustibles. Rosanna has no realm, Rosanna remains compelled by nothing in outward society. I cannot surmount some psychic literary galleon, or build up in my mind some narrative Cibola where gold is found mounting to the stars. But this is no excuse for my continuing impairment, for my penultimate entrapment. I am only expressing signals, torrential aural diamonds, expressing blaze over and beyond limitation as want. Rosanna with fame or gold in her bosom, Rosanna full of spurious cranial apprehension according to saturation as prowess. But what do I mean by prowess? Saturation by valued forms of consensus? Saturation concerning powers which thrive through acquisition as pattern? I think that I can now be understood according to the imploded rhetoric which whispers as an anti-arithmetic. As to confidence, as to memorized insistence, I am brimming. Not as a molecule infused by terminal hubris, but as an energy floating as breath before the Sun door. I occupy nothing but presence, and because of this presence the voluntary realm has been altered. There exists bodily function yes, but there exists another property in my balance, which ceases to imply a replication as expressed through entropy. Therefore I am feeling emergence from this compound interregnum.

As it stands I am contemporaneous with absence, estranged as I am from material duality. Rosanna as vacuum, as erratic mirror in the Pleiades. I understand that the Sun ignites the minerals, that elements of the agave can be chronicled, which at a certain level activates knowledge as monotony. Which condones stabilized criteria in order to establish an Imperial policy towards existence. A province which seeks to erase creative schism by exerting a daunting grip on every tangent. Yet I am always dipping into the turbulence of great tangents never localized as stasis through old kindling. Under silence and depression I know there exists ekstasis, there exists the singing of primeval colouration charged by a brewing alchemical kinetic. A surge, frenetic with distillation, so again, I can advance my own purity with or without the impecunious. Even as a pointless copper heir, copper has no ultimate sway over the energy I incite. I do not create some shaken technical palace in order to prove or disprove a necessitous remoteness. I am revealed in much the way a taut or a charismatic complexity derives itself through emotion. So I can do nothing other than reveal a scattering of fatigue mixed with psychic osmosis.

Yes, I am disabled, yet I am not catastrophic. I'm internally pointing to things as they've been, and what I feel are the energies to come. I'm speaking of the total circumstance as flux. Not in terms of the zodiac as a rhetoric of my behaviour, but in terms of a precipice colliding with itself. In Islamabad, in Shenzhen in China there is catastrophe. In the Sudan, draughts of milk and water. In the old Acoma sky there is loss of philosophy and eagles. This is not the praxis of a stoic symbology, or a theology of storms, but Euphratean dice on a board. I am playing with spells and counter-spells, with conch shells, with bits of gravel with different leanings. And these shells and bits of gravel I call language, and more precisely, language in the service of itself as it grasps at higher spillage. This being gravitas suspended, it means actionless meta-kinetics.

As I sit, molecules spin, and distortions persist and cease to persist, creating interior vibratory impartation. This in turn creates a substance which can imaginate schist, which can fly into stunning avian transmission as inspirational correspondence. So in this sense I am an inspirational practitioner completely removed from the scholarly corpus as triggered scorpion remains. This is something more than dazzling solar explanation. Not grounded by imported Saxon duties, or lulled into detraction, or obscured by a rationally summoned Sun.

In this sense I am no longer tethered to matter. And I mean by matter life re-sundered for consumption. I'm like the phosphorus from angels listening by first instruction. Because mixtures of angels and beings I've come to apply circumstantial gradations which announce themselves not according to suffering, or to states induced by imprisoned dialectics. This is liberty which erupts from various aural constellations.

One hears being before it comes into presence, then what follows are mirrors, and draughts, and various oxygen cycles. So if I am reading my fate from motion which occurs from an old cyclonic barge it means that it carries a subjective flow not unlike the terrain which occurs on Dione, or Tethys, or Mimas.

I'm speaking of essence as it roams occulted ozone, the latter remaining inveigled in me, always attempting to listen to myself for living utopian transmission invoking the dictum of gamblers, always overcoming the odds. One does not have to underscore the embranglement which some describe as loneliness, as if one were a disparate or unenviable elf. I can say that I am unenviable with no palpable connection to a world which seeks to convince itself that the soil upon which it stands is no longer poisoned. This being a litmus which in turn signals my advances. This being a state which has no relation to diamonds or crops. Or to plasmatic monsters formed from methane physiologies. Again, not a theatre of gravity, or token conservations. Certainly this being the opposite of elevated compost, with its unliveable trees, with its broken snow caps missing.

This being the strategy of 'human deafening which equates with an infinity of reverses in nature. In the end, the ozone entangled, with the seasons gone awry. This being removed from Egyptian organicity, with its kinetics, and the counterpart of its kinetics in the invisible. I think of particles ascending to their origin. I think of the coming together of suns in the mind. Then the merging of infinite planes of the mind living as flames in the mysterium.

How does this test the self-definitives of Zomaya? She remains confined to reputation, to Albuquerque as reduction, to her limited psychic projection. As to conversational projection, as to financial embellishment of the concert kingdom, full of Brahms, Haydn, and Lizst. Full of the 19th century with its tainted programming ear. This is the milieu of Zomaya as heiress, of Zomaya as chaste, always living above the inchoate. This is how the West confines biography, to official squares and perfect parallels. Locally one could speak of Alicia Romero, of Josephina Ortega, of Belina Ramirez, as lives perfectly squared upon a pedestal of karma. On the other hand I know that Zomaya has deeper attitudes, a less constrained osmosis. Sharing her body daily, conniving to pit the brutes against themselves, then in her heart of hearts orchestrating rape. This being her unintended half, her involuntary hand, drawing subconscious angst. Of course she does not create in me that all encompassing drive which sustains great poetic spirit. She is a rhetoric gravitised, and praised by spirits condoned to singing infernal hymnlets. And I do not sing infernal hymnlets, nor do I praise those who always threaten themselves with acts they consider as reprehensible. So she is that monster who is fitted to scale, who has become a personage who dwells in the decreased. She, whose action is now the guttering sound of a candle, not unlike a camel whose hide is half destroyed.

I am not speaking of percentages. Of how Zomaya is so much of this, or so much of that. She is a mixture whose percentages vary according to circumstantial pattern. For instance, what is her intention of secrecy? What would be her number as concealment in daylight? I absolutely cannot say, as I am totally devoid of counting, of reaction charted according to abstract numeration.

For instance, Zomaya as lesbian, as conductor of rapes. Or Zomaya in daylight in afternoons through Folkloristica. Of course, these realities counter-balance and burn. And because they burn there can never be any definitive as to either, as to higher or lower chamber as presence. In any life there is always conglomeration, perhaps of heightening, or noise, or brutality. This being Zomaya's status, yet I am not absolving her from evil. Certainly I am not condoning her actions as angelic logarithmics. She remains conditioned by damage. In another era I would say that she is a witch capable of raising lions from the dead. I know she has power, that is why we hold one another in basic annulment. I surprise her, I know that I surprise her. I am her only remaining witness. I am what we'll call an intangible neutron thinker. Someone who fissions, someone who gives off marks from saliva. This is neither good nor bad but only runs parallel to itself. In this sense I do not sponsor chaos, I do not graft to my self-dishevelment a negative mental liquor. It is the centre of my thought beam. And so when it releases itself within time and space it produces the uncanny. It begins to live in people's minds so that they can feel me inside their thinking. This is where Zomaya knows I dwell, even proto to her own thinking. So now I can anticipate her patterns. I can continue to roam inside her patterns like a ghost inside the patterns, much like travelling the Oort dimension when travelling from another solar circle, thereby touching life from great expanse while still respiring on Earth. It is like testing the winds of the unruly. In this sense I exist as patternless light, as roiling penultimate mystery. And I am not saying that I have crossed over, that my nerves have been subsumed in a creatureless spate of starlight. No. I remain semi-entranced by human theatre, and I still possess skills by which the human mean commonly exhibits itself.

Zomaya somehow senses the power in my distraction, and knows that it carries a powerful interior dialectic. My distraction embodies itself in the overworld, burning through other crystals, through other waves of the psycho-kinetic. This is why the society that I carry exists and releases itself in the presently existing so that there exists a cohesion which inscripts the curiously inclement Rosanna. To Zomaya, to those substantially sighted I am much like a sun implying itself below the horizon. I cast both invisible light and invisible dark. And what arrives is a synthesis, an osmotic integration which always suspends conclusion. And because she responds by habit to two opposable dimensions she cannot contend with its energy, or the thought which this energy implies. What is good and what is evil can no longer transfix the power of the Sun with all its subtending forces. For instance, after 300 million years the Sun is still forceful. It still multiplies and multiplies, and multiplies, with its length adding up, to provisional billions. Which means the Earthly geologic is a minor camera of the Sun. This is true. And by saying this I am not entrapping myself as a connoisseur of obscurity, nor do I cast my blankness and transpose its elements as ire to be distributed.

According to the Christians good and evil are unequally distributed. According to laws and the censorship of governments, evil remains the principle operating key. And all doctrine, and all exoteric fulfilment remains in a subtended ozone where life amounts to encompassing hesitation. So where does good exist in such a dimension as this? Where do its minimums accrue? Perhaps in martyrdom. Perhaps in fending for the poor. There is some basis for the latter in the energy of St. Francis. To attempt the combination of the disparate in the wake of the inconvivial carries a positive import. I think of St. John of the Cross, of St. Ursula, or St. Teresa of Avila. Am I granting them evolutionary status? True, there does exist living in their morose elevations. I am saying this because it is true, not because of some ideological referendum, I do not intend to create a commanding oblivion when encountering realities which seem to disfavour me.

So does such instinctive largesse extend to someone of the ilk of Jesus, whom Zomaya on occasion has delimited to the animus of the tapeworm. I can say without frenzy that his cells can advance potential, that his cells can roam as emancipated Suns, should his power escape the culture of gravitas. And I am not being ideal in this regard. Should Zomaya escape her attempts at European embranglement she could equate him with more of the ozone, with the tangibles of Pueblo culture, and intuit from the general melanin of the populace the coming darkness of the species. I am not exporting racial chauvenistics but simply exploring a simple understanding, understanding as I do the general tendency of humanity over time. What I'm saying is not in concert with gross material philanthropy, but with vertiginous flow by teleportational insight, reaching body to body, and zone to zone, thereby creating splendiferous aural theatre.

So am I conducting loneliness as self therapy, as tragic self-incensement? I do not seek to divinise any life long occlusion, or demonized barriers that separate and part. What I've done is open up a bloody anodyne folder, and in it all the crude interiorized perplexity that I've lived. I am asking for nothing. I am seeking a semblance of that which resists itself from concretized self-sabotage. In a word, I am not broken. I am not instigating a peculiar in-saturation which keeps me from listening to myself as peculiar shift through chronicle. Thus, I've never negated my veritable right to speak. I've never lost my right to action, thereby reducing my right to panic. I know my personal historicity, absent as it is of dates, of substantive memorabilia. I know that moons roar, that the Kodiak Bear makes dissonance, that calendars work according to an uneven stasis. Of course this is personal and comes from living as general unrest. Yet I have not panicked, or given to my rivals some ultimate materia to probe and maniacally maintain. Yet there remains bitterness, there remains the fumes of passion and bitterness. Therefore I am working by deprivation, by occult circumstantials. I can never acknowledge any evidence of objective of trust all the while knowing that Zomaya has created in my life unembellished suspicion. She has created in me the wariness of an ocelot or a kinkajou when contending with larger prey. Not that I don't bite, or am incapable of drawing blood, but I've risen above this state, knowing that something exists over and above the terrestrial as lasting conclusion.

It could be easily asked, why do I speculate on planes that the Saints are incapable of rendering? I am not saying that they plagiarised experience, that they rendered incapable models as super-imposed experience. What I'm saying is that they've contained the cellular field within closely structured doctrinal flaws. Not that they had no powers of poignancy, but the Church now claims them as having powers over wolves, and scarabs, and humans. It is like saying that I have sinned and am treacherously ruled by random sparrows. That I have not reached maturation because of failure to succumb to forces enacted by monetary badgers.

The Saints are connected to eclectic strains of nature, codified by the Church and its various kindlings. Say, if I live in Alsace, it is St. Odilia, in Argentina it is Our Lady of Lujan, in Corsica, it is the Immaculate Conception, in Silesia, it is St. Hedwig, in Slovakia, it is Our Lady of Sorrows. And these are what I'll consider as outskirts, as zones no longer concussive in determining collective outcome. But personally I may qualify in evolving to the status of St. Rita. Perhaps I qualify as the equal of St. Odilia. But alas, I remain the poor Rosanna who lives within encryption. Because I have no dates I remain this compound interregnum, this perspicacious figment, who remains curious and blasphemous in origin. According to the mongerers in St. Peter's my sufferings don't configure, therefore there exists no redemption. In a trenchant sense I am less redemptive than a leper. My dates are double question marks. So I am of that order who's been conquered and defanged of principle turning points. I am not of the saved nor of the summoned condoned by the exclusivity of heaven. My name is listed in no pact. I have no listing as contained in carnivorous paradigm.

I have made no concoction so as to reverse the Sun and stir up blazing winters. This is not my ordination, nor have I gained recognition so as to fuel my betterment in the eyes of the heavenly host. I am simply a blank. And because I am a blank I remain a threat to the Holy Writ as issued from St. Peter's. Thus, I am excluded from religious legality. I, who in her current position remains a source of ulterior voltage. A theorem by broken lightning. All this as aspects of sound by me, a broken animal in ambivalence.

So am I the monstrously diabolical?

Am I the food which is cast from demons?

Have I been conscripted by forces derived from hellish sigils? Has my nervous system been prey to other forces of consumption?

What I can say is that Zomaya and the brutes remain separate parties. Of course they are aspects of flummoxed psychosis. So if I mine peculiarities from the moments of the life of Jesus, and attempt to multiply these acts in Esteban, one reaches a similar conclusion in Oraculos, which then can re-stray into the sibling Jesus, then back again to all of the aforesaid who are claimed by ominous uttering. They have thoughts which extend across apocalyptic boundaries erratically soaked in the vindictive. I feel in them no resting points. But if I were so inclined I would be subsumed in each of their separate experiences. So the tendencies in each one of them would prolong and intensify my aboriginal electrics. Let me say though, that next to Zomaya Oraculos has done the most to electrically drain me. Because I know in my thoughts the basic pattern of his sperm. I know the molecules which lull in his perversion. And then there is Esteban, the drunken Esteban, somehow skilled at a brutal randomness. But instead of listening to each personality as Freudian absorption, I've combined their spate of tendencies and condensed them by fundamental insight, thereby knowing their depth of barbarism through drift. And what do I mean by drift? Gaining distance from the actual physical acts so as to transcribe their personas through my genes. So having dwelt with these amoebas I've developed other levels of listening, other powers, other modes of conduction. Their poison has not killed me. As the common saying goes I've actually taken on strength.

As chiropteran I carry no legal energy or pattern. This has allowed me maximum exosmosis, thereby knowing the aleatoric as reason. This is a capacity that Zomaya has no ability to control. I've risen above those powers which reveal themselves through standard inoculation. I am from a hidden race of savants able to focus through arcs of blindness. I've grown through a gruelling calculus of suspense. So therefore I do not listen to myself through previous limit. Because this limit expands day by day by day. Zomaya is always guessing at my seeming outward simplicity. She scours my silence for motives, for a kind of harm which advances these motives. For instance, if the Sun had emptied its powers 12 millennia ago the power of which I speak would continue to post exist. It would move as an episodic maelstrom throughout the cosmos without concern for bodies, or thoughts of bodies. Because each body exists through foundational ruin, as chiropteran, I resurrect the unlimited. I expand dimension and experience as alchemical substrates, as energy which persists through unburnished leaven. As relates to aspects musical, or more specifically Schoenbergian, I am conservatively considered through previous atonalities. Nothing adds or subtracts, it is simple patterns gone astray. As to more complex figuration something supersedes even this containment. On the material plane the vehicular becomes semi-equational with measurement so life then leans away from the known. In common parlance, the unprecedented dwells. That which knows nothing of any prior attempt upon itself. And this is where I stand, without prior attempt upon myself. Therefore, I do not know what's coming. I do not have any definitive forthcoming as relates to what Zomaya may conclude at the border of the next kinetic. Yet I understand her patterns without any definitive forthcoming. Yet if Zomaya could so construe it my body would lapse into the indifferent, and Ornelas, and St. Catherine's, could amply erase my former whereabouts claiming my body as anonymous cargo to be deposed. And in spite of all I've said this possibility remains a threat. It has a greater heightening more than objective annoyance. It remains a scenario, a dangerous conceivability, yet being one of many outcomes. To script any other outcomes would be to convince myself of smoke, and hang lanterns as though I were guided by seeing.

As chiropteran I cannot trace chronic assumptions, though outcomes do exist. I simply feel by porous fresco. This is the intrados, the core, the invisible, through which I fly, glancing off philosophical acidity. Because my mind has not gone public, my eyes with their onyx exteriors always beguile with powers thought to have merged with the impossible. These are eyes that see. Though blind these are eyes that see. Because I have heard so much thought, and listened to so much language, I can simulate seeing through speech. Perhaps at some moment in the future I'll comment on the architectural prowess of Juan de Villanueva, or Ventura Rodriguez in the throes of Bourbon Spain, or comment on Spanish building effects as they accrued in the central Andes.

This is a power which always riddles Zomaya, that I can see without palpable instrumentation. She suspects that I have honed a visual filigree, and further, see her present mental capacity as inner lanterns falling apart. With me, she now accrues no state of safe direction. Because my body has absented the dwelling, pressure from the brutes has increased.

What she has done is constructed an ad hoc Mass telling them that they have lost their personal kingdoms, and through transubstantiation she tells them they can renew their spirits as living events.

I'm surmising that this action issues more from cerebral than visceral psychology. I'm saying this because I now know what my body has meant to her power. I am no longer there to increase her inferno. I am no longer the buffer between her body and the body of the brutes. The atmosphere has changed. She is now the one distorted, she is now the one who absorbs the central pressure. Because she is so weakened I can invade her, I can roam her private investiture knowing in the motion her contorted terrain. Yet at another level she remains implacable, staunch, in her assiduous approach to any disclosure I may embody. Understanding these dynamics she approaches me with caution because I am someone who has gained substantive formidability, as someone who can never be construed as living through infamous leisure. Knowing that she knows that I don't consist of panic, that any outrage I've considered has risen to a new engaging silence having fully superseded the life formally fuelled according to carnivorous effect. It is a level that the dualistic mind cannot counter. I sit, I accrue no seeming experience. In contradiction she is seeking to dislodge matter. Because I have left no record at some prior position or stratification I unnerve her, I de-kindle strength so she takes on a quaking which promotes an unsettled balance in her waking. As I've said she remains to all general concern absolutely implacable, always arriving daily like a clock. In this regard she is not unlike Immanuel Kant honed by methodology. At 11:30 Zomaya arrives. After a condensed and unstable hour she leaves. This is a figment of course, but knowing this figment is like arriving at a signal which alerts all principle action in my body. I feel the energy of her diligence, as well as accursed fear. The two take on a symbolical ether which scatters its own cohesion. True, there is an invisible signature that I smell, a tendency, a mental gait which cross-philosophises. Thus, her visits ignite my volcanic dossier.

And everything returns to ineluctable synecdoche, to a daring crucible which confounds and opens at the boundary of limit. As chiropteran, this is like releasing from my coils a flood of ink, making to some degree a pernicious array of markings, as if I were sighted and testing black silver. Sitting, I do not wear investigative apparel, or weave with my voice in-reductive ice. Which further translates to hoarseness, to the contested by in-ocular speech. Yet I am clear in this regard without morose or corrosive embellishment. Which means I can see Esteban when I name him. A life doubled over in drinking, always exposing the sex on his breath. Always contending with unfortunate accounts. This, of course, is turbulent mental weather by which storms are marked, suns disrupt, and moons resist conjunction. This remains Esteban. As for Jesus, there remains other catastrophic examples.

As for Oraculos, the cells understand his poisoning, the result of his inference. This remains the utter direness of the zone through which I've passed. Perhaps it could be said that my speech is akin to nervous wafting, to that which ceases its own configuration. A void, or perhaps a less complex interregnum. I do not cling to voided emanations, to fetid scrolls, to distasteful benchmarks. And I do say these things in paradox in order to reinforce an outmoded syntax. No deeper issue can be reached in this manner. Above all there exist in one's fate fire, along with the fortuitous soil of interior combinations. Then of course one must listen to scales in one's emotional prairies. One must understand oneself as suggestive animation, coming to acme as lawless intestinal proof. It is in this way that I confide within myself, through which I etch the fundamental ground with my talons. As chiropteran I'm considered as skilless, without linkage, without the engenderment to bleed as ideology. But what I've come to is luminosity by error, by conditionings which seem to fail, and disembody, and then retreat in themselves. This is how I fly, seemingly tilted at angles, abrupt with disintegration and renewal, This is where Zomaya breaks, this is where her psyche parts, this is where her fate falls down from the Sun.

Dense and as cruelly tethered as she is, she has some need of order. This is why Sister Ornelas can time her visits with precision. This is why the nuns mark her with prominence not only for the funds she imparts, but for the discipline she seems to pursue. Her energy in the face of these confines impresses. She understands my surreptitious energy as challenge. But for me, the events imparted have never been about analysis, but about feeling.

About the somatic realms and how they conspire. So my conspiration spins, and reticulates and connects by transfunction. Having overcome the conscripted as dilemma there has erupted in me a sense that has fused with the unmistakable. With that which creates through itself something other than matching simulations. Simulation is not the secrecy of mirroring through which I've felt the parallel of sorcery in my heart. As if one were listening to ravens created from flecks of the Sun. And in their parallels I can feel the invisible state of my movement. This being the uranian element which dominates my flux. So when Zomaya perceives me of being in coma, it is the other side of the Sun that she's seeing. I become in these states a stunning camouflage of vacuums. At one level I am both camouflage and ruin, at another level there is a stunning amalgam fuelled by animations which create from the blood centripetal flares. Which ignites my presence with inseparable teeming. That I live and cross circulate as chiropteran I distance myself from Zomaya, capable as she is of empowering stunning separable fixation. In the West, the mind seems to travel no further than the bizarre, it can never chase from itself the harassment which inflames through phenomena. Any deeper merging is only catalogued with the listless, with the seemingly superstitious, with that which has no effect. What Zomaya is attempting to do is to seize my personality and claim it, and keep it scrolled within the tenseness of her purview. And like the majority in the West she cannot claim the more recondite habitations. She cannot claim my presence or even leap to the plane where miracles are enacted. For her, there is absence and the teeming of absence. And this teeming of absence is what compels her, is what magnetizes her very sense of effort, yet what I am able to emanate comes from a realm which no measurement can explore. To the replicating mind I am abandoned so common recall can't confine me. It is like a river seemingly haunted by instigation from which no direction can be formed. My spirit is not a house constructed of plaster and diamonds, and my mind is not built by lumber and barter. There exists no terseness in my power. Always the amplitudes persist. There is no limit to the energy which circles through me. Yes, a chiropteran, but also a leaf, a root, a spider, those parallel aforementioned ravens. All these relations being of subconscious sonar. Just the opposite of someone like Vespucci seeking to colonize nativity. Because I exist through adumbration my body can be fitfully explained by dazed accumulation, as if one could stack up sucrose in one's sleep. Again, my realia can't be measured. Across this inner condition I am not a chiropteran who feeds on summary olfaction: in this regard I do not attempt Zomaya in order to extract faeces or blood. I am not an enemy to her senses, but to the tedium which enthrals her senses. And it is this tedium which leads to deeper and deeper negation. And by negation, I mean negation of spontaneous occurrence. Zomaya has created a criminal rationality. I know her mind, it can orchestrate in listlessness. It can take someone like Jesus and direct his derangement according to the surrounding collectivity. Which means she's adept at magnetically harnessing a general point towards which the proximate bodies cascade. She justifies annealment to a pre-existing limit embellished by current circumstance. But on the other hand it can work against her. As in my case, it can turn to psychic squalls, to meta-dimensional spirals, as if the Sun had expanded beyond its distance. Naturally Zomaya leans to what she has known, to what allowed her scandalous priority. Exacting creatural comfort, specific social escalation.

From what I gather, Edmundo grew to term in Canones or El Valle, where all the roads were dirt, the populace conscripted by poverty. Having gained from unsavoury windfall, Edmundo continued to intensify his coffers. As his status increased Zomaya and Catalina became an unspoken presence amongst the New Mexican Conquistadores. They became accepted as conservationists of the order. So by allowance of their social advancement, they felt, as their God given persona, the private right to indulge in all manner of depravity. Being privy to the enormous bouts of Catalina and Edmundo in private, she has developed a stark dualism which craves lucidity on the one hand, and a sensuous cruelty on the other. I cannot say that she occupies greed, but she places maximum effort upon centrality of station. This is why I exist in this state, hidden away, dazzling with occlusion. Being consumed by the fear of status she is consumed by the paltry enclave of systems. It could be said that I am virgin in the sense that I have never been tempted, or had to withstand the beast which proliferates in the form of social pressure. I understand this, but there are other creatures, other burnings which attempt to ensnare me in their welters. Perhaps me as a fragile vampire willow as psychic prey to a flat nosed bear secreted in an obscure uranian warren. Certainly, I cannot claim like Zomaya to have my name inscribed by ecumenical burin. I admit the profundity of my hovering, of my dispersed syntactics. On the other hand she is in no position to admit the depth of her carnality, conjoined as she is by duplicitous conjuration. Much like a priest in his dual monstrosity conducting masses in secret condoned by obsolescence and murder. Holding her at bay I remain the oblique tactician, understanding all the curious and indelible combinations.

Because I have never uttered ascent to the Christos, I am freed from superfluous entanglement. I practice no crude conjoinment with any pointless intercessionist seeking to negotiate my spirit with endless shifts of eternity. Such converse is not possible. The priest or intercessionist's concerns only encapsulates assumptions within a conscious point in time. It then accrues as belief that which has no key to the stunning gulfs which surround the haunted persona. It has no power to quell the psychic fires when the outer forces take root. And I am speaking of the root of new Suns spinning with voracious inevitability. After sleeping I always wake to the mounting chaos of stars. Yet beyond the phenomena of these Suns I feel surges which accrue and suffuse my nervous reach with a sound which suggests a wayward and profound alchemical instigation. Now I more profoundly understand the universe and its ecology of treason. For instance, cosmologists seem hampered by the transition of humans and the dice of events. And so within the dice of phenomena I am still the cause of the unstilled leper, a subset of subsets, brokering in myself something other than the powers which peak from human transition. As subset I am reduced. So even for the European cosmologist I tend towards alien energy when they tend to objective ideas attempting to break the glass of the planes as proof by quantification. I'm speaking in this regard of my own authenticity as ghost. I see eternity as a parallel somatic tincture, and so I am of that race of beings who extend to other planes under the guise of other energies. So how else speak of a prolapse on Neptune, or gather intuitive events concerning catalytic volcanoes as they occur across the galaxy. The psyche as pan-spermia, always eclipsing its own state. Therefore I have been able to shift inside myself between known and unknown lumens, as if I shifted between a zone like Sogdiana, and one of the poles of the moons of Saturn. Not random and oblique, yet at the same time random and oblique. A most excruciating in-sovereignty. Not that I am bemoaning a former perception of sovereignty; this is certainly not the case, knowing all that I have known, by superseding all that I have known.

Alienated ray?

Intervallic raptor?

If I revert and inundate myself as Rosanna, then one may start to cycle the vocables which maintain the titanic through the suicidal. My circumstance would be more fully enumerable concerning guilt and the tragic moral psyche. The duty of censure, self blame, truncated obsessional reach. Instead of darting as chiropteran, I would weep in my broken habitat compressed by the power of self-haunting. I would be in-solstitial, laboured, having less than the powers of interrogated phantoms. But because I occupy randomity I am without the nexus which implants itself according to formal embarkation, according to plummeted electrical prognosis.

Do I carry neutrality as regards basic dwelling as depression? Has depression been falsely occluded by neutrality so as to become an in-genuine psychic buffer? Am I stealing forms from myself in order to withstand myself? I must admit that this day I am blank. That the feeling I once renewed seems absent on this day. That pointlessness reigns. Should Zomaya now punctuate my presence, I would present myself through curiously looming weakness, as if the solar form had never visited my substance. I am liminal, fraught with ulterior unravelling. I have nothing in keeping with the general focus of the Empire. And by traitorous it is understood that matter remains the dominant exclusivity as barrier which resists as the single isle of being. As ultimate test I am surrounded by the infected, by those whose gross appeal roars like an Imperial fragmentary lion. So I am surrounded by these Imperial fragmentary lions. Always gnawing away at my rootings, always suggesting that my impalpable yield is no more than the scarce result of fraudulent apprehension.

There are days when the invisible refuses answer, when one is left tortured within a materially defined anachronism. Then the rancid fuels attempt enactment of the psychic pores. One is then struck by the untranslatable as tongue. So I feel this crushing in-support as if listening to myself on Dion or Mimas. I practise as singular habitat, as the one chiropteran who exists, who has left all other chiropteran, who seems swallowed by the oblivious. And Zomaya and Ornelas seem more and more consumed by the oblivious. That region of being that the living and the dead pronounce as oblivious. In other words, ornaments, which render the seeming presentness of things. Which means I am no longer part of consensus laterality. And this is not of stylistic manufacture, but something which lives as substantive sigil.

Am I reducing in the process others who exist as psychic chiropterans, who aurally interrogate folly?

Am I positing myself as sum as highest highest? Have I so removed my remains so as to increase the rest to pointless giaours or infidels?

Let me say, I know no literary posture, no baffling charades as they pose for themselves through intellectual posture. Therefore I am without prior posture as regards any conscious underpinning. Not bounded by parentheticals there doesn't exist for me theory, or the compound or complex as regards thought preceding thought which accrues as political orchestration. Yet I have not procured evidence that can be pursued within the psychological constructs imposed by mediocrity. I cannot enmesh a perfected enunciation in order to create an authenticity with a public derived and contracted by the aforesaid mediocrity. And I am not saying that the body does not exist, that ciphers don't circulate through matter. I am not negating ignitions as they occur in the feelings. I've felt markings on the body as if burned by glass, feeling the scent of upheaving planes in my being. Everyday uncertainty, and with that uncertainty constant strain etched by emotional plague.

But in spite of everything kept a-blaze as accusation, the brutes were born by spontaneous mammalian combustion. Just because Zomaya was crowned by nefarious induction does not mean that she or the brutes remain consumed by static appearance. I do not look at them as a complexity to be suddenly solved. They all live. And quite possibly Zomaya could ruthlessly portray me as someone who breathes as living moral corruption. As someone who has lured Jesus, and because of that luring has forced Zomaya to beat him, to constantly charge him with unseasonable calumny, convinced that his darkness is sorcery bred by untenable Olmec. She could say that I've bred the Olmec in him, that I've caused the pestilence to rise from the vapour of his bedding. By further illustration she could say that I've cast a ruse upon Oraculos so that he desired his own daughter, and that Esteban followed suit by the sheer fact of my presence. And of course the whole of them could concertise these charges expressive of the danger I've engendered. I do not say that the brutes are personal clauses that I've scattered across my teeming ravine. It is not sorcery, nor is it wisdom which I wilfully construct as this damaged family portrait. Yet I've registered in my depths the oppression they've embodied in me, and thereby feel the need for insurrection which my mind continuously calls for.

My stamina has to do with a particular kind of judgement. And I say this because I weigh my mind like a blasphemous kind of algebra. Again, not a necromancer's hoax, or an eeriness displayed through power as ironical codex, but a wayward instigator's physics which implies rapturous conjuration. A conjuration over and beyond contentious operation. Not a momentary dalliance which lives without energy, but a realia like a tribe of eagles haunting phenomena with proto-electrical heat. You ask, why does a chiropteran speak of eagles, why do I as occlusion speak of flight as relates to optical exposure? Then, as relates to Zomaya, am I showing compassion as if she were forced to breathe beneath ammoniated crags? Because I'm seeing Zomaya and the brutes as perpetually trapped as Homo Sapiens Sapiens. Add to this the fact that I have as chiropteran reached alterity in the Divine. Of course this implies gradations between Homo Sapiens Sapiens and Rosanna the chiropteran who flies inside the solar current of Sun-struck rivers. I'm speaking here of compressed tremendums, of vertical densification, living as clairaudient intensity, which advances as struggle on the anomalous plane. Perhaps birth has granted me this lone survivability, this daunting research of the inviolable, which allows me access to the spellbinding centricality of all possible myrioramas. And so since I've been privy to thoughts outside the cosmos it can be understood how I have objectively probed the value of social standing in the world. Whether I've socially engaged as a breathing body, or as occurred so far in my odyssey, left to dwell as chronic invalidation, ultimately means nothing in the total drift of things. Now I profoundly understand this planet filled with conscious beings staggering in the void, chronically transmixed with mystery. So in this sense what does it mean to be a king, or leader of a planet? Even if one fled to a translocated moon what would it mean to erupting stellar nurseries as I speak? What would it be to their rampant plutocracies floating within a corrupted cellular mean?

There exist no answers in terms of belief or behaviour, the latter seeming to convince according to atomic fixation. The sighted cling to belief as an unalterable plinth, where the mind locates its fervour in prejudice. If I accepted Mary Magdalene as my only honour I would locate according to de-limited respiration. According to the arthritic which can only relate to a former condition of itself. How can this bring the stellar implications into presence? How can this unite the unknowable with its incessant cipherisation? Having said this I am convinced that there exists no outcome according to conscious or rational leaven. Of course I have abandoned systems, simultaneously merging with and becoming chiropteran. Again, an instinctual power which understands itself over and beyond any notion of itself. I exist, and because I exist there can be no other outcome than the simultaneous notions which parallel themselves. It is like an energy which concludes and quickly unravels that conclusion. Thus, I can announce to the sighted that the Gods are disfigured landmarks, and have come to figure as a prime example of unintelligible figurines. In this sense they are impediments charged with uninhabitable foundations. Beyond bare existence there exists a facelessness which impalpably hisses. Pure energy, yes. And from this energy a continuous permutability. Because the Sun is resonant with this fertility I equal on its behalf a clause of barren snow which burns and reflects as its power light as a merciless cinema. I'm speaking of dialectical alteration, where the nervous system becomes a creative neology tending to lean beyond the tenebrous. In the deepest sense I travel an unalterable thunder course, those navigational sums which gain through deeper and deeper relativity. As for now I evoke the blind plane of lightning, and because I evoke the blind plane of lightning I understand my situation not as some absolute or unchanging horror, but a zone that will dispel through intuitive approximation becoming existential animation. Of course I can argue without cease the in-benefit of Zomaya, the in-benefit of corrosive Catholic penance, but they too are merely particles subsumed by the eons. Because the eons and Holocene seem incommensurate it gives me subjective grasp of gargantua. As particle in the eons, spawned in the vastitudes, I understand that a zone will exist when nothing will occur.

I am not bemoaning the sands in my body. I am not bemoaning the power of previous cruelties, memorialising some fleeting thought of Edmundo and Catalina involved in a gluttonous tryst at the Alvarado Hotel. Which become thoughts extending themselves through consumption. Thus the Sun as transpicuous fire extends through human psychic consolidation. I, Rosanna, exquisite in my own delirium can tell you that I feel a powerful quality in my haunting. A sidereal internality etching my soma as exports to other dimensions. And from these exports other somas coalesce and parallel to terrains that the present Earth cannot withstand. To attempt Napoleonic conjunction at this level becomes no more than a spectral absurdity. To speak of one Napoleonic is to implement regression, is to speak of one who lessens and lessens and lessens like flames from aborted stars. I'm signalling out Napoleon as the one example in 4000 years, because history in its greater quantity has devolved around nepotistic dissolution. The upper classes who disrupt and destroy. The Spaniards who condone themselves by whiteness. Never condoned by European absolutes I am proud to say I am Indian derived from the Pharaohs, if I say I am Mescalero and Olmec, it more expresses my gifts as they continue to drift from Asiatic sands, from Afro-Dravidian summits-mystically south of Sumer. My essence being not of the Northern regimes, or of the fumes of their pessimistic jargons filled as they are with belligerence and bloodshed. This has been the strain, the general mark that Zomaya has compounded. Her ferocity, according to Northern lack, according to life long composition by error. This remains a curious testing point for me. In this sense I am always alerted by discomfort. Thus, my power constricts through incentive. But then hypothetical injunction induces flight through constant tremor. One clings to savage posture ironically blessed by partial impairment. And what better example than I, Rosanna, the cosmic reject from the sea. And because of this velocity of isolation my neural structure weakens and disappears only to re-arise and spin as nouveau planetary option.

The toxicity which seems to generally advance cannot cast pressure on the winged. Because I advance through collapse, my flight through imperial fatigue does not mean that I exist through impartial workings, workings which connect and erase, and connect and erase, as if I were other than a living momentum. I call the latter Cartesian physiology which I associate with the breakage of the mind, prone at the surface to aspects which lend themselves to mechanical registration.

Let me ask the question; is the body prone to biological psychiatry?

Can it recall all remembrance of its ancient metamorphosis?

I can only say that the invisible suffices, that animation precedes measurable tectonics. The source can never be concluded as isolate fragment. It is like saying, that I, Rosanna as temporal personality exists as the whole of the psychic energy field. This is why I can never conclude as the anonymous impersonal figment. Being a blind Mrs. Vargas whose typical conclusion only evinces a smile. A limitation of one who curtails her responses to limitation and is thereby seen as a citizen whose upright advances shepherds authority. Who keeps to herself and defends at all costs official pronouncement.

I know that I've already advanced this response, responding to Mrs. Vargas and her consuming retrogression. I'm concerned with skills which transcend the soma, which imply the skills passed down from the mother's mitochondria. In the case of a Mrs. Vargas there exists a dominant mitochondria which advances unintelligence. This tends towards the collective model which always fails to advance itself through insight.

In rarer response, fire from the cytoplasm soars as imaginal contagion. I'm speaking of the arts of the mind. Those fuels which evolve through dendritic inter-meshings which ascertains findings far beyond pedestrian groundings in soma.

So do I thank Zomaya for her genetic mitochondria?

Do I revere her power through retro-causal prayer?

In answer to the latter two questions I've found no conscious energy in my being. No diagrammatic model to refer to. So what I'm experiencing to a greater and greater degree is independence from regression, independence from fear which cancels combusting ambrosia. These words coming from a body which has always been vacant, and which stares from its unstable infinites. Being chiropteran I am a source which flits between densities, who emerges and de-emerges as simultaneous emission. Because of this emergence and de-emergence I emit no linearity. The cells cross-pollinate and rise and extinguish. This again creates psychic tremor which translates across physical proximity. For Zomaya this translates as unease because it creates no sovereign motion, no equational surfeit which issues connecting lines and sparks. No one can know in which direction I'll combine. Therefore Zomaya concurs within draught. Because I have no social concurrence I appear to her as a curiously exposed cipher. Moreover I know she mentally weighs my cipher as a test of the unclean. Therefore I persist as despicable anecdote. So I am speaking as one who opens implicate insurrections, as if I sat here waiting for some small recognitions of my outcome, yet at times I scream, I bite my wrists in anger. This is why I understand how hurricanes act as messengers of work. They pass in and out of vertigo as simooms and anti-simooms, erratic, prone, multiple, violent. Then the calm which understands itself as morphological turquoise. And this turquoise exists as a ravishing phonology, a phonology intrinsic to the way I intensify, to the way my molecules ignite and spin about themselves, as if the body were a coded bell, or a soporific index, or a therapeutic spiral. I do not speak according to auditory scripture as though I had developed ghosts by causation. Yet these ghosts are always posing questions about the given, about the flaws which continue to post-erupt from the earliest proto-suns. As chiropteran such questions flow through me. Because I do not disturb myself with intellect which disturbs its own electrics by always maintaining a halting circumnavigation. And I mean by this those mental constructs which deflect and give off restraint as pointless secondary chatter. Ultimately, Ornelas and Zomaya can go no further than the heights of a garrulous secondary chatter. Always they pursue a boundless in-direction concerning the imminent power of things. Codification through samsara, which leads to action mired in psychic statutory trauma. In scorched contusive powers which mingle inside motifs which neurologically dazzle and then settle into half-wrought meiosis. In this state questions can never convince themselves of their own energetics. And so they replicate and self-replicate and fall into fatigue. For me, these are energies which burn in error. In themselves they are not the ultimate defeat of balance, yet they echo proof of impoverishment, of grasp which curiously dissolves at contact with living kinetics.

I call these flaws; I call these circumstantial groundings in the being. They treat the human condition as if I fed them ropes and candles. As if the species were still rooted in phantasmagoria. In contrast, such rooting takes place at a depth no deeper than the surface of auricular skin life. What I'm doing is calling on the vastness which hovers in the levitated question, its abstract ignition through distance commanding both a primal and a secondary energy being both separate and unextended from the soma. Essential organicity is of course lessened. Then the great questions founder in compounded dimness. This is a dimness which as chiropteran I tend to decipher. I echolocate its rays, and understand their depth through elliptical in-direction. Which are rays which rankle, which extend through aporia. It is like listening to sound in splintered aural mazes. To the less perceptive mind such mazes take on the air of fixation, as if one prophet, one law were responsible for created gargantua. As if one desert yielded the whole bitterness of the cosmos through the voice of one prophetic extension.

To pose questions which reek of impossible scale creates in the soma a frenzy of ghosts. These are abstract lightnings from gulfs of concussive data. Micro-tonal centipedes creating an energy parallel to true self-effacing emotion. Ultimately I'm speaking of the question as posing binaries based on rising above yes or no commands. Saying this, I am not negating forms of guidance, but at the same time I've suspended those levels of the given subject as they tend towards oppressive cultural dictation. I mean the question as posed according to the monomial advanced in the service of say, a poisonous Euro-electrical invasion, with its need to promulgate reduction, with its need to promulgate reaction according to its fear. I can in no way tolerate such reduction, I can in no way cultivate its prescient adage which always announces a dry foretelling as matter. Someone like Zomaya can see that I'm psychically fused by the primeval as resistance. As one who has soared beyond all need for resuscitation. As one who has exhibited none of the omens of thinking. As if I had absconded links to human registration. Perhaps she feels me as coelacanth or water owl. A being for whom communion is unmentionable. A being who ironically blazes deficit by deficit so that my appearance to her daily must take on the cast of an in-germinate cipher. And this remains to her reflexive response as the equation of ciphers with their corresponding energy as silence.

For me, life remains seasonal as distance. It is like an invisible grace, not unlike 20,000 years brewing a curious vapour from voltage. Not the voltage as I'm told which smoulders in meadows, but as growth transpersonal with methane and shaking. And it is because my blindness wanders inside this methane I am able to evince a primeval glossary laden with saliva. Therefore I've ignited a seeming synoptic fictional largesse. A panoply of wrath blessed with a memory of the Sun as it leaks into the Sun. Raw, like a poetically derived Cimmerian trout, implying kelp, and maize, and various forms of helium, so if I attempt to break open gourds, if I attempt to activate my torso in another living continuum it is because of my cortical spells which remain torrential in their struggles. I call this fate emboldened inequity having left vernacular understanding in its metier of dishonour. It is like saying that I've glottalised brilliance, that I've unleashed its tropical honings and transmixed in-location with rotational oneirics. These are my travels that Zomaya cites as distance, outside the mysterious planes which seem to govern the stupendous. Of course I'm saying this as being more than the frayed eater, or as Rosanna the orphan, portrayed through her curious lexical priorities. I am more than a terminal body which rivets, more than a disabled mistress who slumbers. Now I cast this rimless electrical field, this drama which electrifies tremendums. For Zomaya, it is like facing a limitless convexity. It is an energy which contends with in-canonical turbulence, with a flux of stars and gases, with I, Rosanna, as its microscopic plinth, its gnawing cellular abyss. Yet as both plinth and abyss I am neither, being parallel by intangible, and by that again which surmounts itself in the intangible. It must be understood that I've reversed the hypnotism, that I've gone beyond the bounds of the appropriated. No longer does my energy respond to the dialectics of the expected. Furthermore I am not a mystic who associates her affairs with any previous enunciation. I have not allotted my stores to Christian or Islamic inference. My current ignites the powers which prevailed before Menes. I can only say that I was born and imploded with a given name. Not an implosional core, but something random, ad hoc, in-tenacious.

Can I say that Zomaya wrought my ad hoc appellation? Or was, it Oraculos prone and mumbling out names after one of his steadfast drinking bouts? All I know is that the name appeared and has acted upon me as no more than a tangential compulsion. By my experience in these latter days I have come to feel more transmixed by its exposure, so that Rosanna has become a symbol which aligns me with compelling depths. It is a spark, a relay which ignites a liminal balance between the visible and the invisible. So whatever Zomaya or Oraculos intended no longer has a source in existence. What seems curious is the lacuna between my birth and Zomaya's subsequent vaginal healing. Were the brutes doused with sleep inducing syrups? Or were they sexually ciphered due to miraculous moral incantation? From what I ascertain the body of the den was maintained, compulsive alternation was forgone. So my name is circumstance and I've gained neutrality over my circumstance. Therefore I have placed no restriction on Sister Ornelas in calling out my name. This not only guards against triggering depression, but its vocalization rises and keeps me seminal with balance. Of course my humanity hallucinates, and both levitates and self-depresses. So in the objective sense I have no status, my condition is joined to nothing. If I were sighted I would walk at the very bottom of mirrors so as to deflect my own grimness vis-à-vis what I feel and what I know of what I feel. Since I am feeling only part of my marrow as I speak many of the episodes in my body riot and spell out to me a tracery of my own discomfort.

This is not something I'm hiding. It is an energy which Zomaya has faced with its un-intended neurology. It is a neurology which she can no longer track in me. It is like tracing an occulted thread inside obnubilation. Not being able to affirm this tracery of mystery she understands in herself that I have wakened to incalcable astonishment. Having embraced this condition I know nothing other than shifts of lightning in the body. Because I am primeval there are always phases of lightning in the body. It is nothing less than a language which shifts like a lower or higher Wolof making of itself vatic insinuation of that which has no boundaries. If I were bounded by Rosanna I would be truly inconsolable. Surrounded by consensus palpability I would truly be engaged by myself as nothing less than collapse. And I'm not speaking of fuel from a strictly chemical state. I'm speaking of the way depression conjoins with a treated galvanics. At this point how can medicinals conjoin me?

How can its modes align my depths with parcelled dopomine? The physicians would mechanically note the crime of my position going no further than producing chemical alternation in my system so as to describe my illness as a vapour, and make me party to the peregrinations of the subjected. The wage mongrels, the chemically depressed, the quotidian loyalists. But resistance explodes from the sum of my marrow. This is not Rosanna the exploited little daughter seeking placement on the roster of those who toil, who defend the given as they would a commandment. I do not anticipate any neo-acculturation creating in me the urge to walk out blind singing to the neo-Roman media that I was once misled, and am now ready to join them in their pointless conquest of the soul. I laugh because my spirit is chiropteran, and is rife with intangible ferocity. A ferocity which commences by emitting no current. Therefore I am she who conjoins no answer, thereby sealing myself against buffeted exteriors. My pattern is like trying to rationally trace the motion of moons as they explode inside a spleen. No order exists. No moral diagnosis of any disruption of pattern.

So am I speaking of agonized deterrents, situational debilities? It seems I live in mathematically cracked mirrors, that I've transmuted loathing through my curvature of breathing. This is the scope I desire, this is the mountain that I travel. Because my system de-emphasizes governing uniformity I'll fly through a zone which gathers from itself a palatial mansion of moths, while following the astral slope of a hidden tumbleweed current. This is why I vanish and re-populate my aura with wings which rise from metempsychotic dimensions, so as to irrigate movement as something other than the mortal as sensorium. Therefore I have no need to panic during the hours that my voice enunciates itself to itself. I have no need to covet exotica hailing in my quest aurifically burning owls. True, I am entered by nerves, by olfactory thrusts, by salacious dysentery models. So at times this is how Zomaya attempts to view me, as if I were a skink, or a common oedipal bear. She would like to remind me of Jesus' entry into my body, or conjure the whispers of Esteban before his swallowing up of my menses. Of course this is a rancid poll of her domestic gnemonics. Further, a whole catalogue of her despicable light could emerge as signs of ink on a page. A book of nefarious twisting, of infamous comradery imploding through New Mexico's other considerations. Zomaya would then exist as a new development beneath the Sun. But in this regard she is less bold than I, she has less grasp of the secret of transpersonal struggle. She is unable to see the possible good in her pestilence. She could publicly lavish herself with crime and thereby gather a following completely conversant with her failure. She could then erupt into the world as an incredulous monster. Perhaps this attention would find its way into texts which extol primeval conundrums. She could freely speak of erotica and oil, of milk which erupts from the nipples. But alas, it has been left to me to advance the power of my own speaking. Because I have been able to describe Zomaya according to a dulcet kind of murder I've been able to implicate the proto-suicides she engenders which always commences through psychic suffocation. Knowing for a fact that Oraculos my father, who, along with Zomaya, has fostered in me darkness, who implanted in my eyes Ophthalmia Neonatorum, a blindness resulting from incestual gonorrhoea. At times I feel its organisms alight like flies in my psyche. Yet to some oblivious expert I am nothing more than suffering affliction from enduring trachoma, that I am result of dark genetic gangrene.

Perhaps because I am psychic Seminole and Mexican it will be concluded that I suffer from onchocerciasis full of darkened filarial deposits fully formed in disrupted nervous fibres. Thus, the odyssey of Rosanna as urchin, as reactive concubine from hell. A Christian medium would conclude that I've come from broken cobra's locales, or from the elliptical ire researched in the works of Juan Liscano or Vincente Gerbasi. Yet to actively speak with someone fully rooted in oppressive conclusion would only affix my behaviour to an endless cycle of venereal osmosis. That I would create from my presence an atmosphere of deltas full of Sunless days. Or more specifically put, an atmosphere which lurks without warning on 44 Sun drained days. Thus the cells as rotational dioxide, as vivified alburnums, as prior Venusian peristaltics, ruining vegetation by upsetting winds above the Fahrenheit of neon. For me, I will always be chronological as heresy, as a dazed rabbinical hull, only giving me hope as self-evidence by bribery.

As to the chair from which I speak I have gotten used to the sores the urination produces. Tonight I suffer as a viscous microbe, as an overcast molecule. Ambulation is seldom probed, so I sit like a terse microscopic contact point existing between a double layer of haze. Perhaps one could dissolve me as a median droplet of acid being a gaseous stain in a subconscious valley. As to tectonic canyons I can only answer through a non-existent oxygen. Again, I am puzzling, part chiropteran, part human through molecule. So for someone looking for themselves in me I am rife with amphibology. True, there is heat trapped inside my puzzling depression. As for the jealousy which dwells in the atmosphere I know my presence traps my name inside its borders. On more than one occasion Zomaya became embroiled with Oraculos concerning beauty versus beauty. On many days I held the more preferable crown. It would exhaust Zomaya. Here I was the dextrous underling working on her behalf, yet overtaking her wiles while maintaining volcanic indifference. To her I was no more than annoying contraband evoking a virulent foment. Yet then as now there was gain on my behalf as I was curiously absorbed by neutralized potentia. Of course, there was never any overt resolution. I was always balanced by my teeming neutrality, keeping all the forces at bay giving me time to advance the sceptical devastation of my thinking.

Here I am with the arguments of a leper not craving the salt of any prior justification. Or signalling any Pentecostal forgery as if I were brazen and uncrafted to begin with. As if I had never sought the authentic in my droplets always minus the ire of true conviction. This ire is something Zomaya always senses. It is akin to a phantasmal quality which appears and begins to ambulate in her system. She knows this, she knows my arcane respirations so much so that her cells begin to mimic themselves through pedagogical oscillation. To her I've now approached a summed and torrential beginning. A beginning which overcomes the approach she invigorates through disfigured guises. I have appeared. So the eschatology I emit is something which lives in her as serious encounter. There can be no consolation in this challenge. My Braille configures an in-climatology which leads to further heightening above neurology. Which leads to pre-obtaining causes, which leads to clairaudient water in the genes. This is where the rains dislodge and re-commingle with mystery. It is through such sensing that one can speak of the weight of mist, of a soil so enlivened that its particles erupt according to continuous transparency. This is why my vocal irregularity threatens. No one knows what I say. I myself cannot know what I say. And when I say this there exists no form of deception, no pre-concluded spectre burnishing a rational code for ingestion. Because Zomaya's thoughts can go no further than her fetid blizzard house, no further than the contracted property, she simply seeks to endure.

In the hacienda there exists an archipelago of lapse rates, of complex denigrations, as if listening to rays from damaged botany. As in a seasonal lagoon there are minerals of commingled laterality not unlike a fractured calculus in a garish den. I remember the sounds from the rooms like a rush of aural integers not unlike the sounds of captured jaguars in Tenochtitlan. An almost mystical ferocity. Yet this remains symbolic of the clan with its baleful in-documentation. Again, I, the damaged diva, I, the pubescent suffragette, dazzling, ensconced in seeming paranoia. Every element in my life has been sickened by duress. Every luminosity has somehow instructed its own renewal in entanglement. So in spite of my age I am worn, my body clouds, it has forgotten its original patterns. So perhaps this is the subtext of why Zomaya now complies with my wishes. She sees my exposed scales, she sees the code in my in-operative balance. In her mind she adds up the scale of rapes, her own personal assaults, add to this, my irregular nourishment during her regime, and you have a being consumed by the physical scale of her actions. Conversely, my body begins to shake like an oracle during speech. So Zomaya in her heart of hearts knows this, and so she lobbies in her prayers for my collapse. Therefore she counts anonymous damage in her thinking. She calculates that through the testing of time a fabulous weakening will betray me, and she will awake one dawn and curiously approach Sister Ornelas, and the latter will confirm that my body has stilled during slumber. The relief would be palpable. The tapes confiscated, all record of my appearance stilled, even in the eyes of my former beholders. So as of now, I am balanced on damaged grain. Days arise and they set. And I know that this ordeal is not only my own but also all of the bodies which populate this mill. And I mean by this mill this unending roulette. And I mean by the latter all the beings in this drama of this unending roulette. Each individual implying death by draconian figment. For Jesus a dour eponymous dimension. For Oraculos the same, but of a more complex debasement. As for Esteban, biography as drain, as desolation fostered by imbibing. For Zomaya, the provincial misread through the catastrophe of power. It is a sum which continues to subvert her very dimension. Within this condition she is parallel to the worker who boils grapes, who cleans tiles for municipalities. This being the absolute maintenance of monotony.

Every day that Zomaya invades St. Catherine's it signals the assiduous maintenance of her nothingness. What accrues from monitored abstraction is precarious taint. Certainly not behavioural insurrection, but maintenance, as the lowest law of moral squalor. At best it could be seen as spinning phenomena by dice. What I've found is that the indefinite continues and mimics the human minimum as psycho-geology. This minimum I consider to be the amplification of error, of strife condoned by the habitual. This is the way that hierarchies live. This is rulership by stasis. Because the higher mind is generally stunted in these conditions the rulers are stricken vis-à-vis eternity. From this follows the emblems, the code words, the killings. Which results in the ownership of metals and lands. The latter evincing Edmundo and Catalina. Because everything for them was dictated by starkness. There was never in their minds any moral or electrical complication. The consuming obscuration of the brutes became to them an assimilated manoeuvre. Because they were hidden and psychologically caged, Edmundo could enjoy the status of the newly minted. By the time of his genuine social recognition Zomaya was of age, and since they had been born there was no inkling of their existence, no susurrations expelled regarding the general smell of their existence. The old Acoma helpers were compensated for their silence. To insular society there remained Edmundo and Catalina and Zomaya, as triangular hatchlings, as civic models whose destiny was approved by hard work. They existed as the perfect measure in no way consumed by misfortune. Their status was set. They had secured their implosive corner. It was a New Mexico unspent by the death ledgers at Almagordo, or the human experiment at the compound at Dulce. They were the perfect evidence of a comatose social setting. Yet this is corruption as legacy, as an on-going past tainted by genetic provocation. Reaching into what I'll call the poisonous onyx furnace. And the onyx furnace is the instinctive beguiling of the cells which feeds from primordial exhaustion. A lineage of error, of transient moral interpretation, somehow closed to the lakes of primordial respiration. What I'm evincing is not some pre-claimed ballet, some registered aesthetic formulaic with perfection. It is an understanding that deeper waters persist, that certain instinctual toxins can no longer persist.

So am I evolving myself as arcane utensil of use to levels completely devoid of the human?

Is this why I concur as chiropteran?

Is this the reason that I always feel power through obvious flames of desperation?

I understand the complete system of prey. And because I know its interior brevity through misfortune I can always sense its noisome nervous linkage, its spells which intensify synaptic toxicity. So in this sense Zomaya is its vermiculate transducer, like an old Jurassic spider spreading poison from a contained and insular velum. It's her exported colonization. I was always matched with Jesus as we were seen to respire through dialectical self-hatred. Because she is replete with a portion of self-hatred, I've come to be seen as the one most magnetic to these feelings. By attempting to devour the life I've had to offer she has advanced rather deeply into her performing schizophrenia. On the mental plane, assault upon my person was an attempt to exorcise the self-transgression in her spirit, and on the physical plane it was the animal in her so deviously culled from her infamous inclusion in the unseemly acts of Edmundo and Catalina. What she feels is always doubt of the perpetrator. Therefore there always exists schisms in the reasoning. And with schism comes weakening. And so sitting amidst the auricular circumstance which so envelops me I rush into the squall of her intervallic minimums further de-structuring her grasp by feeling myself through greater and greater exhibit. And because there is no precedent for my existing I feel her secreting toxins which go to waste in her general atmosphere. Yet it is not a cleansing which transpires, but a blunted attempt at post-occurring re-ingestion. As if she were taking on squandered poison, further stilling the voracious impetuosity which comes from an adder's authority.

So is Zomaya civilization?

Is Zomaya the whole species?

I'll say this: she replicates, she schisms, she turns around in her waste. She represents a species which presently fishes from crumbling ocean bottoms. This is what I'll call the Spaniard in her, the photonic European in declension. She who attempts to maintain a degenerate fiduciary kingdom. As if she controlled a ring of lessened circus beasts. As if she tried to hold in place a cracking meteor door. And day by day she feels me knocking on her meteor door raising up from the Earth otopathic spellbinder's castles. And these castles under the power of auric instigation emanating heraldic premonitions concerning loss at human boundary for supremacy of thought. And this is not simply a private concern, but a power unconcerned with Richters or measurement. Again I am speaking through primordial respiration alive with my compliance with the unfathomed, with cartographical ambrosia. I am not someone whose calm consists of ordinary thinking. Not the way that shoes are strapped, or gardens are disposed of. In this sense I am not confined to the syllabus of the senses. So to those of conscripted annums my thought will thrive as disturbing liquid, as anti-coagulant saliva which erupts from the vampire as chiropteran. Which means that I eat through annihilated posts, this being the symbol of energy emptied and non-standing. Which has nothing in common with law abiding summary. Something not quite in keeping with a protracted summons. This is not a bell perceived in doorways, or a sculpted bird screeching from a tower. I am not trying to advance a teeming social satisfaction by swearing on my grave, and even less am I replete as monarch who seems to hail over progressive forces. But here, something has set in over and beyond all known timing and protest. So if I said that I would protest the cells for another 300 years and then live as a blinding presence for another self-sustaining duration, this would be seen as taking on criminal exuberance, as fostering fantastical remoteness, deriving from a point no stronger than circuitous anonymity. Then the analysis would centre on displaced revenge, of raising myself to the level of indomitable consequence creating a thirst for many to behold. I am not trying to convince as though I had discovered my own movement through accrual from in-velocity, as though this in-velocity had created sustaining miracles. Believe me, I have nothing created that will re-shape Zomaya, that will create inside her spiritual hue reaction to religious commandments. No, not an explosion of salt which suddenly entrances the world to fall down in burning prayer. So I have not so simple a struggle when challenging the modes which prevail at the hacienda. There is an energy at risk. Something not perceived, yet occulted, veiled. Perhaps it is only I, the tense recipient of such gain, only I, the unvanquished sorceress who takes on other strategies of breathing. For me, the body and the mind are not of complete summation. Its tempestuous combination does not reveal complete evolvement or embody totalic integer which equates as palpable perfection. Perhaps in saying this I am hoarding directional nuance, or walking step by step beyond a quantifying ray. I am only saying that I have no consensus example to emit. I've seemed to go no further than pointless in-settlement procuring for myself nothing other than in-requisite living. It is another date, and another racing through mortality. And I sit as the urinating blind girl, and Zomaya comes and goes, and the brothers remain the same. They do not claw at new experience. What they do is return day after day to a core which enacts a central necrosis. Of course this means withdrawal from living energy. But in contradistinction how long I will persist as this body of existing rubble no one can tell. If it is God who funnels through the voice that I speak with, he fails to know within the structure of his exoteric power. There is no exteriority by which to weigh myself, by which to anoint my own unleashing. I only advance through my voice a new parabola of spells, which holds me, which allows me to trans-personalize the wealth of my own dilemma. What is for certain is that there exists a scurrilous temporal weather in the mind. Not a cold or childish summoning, but seeming fate as regards general mental abstraction. And I mean abstraction as it exists under day to day materialist's concerns. What persists for me is a condemned neurology which rises up and infects the psycho-chemical as posture. This neurology not carrying whole value becomes alive in itself as furious ambivalence. Feelings transpire as accuracy by dust. Then the mind is always given spurious fumes to imbibe. There exists in the depths no accuracy to one's banter. Under such pallor there exists no lingering assessment, no swan which speaks beyond calendrical saliva. But for some of us a great moment appears where a true amassing erupts and creative quivering appears. Of course this is not the psycho-physical as concrete, as bodily laws which occur, such as Esteban, Jesus, and Oraculos. What I'm speaking is an amassing above such figments, knowing these figments to be in keeping with Buddhist samsara. I mean the rattling of the bones overwhelmed by the body as the core of arresting tonnage. In response to this I feel myself as if surrounded by the flux of kelp taken away from the hive of detritus. In one dimension my residue exists as philosophical yeast, in another, as energy through quavering suggestion. Certainly not breath through simulation, but immunity from minds as they opt and opt again for terrestrial conclusion. Thus, I am the form which is gathering distance, which is moving away into the source of an unknown imminence. Imminence on this plane reacts like a susurrant separation of ice. A sound revealed through spontaneous unfolding analogous to diving, slowly bracing oneself in order to reach jagged underwater ranges, which corresponds to dangers ignited by butane and hazard. One always risks destruction. As for the seven stings of danger, I call them glass, pillage, rupture, asylum, spoilage, brain death, breakage. As for provisional definition I relate to glass as knives come to stasis according to a geology of phantoms. Pillage transmits for me mirage as proto-ambulate piracy. As for rupture, I think of the breakage of veins in one's river. As for asylum, the body as struggling glacial insensation. Spoilage relates to the harbour of waste which reeks in the spirit. Brain death relates to a ghost which is moored in broken haciendas. Breakage reveals the sudden giving up of the breath.

And I feel all of the above as gross enemy of the cells. But in another way perhaps ironical forms of surfeit. All I can say is that these are not absolutes, nor do they figure throughout the thought stream as unintended reasonings. They remain ambivalent reckonings along the way. For me, curious aural traceries within the system. If I were able to see the planets rise, at first, I would stagger over Venus, I would cool its verdet to a manageable degree so as to randomly transpose with certain crevasses on Mars. For the less discerning mind this is nothing but a code for revealing the supercilious, as if Olympus Mons had implanted itself on the lava fields of Venus. Then by extension I would move the Sun to a slightly less favourable distance so that a different planetary make up could apply. So you see what I'm leaning towards. What if Earth was not here? What if its spatial distillation had vanished? Would instinctive nitrogen still apply?

Perhaps I've created a childish transposition as if this were that and that were this, as if Rosanna had transposed the sequence of stars in her auspices as God. Yet what seems firmly rooted is the Sun and its local family revolving through explosive chance. Who says the distance from the Earth to the Sun has anything to do with a hand fixed hegemony? I'm speaking in this vein of stability as conjecture. Measurement in its latter manifestations has become nothing more than a fraudulent summary. It becomes a motif which enervates creative injunction. This is why I play with parsecs, this is why the realia of zones is always something other than persistence through reasoned abstraction. This is the spur to new discovery and view. This is why Kepler kept the Sun a secret. He had un-wrought consensus perception. It could be said that I have also turned the Sun around. In this degree I've more than courted the telepathic. If anything I am waving a nerveless banner, I'm sending out unspoken signals from my soma. Because of this I can walk along slopes on Venus, I can recreate topography by placing a double Sun in orbit. Here I'm not exhibiting a circumstantial prowess, or employing an exerted referendum on my ability to exercise the limits of being. Saying this, does my energy linger in other persons? Does it circulate in the likes of Oraculos? I know at some level he craves the hidden activity of certain psychic gifts, that he has made an obscuring appraisal for a second life on a nearby planet. This latter being the germ which exhausts itself in me. At times I stumble through my facts in the dark. And at times I must convey the fact that my energy works upon rumour. There is an intellectual fever which persists at the hacienda. I know that Oraculos cradles himself in his studies. I know that he is rampant with exploration when it comes to the heavens. A feral planet, a transgressive comet, embalms him in distance so that he can absent this portion of his being from the onslaught of bodies. Sometimes Zomaya may be engaged with Jesus, or in the outer world creating a stable picture of herself in the eyes of society. He does not enter her mind so he attempts to heal on those days. At certain hours he takes up terms on psycho-pharmacology, and combines them with study on the rotations of Uranus, thereby creating a chart, provisionally condoned by Hebrew magicians. Under different conditions I could feel him composing poems on the nature of great circumstance. On understanding the depth of various oblivions. Given these terms he is not so caustic, or irrelevant, or aloof. Within such behavioural sliver he is not the brutish field hand I once evoked. So there exists in him a testament to certain brewings of beauty. And I cannot say that Zomaya is averse to the ritual of study. As for Jesus, there exists articulation from pain. And as for Esteban, always menace and fever through his intellectual beckoning. None of them, but none of them seems prompted by the illiterate. Although dominated by the absurd, they remain perfectly understandable in this degree. Although Spanish suffuses the general locale Zomaya has made English the law. She says that it takes us away from cultural dearth, and allows us greater power in the region. I have never had instruction in Spanish. As far as I can tell the brutes understand a broken dimension of its usage. As for Zomaya, I know she speaks Castilian having had it drummed in her by the private fuels which stung Edmundo and Catalina. Edmundo, so desperate to distance himself from the penurious, from the dust of general Indian conclusion, provoked in him the need to explore a stilted Spanish, which Catalina approved, and which Zomaya absorbed from the habits of private education. But I, as the increasing victim, was only given the language which stemmed from Zomaya's law. I, the English speaking Seminole, I, the renegado, who darkens the English voice, so that I proceed by perpetual clauses. In this, I am never linked to direct usage, to absolute certainty or claim. For me, there is always the parenthetical as causation, as if I were always shaping with my hands sounds from invidious foil. It's like a secondary contact, or a poised yet bothersome distraction. As for nouns or verbs I only understand a minimum functionality. The same is true with the parts of speech, as well as adjectives and their various groundings. I cannot increase or reduce my acquisition in this regard. I am destabilized by volitional exhaustion, I do not throw my voice from the ramparts so that all will know what I'm saying. I am furtive, I seem to mumble beneath the moon so that my volitional engendering is my form of flailing and seeing. Because by speaking into these tapes it has become my first accrual of thought, the first essential ownership I've conveyed. I use shards of life as modes of energy within life. Certainly I do not comport myself through chastity, or convey an anger which constricts osmosis. I live a life through marginalia, through old suggestions which increase the tempestuous. Not a world contained by the pressure of gloating, or by praising my singular circumstance as I uproot myself from Zomaya. Again, I am not pacing myself through delirium, casting my code according to tragic reclamation. Yet at times my nerves ache, the power in my flesh seems crippled. But knowing the difference between the day and the night I feel my voice rising when the moon begins to fill my blood. It becomes the aural tincture of a double mind. There exists no official pacing to how I think, no rhetoric which dissolves me as invalid. I am merely one of the animals of divine absurdity. For me, there is a blizzard which crowns itself through insight. Not the pressure from sobriety, but a power which sustains itself, flaw by suggestive flaw. I feel that when I speak I am testing the crucial elements of oxygen, breeding new and uncountable sustainabilities. This is how the cells transpire under fresh vibrational eloquence. Not law, not persistent social quandary, but the high transparency of wonder spinning as tornadoes in the body. This is why I sometimes shake in silence. This is why I sometimes breathe as if I were hearing a completely new complicity. A kind of yoga, yes, but one without the action of immediate variety. So when I next speak to Ornelas I do not expect a report that Zomaya has dissolved, or that Zomaya has changed forms. I do not expect my suspension to randomly impact Jesus, to change his stature, or finesse elements of his mind from savagery or withdrawal. Therefore, the deeper parts of the mind do not respond to undue physical immediacy. Never a short term event, but geology in terms of the state of human change and renewal.

True life at the hacienda never existed. I was Zomaya's brand. I was the curious intra-foundling who ignited violence and limitation. But Zomaya knows that phase is gone and has absorbed abstraction in her mind, creating in her a deafness through human layering. What makes this so interesting is that the brutes have been entrapped inside this layering. The outcome to this entrapment could be attributed to heroin and liquor, to early debacle by means of estrangement. Nevertheless they enhance the provincial. They've become a sum of chaotic tools, always keeping their functions alive by continuous praxis as demise. They are soldiers marching to the inhospitable, drugged as they are on the methane of failure. And it is this failure which continues to haunt the human constitution. Behaviour according to repetitive poison. Again, behaviour which burns and investigates demise. This being the imperative of the civilized system as I've known it. And Zomaya continues to repeat this system with no other impact than fatigue superseding fatigue. The whole lot becoming a repetitive carnage of themselves.

Because Zomaya always knew her terrain she always took as her method the power of scrutiny. She always examined all the possibles and sub-possibles in order to ensure that all the forces were controlled. By examining all the hidden potentials she could ambulate the unpredictable. But this is what now destroys her. She no longer knows me. I've extended provocation by disappearing inside my being. I am not Jesus condemned by general self-loathing, or the unplotted syllables of Esteban, or the slurred misanthrope that my nightmares openly code as Oraculos. I've broken away from the timing she possesses, so when she blatantly attempts to possess me I give off the uncanny, enhanced by the vertiginous as kinetic. It is an alien temperature as if I were a rising sea on the moon. Because as chiropteran I echo and re-echo on this moon and emit to Zomaya an evaporated witness.

So as of now I'm not locatable, something a medium would equate with post-existing. Or perhaps as Rosanna I am analogous to Zomaya as a fish on a curious sea floor none has ever seen. Between chiropteran and chiropteran there exists a void, a seminal tincture which obfuscates the exoteric as motion. This is what Zomaya attempts to grasp, something from a strange lesion in existence. I, too, understand myself to be something other than what's been previously known. Not in terms of hubris, or understanding according to devolutics. This amounts to an energy which hovers, which chaotically respirates at a level beyond plausible dialectics. Vibrational effects which are somehow not beholden to the electro-chemistry of the nerves. One then shifts beyond the powers perpetual in human conditioning. A daunting vascular language which sends a stormy micro-climate throughout the body. The blood descends three caverns. The heart rate dulls, then extends by means of suffusing transparency. This is now the new magnetics which haunts her, which shifts in all directions. And I'm sure this is something that Ornelas has encountered but not to the degree that Zomaya has experienced. This is the effect of the cells in transition. The first stirrings, the first phenomena which is other than the senses. Having entered this realm I know that the past and the future are intrinsically altered in the depths. Shiftings begin transpiring on the surface. All former certainty takes as its substance the trajectory of the riddle. What once engulfed the mind no longer inflames. One becomes dazed in a cryptic maze of sigils. One's former command becomes shaken, the thoughts weaken only to further diminish in themselves which thereby intensifies the riddle. Nothing formerly known is obvious, an in-lucidity begins to prevail.

Death is no longer the progenitor that it was. The body takes on experience not unlike the chiropteran in movement. Unlike the domain of the former personality, interiority ignites, the inclement strengthens. One is then singed by bouts of disappearance, one's vocables extend as though one were collapsed by imponderables.

These are not powers evolved to fight quotidian social arrangement. One would think my power over Zomaya would be an end in itself. Power then carries no farther than an extra judicial malevolence. It becomes call and response from an agitated warren. Say, on a certain Thursday afternoon I would wake with a deadly mnemonics focused on Esteban; or perhaps on a following Tuesday focus my old despair upon an unsuspecting Jesus, I would only enrich calamity. As for complex motivation, it would only parallel the transhuman. I would only increase the energy of a classic chiropteran compelled by nothing more than a bevy of animal parts. But since I've mined the ethers of these parts my energy has gained the unlocatable as presence, giving further stimulus to the state I'll simply call unlimited evolvement.

It must be remembered that I've travelled through dazed experiment, that I've opened the blankness of a psychic double species. There's been only transition without respite. So in the deepest sense I feel I only live through the fecundity of experiment. Unlike the Chupacabra I seem separate from the land, inhaling spores from unstabilised vampirics. Something which has never appeared according to the chronicles of experiment. Something outside of chronic anchoring flaw. And I mean by this specificity of species according to forgone definition. Certainly to Zomaya and to all who view me, I am strange. I, who cast no seeming definition. A girl who seems impregnable, who is immoderate, who at the same time reeks of the angelic. Who solicits from herself no background, who seeks to conjure from tension no audience. Therefore, I am indeterminate as solar jewel, as sapphire, as ruby. This is my true inclemency, to withstand the power of my own chronic saturation. Which respires as a sudden insular daring rising as a flame from co-habited dust. Even when doubt assails me I can speak of no final defeat, no geographical dimension which makes of me a cannibalized injunction. So any power that scolds me, or defends me, creates in my ascendance a stunning creatural spur, allowing my transcendence of inner war, and its attending torture which collapses.

These are brushes with existence. Self ingested forms plummeted into cusps. And these cusps keep one angled, vociferous, desolate eerie conditions persist. It is like feeling a treeless sensory delta consumed by worms and ravens. This is loneliness at its most en-fixed. And it is in this state that the most merciless dangers persist, always feeling around me curtains of torn anemones. It is knowing that powers are construed through elemental ambush. One is always unsafe.

I'll admit there are days when I am diacritically reduced, when I strain against compression. It seems I am emptied of possibility, that I am fractionally conversant with the quicksand which runs about me. Because I am not resolved by stupor, or claimed by grainy indices rates I seem overwhelmed by absence, by thoughtless nautical samsara, always entangled by impending outcome. With Zomaya and the Myrmidons I felt I was born into parlous solar bickering always insisting on crime and seeming personal obfuscation, on the after effects of imploded solar tautologies. As if I were onierically captured by a plutonian midwife only to be released to the crows over and over again. Therefore a sacrificed property in a sullen anti-bohemia. The hacienda seemed sculpted from a poisoned masonry of sugars as if gathered from exploded kivas. This is the New Mexico of Don Diego de Vargas, with his Indian slaughter, with his massacre of innocents, the land held to his laws which have descended to Zomaya as massive fragmentary roping, laws which anneal themselves to jaded burial foundations. And the hacienda was and remains a jaded burial foundation. I've felt the fumes rising from its burial foundation. Perhaps these are fumes from Don Diego transmixed with the seed of

Edmundo. A psycho-genetic intaglio. These fumes are not the result of neutered scatterings, no, they've created a virulent oscillation in the run of things. Jesus, and Esteban, and Oraculos, each carry a particular strain of this virulence. All of them warped by genetic super-imposition. Jesus, withdrawn, brutish in demeanour, Oraculos, the dandy, the psychically impoverished scholar, and Esteban the drunken dastardly medium, always active with the power of insult. I call them the various spirits of Edmundo and Don Diego. In my mind Edmundo and Don Diego combine in intra-cohabitation with Catalina. And quite naturally the offspring, alive with punishing cholera, with a sumptuous array of toxins. I'm not saying that the crimes of the hacienda exist as exclusive portrayal. I am speaking of a condition which exists in the Yuga at the end of Yugas with its downward spiral into general psychic disaster. The Gods so recently conceived are creations which impose the implausible, who furtively impel this disaster. They tend to create in the populace a reprehensible frenzy for which no known antidote can be found. For instance, the power in rocks or volcanoes carry within themselves true mystical clarity. The same cannot be said for Pisian mental configurations, Gods who are jealous, who maintain schizophrenia. Using these criteria perhaps Don Diego is God and created a calling in Edmundo that was overwhelming and irresistible. A suffocation which ensued in Edmundo allowing him to fully subscribe to his hatred of the Indian in him, moving him to claim the personal genetics of a European Spaniard. And God became no different to the like minded Catalina wanting to never know the roots of the Mescalaro within her. So they convened a pact between them of re-creation and denial. As if they had sprung fully formed from the land of the Spaniards. And building from their fortuitous copper windfall they took on the trappings of local ersatz aristocracy. Zomaya and the Myrmidons blaze with these poisons creating from this myth the pathological traits of assassins. At the out-start I'm sure Zomaya understood the design of Edmundo and Catalina. Keep a concrete formation intact. Create for the world an accessible portrait. A small family unit without seeming tension. No sprawling array of siblings, no backdrop of in-order. As is known, the reality of the brutes was kept shuttered. Not even the slightest scent came from their absence. Zomaya was the only sibling. The only child as the perfect ideal. From what I gather her education was enormous, was advanced in a way that an ambassadress was urged to study. To know the rule and law of continents, to know eclectic thinking patterns, to create new points in the literature of behaviour. And it is on this latter point that Zomaya held sway at the hacienda. How to sway Esteban towards Jesus, or how to make Jesus commune with Esteban through Oraculos. She established a reigning behavioural tonality. She worked by means of informational duality. Or better, of working with different mathematical weights as they formed at various moments in the odyssey of the differing personalities. She knew how the ardour of Jesus interacted with her menses. Of how she directed Oraculos by means of perfectly timed flirtations with Esteban while in the throes of his behavioural drowning. All this crowned by whispers from an orchestrated turbulence. At times, its wrath, or in other dimensions its concentrated sniping. This is the backdrop of my youthful devastation, having all of my nascent assets robbed. I being prey, who was forced to function beyond my self-functioning limit. I was woman, maid, memorizer of randomness, raconteur, formal verbal entertainer, mistress, ghost, in-celibate scholar. The list pullulates and goes beyond its own rejuvenated terror.

This is why I sit having gone through all the motions of imbalance. When such irregular motion has been breached the void dawns, the seeming universe appears. Not in terms of common ocular tenets, but of the way the Sun equates to neurological inkling. Its light then shifts in the neurons, in a form which no longer inheres to stabilized procreation. Thus, this is not a memoir which mirrors quantifiable lagoons. It is an energy which supplants itself as integer becoming suffused as intangible mantra. Therefore I am no longer Rosanna who functions at the behest of a controlling samsara. And it is through this understanding that I understand Zomaya to be a controlling void in samsara. Yes, a maniacal beast, a portentous infidel, but something other, than these powers which seem to code themselves with repletion. And these codes are signs which seem to enmesh themselves in human events. They then become to common perception structures of historical wrought iron, weighted mental postings, chimerical rallies and labour which narrate the general dilemma. And each nation and each mist of nations creates priority and claim and momentary rule over samsara. As chiropteran and Rosanna, I also partake of samsara and its findings. I was born, I breathe, I partake of the forms which project from its lurking phantasmata. Yet there is something which exists as general generating nuance. Not something we can equate with tenaciousness and substance. Not a ferocity which gains on itself, but something other, something which dispels while opening interregnums. This dawn, this night, this opening in my genetics remains the zone of interregnums. Not a state compelled by forensics, branding the mind argument by compelling argument. No, I am not clamouring in my confine seeking to create in its wake an effortless mystical seismology, but to create from the cells a spate of light which connects the higher states to the ambulating body. This latter state is not the equity of Nirvana with its escape to the sum of impalpables. I sit here infused with levitational salt, feeling a source of light which writhes inside the body, not totally unalike a powerful interior rotation. Therefore, no one can say that my body is mirage, or shifts as a vacuum which occludes itself from the intrinsic nature of itself.

A hubristic explanation?

A voice uneven with folly?

There always remains comparison to the human mean as compunction, to the body as civilian compost and its division from an unseen voltage.

It is assumed from common assignation that I am the vampire which feeds from higher or lower suggestion. Who feeds from invisible bursts, from angelic para-normality. So is this motion from a dominating gravesite? Or does it remain a ritual burdened by the rancour of mortal remains? The latter questions conjoin to enlivened materiality, to corpus in the West concerned with obsessive materiality. Vis-à-vis this obsession I feel I have revealed to myself a ghost fire, a fire between states. I've stated those questions because I exist at another remove. A remove outside the Western proportion of dialectical consistency. But for me the dialectic is composed of breathing and divination. Yet I do not assume such oscillation as if I had gained upon myself through abstract pattern as reasoning. As though I had conquered my status as a recipe for mystery. This is a level which human interaction can't explain. This is why all the summations from the hacienda can never explain me. If I summon every detail from every part of my life nothing can explain me. I cannot return to those moments as the entangled Scheherazade keeping swarming perversions at bay. I cannot return to the Zomaya who fuelled poison, who continuously fuelled stealth, much like a cunning mother Roman lizard. I've experienced a particular devastation. Having never had any childhood companionship this is my first extended converse with myself. And it can be said that this is my first attempt to know myself to myself, to extend a hand to myself so as to blindly trace my own abstentia. I do understand that one can never know oneself even when eschewing the brokered outskirts of reason. First of all I am amazed that I continue to live, that I continue to vocalize symbols. Yet I cannot conclude upon solace. In some depth of her contorted witness Zomaya must still desire me. Oraculos would always whisper that my body even in its reluctance exuded kinematics. That my temperature sustained its power more than did Zomaya's. During one of his stupors Jesus called me Mexican and Seminole. And he meant this in the sense that my body was both resistant and electric. As for Esteban he too always compared me to Zomaya so jealousy completely consumed her, so what now issues between us is chronic morass and suspicion. In the politics of life it is like the second in command being stronger than the ruler. In my situation it is being born into envy. That simply by being parallel in gender Zomaya could feel the future and my challenge to her destructive in-gemination. That I summoned other gifts from the mind, and had as my potentia a dominance which could emit itself through charisma. She senses things. This is the depth that she carries about her. She is no mean person and

I understand her to be someone in extremis who desperately holds onto convention. It has created great tension, so as a means in this life I have always been forced to embody dissonance. If indeed my thoughts come out jutted, this is the soil in which my seeds have been engendered. On the other hand it is the power which accrues from great strife. There exists this war inside my solar plexus as if storms were always brewing. The cycles which exist in zones before eruptions. As with proto-eruptions there are tremblings, sluices of Earth which slip, while listening to rabbits and Earth dogs sending out signals. This is eruption with its Lahars and proto-Lahars. So always in the hacienda there remained the tension of a proto-Lahar. A silence through which quaking could extend. So when Oraculos would suddenly appear then feeling his shape upon me, dread would infuse me, my breath would take on partial quaking. Never knowing the way that he would seek to use my body. What I can say is that his penetrations tended more to erotica and deliberation, whereas Jesus was more brutish and tense in the form of his invasives. The body understands differences. Even the body of a girl understands differences. Esteban would apply torment with his crushings. Not so much in terms of physical dishonour, but the way he approached my current with the timing of his voice; with his curses, his deprecations, his threats. I was always a psychic pilgrim always forced to wear a desolated scarf. I existed as a deafening cipher adrift in a locale compelled by consternation. This prior consternation has morphed. Yet in contra-distinction there is triumphal assuagement in the way my voice issues, in the way my voice erupts and clears itself for greater and greater eruption. This has allowed me a less inclement distribution of my senses. The body of the girl is now complicit with inherent constellations. Not a utopian respiration, but certainly a respiration filled with interiority, with gulfs of psychic resplendence. So when Zomaya appears, there exists, yes, traces of old scoldings, but I am renewed every time the moon creates its dawn. Perhaps I am coming to the level where my mind can fully extend into subconscious civilization. Because the galaxy more fully empowers me I can commune with stars such as Mirach, or with the Sun named by the Moorish, El Nath. I know as savant that they provoke the carbohydrates of hearing. And I know that I am nearer and nearer these Suns because I can hear my blood fill with light, I can hear its protein heightening, with its summations flaring into vertiginous symbologies. This is where the blood transmutes and takes on a character I can't quite configure. Under this liminal power I can consecrate no certainty, I cannot quote definitives to those who emphasize regression. And it is this regression which ultimately empowers St. Catherine's. A singular force which we are told erupted from the provincial habitation of Galilee. We are told that the Christos exhibited the bravery of mortals and remains an extrinsic sigil as the central conduit to heaven.

In her deepest resources I know Zomaya continues to carry this issue with God. Will or will he not as Christ the Saviour condemn her as God. Condemn her for the duration of the cosmos. And within this dramatization I have become the central linkage which can utter yea or nay to her fate. Should I utter calliopes of poison it would set in motion a satanic cabal. Should I exercise a less tempestuous vocalization she may sigh in relief upon gaining the purgatorial as her fate. Which means she remains fundamentally divided, as does Ornelas and the whole of St. Catherine's. Not a final judgement, not a private prerogative only consummate with Zomaya and her specific undoing. Let me say that Zomaya's undoing held priority for me at an earlier time, now I understand the potentia of my utterance as only a means. It allows me the liberty to utter, to live and breathe without the threat of attack. As of now it takes on the character of a cautionary silence which minimizes demise at this hour. But I know it has created a shift at the hacienda. When Zomaya thirsts for my fluids, or when Oraculos wakes in the night and finds only Zomaya, a former density is abandoned, an uncertainty begins to sculpt the routine. It must be understood that I am not a cannibal, or a person whose principle priority is the inchoate who claims a childish turbulence inside her. What I can say of Zomaya, or Ignatius Loyola is that they are equally concerned with naming Zomaya within the ambits and the limits of the hacienda, and the latter naming the Catholic faith as a universal tenet, contiguous on Earth to degenerate savages, to a host of random infidels.

I'll say that both are haunted by the burning criterion of control. And this control remains the burning ideal which degenerates, which casts mountainous shadows across the mind. I have no linkage vis-à-vis their shadows. As for being the culminate degenerate, Zomaya knows that I've been imbued with resistance. I can never be cast as an instinctive monster vomited out of sulphur. She knows this. I am not the animal that she would have liked me to become. I cannot possibly function as an excuse for her. She has authored the culminate texts on degenerates. Because she knows that I know this she cannot launch an umbilical tirade against me hoping to reduce me so that I can begin again to turn around inside her private projection of power. She knows at this depth that I have surmounted a regal tournament of angels. Because of this surmounting I cannot replicate state from the unsought state. Every day she comes to me like a haunted miner hoping to dig up buried saffron. She is desperate. Unlike Sister Ornelas or the other nuns at St. Catherine's she feels a fresh resonance from her crimes. So no matter how much she is consoled by this priest or that father she will always remain palpable with guilt. No matter the surgical wealth of her confessions she can never extirpate the voice which voids her continuously. Confession for her can never be a dizzying game which allows for contorted verbal gambits imploded with duplicity. This is the magnification that she suffers, her praxis intrinsically understood as having connivance with demons. She being of substance which can never retreat from poison. So am I revelling in her fixation? Am I gloating with her saturate and in-saturate dilemma?

She knows the fuels which brush against me. She knows when she sees me that they dominate the room. They engulf her priority with vapour. These are fuels which have emerged from the cells. Fuels which advance from specific combinations. A turbulence which combines from approximate ascensions and descensions. Ascension in the general state of the psycho-physical, and the descending force puissant with lightning. This being a grammar capable of exploring other conditions of being. Conditions which the limits of matter can't explain. I prefer to call it experience at the transhuman boundary. In this sense I am not an eroded creature, something more or less extinct. So again, Zomaya cannot address me as some issue trapped within the tenets of infection.

I've ascended from this zone of the brutish, I've revealed over and over the quandary within its failings, therefore I am not to be gathered as a dismembered persona. She would love to say to herself that she has placed me here because I rival Jesus in oblivion. And I mean the sluggish Jesus contained by cups of heroin. Because the traits of the brutes has not persisted in me she cannot elucidate my face in a skillet of rum and say, here she exists condoned by inebriation. As to my memoir as infidel she would like to believe that my menses remain tainted by all of the actions exposed in the hacienda. She would like to feel from me an uncleansed debauchery, a kindled filth as issued from a sinister urchin. She would like to think that I've caused all the smells to rise from the semen, and of how Esteban sometimes claimed these smells as if he were king of an oracular harem. She could then assault the reason in my hibernation, of Rosanna as pathetic, being of morose and transmogrifying stain. Thus I would be the unbearable doyen in reverse, carrying the thought of an anaemic mental sow. She could then somehow ascribe the plague of the hacienda to my incinerated thinking. This exists as her reclusive provisional ballast. This is dishonour. This is the threadless shaken by the threadless. It is energy which dwells in toxic Saxon metier. Knowing the Kivas were ransacked by Coronado she's remained historically favourable to the ilk of Coronado. To his decisive violence in the name of the Christos. She, like Edmundo and Catalina consider the Christian creed to be the essential climacteric. It is an Imperial diagnosis which announces itself as liberty. A liberty as modern asset. I can only conclude such assessment as a rapturous misery. Less wily and polished than Zomaya, I am certain that someone of Edmundo's ilk would have me gone missing, and searches for my body wilfully called off.

I cannot be far mistaken as I surmise him to have voided rum in his sleep. To me, he remains an animal who wrought soil from raw density. To me, this is the way that guano behaves. Yet it could be said that I'm deliberately assaultive, that I persecute the dead with revenge. This could or could not be the case. In any event I refuse to dwell within this zone. I refuse to internally space my cards as if I were pro-active as a medium consummate with belladonna. I cannot be limited to such. Yet this is what the general heritage has called for. Attack by umbilical attack. The offspring attacks her own gene stores as if entangled with saliva in her hands, as if one were caught in a tidal wave of treason. Yet for me, Edmundo remains the leper who inspired all moral reverses, having plotted with Catalina to inveigle their own daughter in a hive of infortuitious frenzy.

Zomaya became tethered to ungainly endocrine suppression. Catalina inflamed her with suggestiveness and soon she became the psychically disfigured wife of Edmundo. This was further stimulus for Catalina who then sought the use of her own sons. Edmundo being riotously jealous of this distinction was strategically blunted by Catalina, who on occasion would carve Edmundo's rum with narcotics wantonly provoking the sons with carnivorous indulgence. The brutes were bred as sexual carnivores not unlike the great male cats who have tasted human flesh. This is how their dangerous addictions began spinning. Zomaya simply extends their haunted thirsts, keeping them mired in suicidal eclectics.

I have thus become the saved and abandoned daughter whose gift is deep time. Whose balance is tilted to a void more distant than the Carboniferous. I understand myself as human fire semi-aurulent with prowling. If I lecture like an effigy let me say this, the Egyptians left to climb unbroken from explorational kinetics may have already visited anomalous regions of the void, and come to know in the void the dialectic of the unknown ocean bottoms. Breathing from the era of both seas they may have merged with the powers of an effortless totalic. Having come to full immersion in the effortless secrets of death, having surmounted the human physical tree. Blankness would have advanced, the unobstructed body would have faultlessly occurred. I'm speaking of 7000 years of intensity. Of 7000 years without corrosive fault and interruption. Then the soma could live as a blinded dowsing rod connecting and exploring that which increases like a star which suddenly ignites the dark with great electrical grace.

So when coming back to someone on the order of Oraculos one understands that his skin has been drained and parched by insubstantials. He knows he is depraved and feasts on that depravity. I know this, but knowing this in deeper and deeper increments allows me to call out my name 10 to 20 times during uncommitted hours. It gives me power. A suddenness ascends from the intake of Duende, which allows me to hear the Sun.

I who understand the mode in impulsive self-governing. For me, all the ink and the acts of ink understand themselves as implosional dioramas. And these implosional dioramas allow me to listen to the secrets of the dead. This is why I understand Edmundo and Catalina so strongly. I write in the ink of the mind which allows vacuums to interact and appear. And of course I am not insisting on individual bodily emission, but upon psychic odours and how they orchestrated ruin. As chiropteran I know each individual's governing smells. I know the different forms of rot that they issued. As for Zomaya, she carries multiple layers of burden in this regard. This is why I've deciphered her palaeontology impelled by phobic reaction. Her dazed foundational atoms which coalesce with the atomic in-calescence of Edmundo, with Catalina in post-nigredo, these states are what I'll call the ashes of Edmundo and Catalina. Having been forced to cohabit with Zomaya I immediately knew her levels of energy as accrued from Catalina, or the halting combinations which befitted Edmundo. From these obscure and frightful contacts I've understood a frayed orchestral tumult composed of salt, gross humidity, and exhaustion. Therefore, one understands how ghosts accrue through ghosts. For instance, the tenor of Edmundo in the writhing of Zomaya, or the way she would respond as Catalina at the acme of libidinous peaks. When my tongue would scorch her throat the ghosts would swelter. But of course I have many examples to burn, other incidents which evoke true distortion. But the above remain my general incidentals, which continues living in a toxic land, encapsulating poison.

Which now allows me to speak of my alphabet of glass. And it is asked, what is an alphabet of glass? How does it let me roam with my feelings? How does it speak to itself through intervallic struggles?

Let me speak of Hindu psychology, of the sparks which roam the sattvic. Not that I attempt to evoke its essence through foliage or schooners, but to advance utterance by utterance according to unmistakable telepathy. I call it a code of immolations where Akashic transmutation begets Akashic transmutation. Therefore the energy of burial is unfounded. No sound is advanced or delimited according to the tenets in cortical reasoning. Everything uttered becomes new mystical salt. Each mark is experienced as developmental burst, as transmuted eruption. Which occurs within my personal ravelment as verbal transparence. Essence leaps and conjoins its own leaping, producing in its wake a weather of spells. The hypnotic conjoins with living so that there never occurs rational occultation where sound is divided in order to provoke its fragments on the plane of matter. Therefore I am always listening, I am always rife with arisen complication. The voice then configures as unmistakable priority. It transposes its vibration as ubiquitous colouration. I'm speaking here of the power of climate, of looming vertical instigation. Within this state there is no weak or insignificant molecular timing. No, I'm not thinking of something as shrewd as pontifical Gaelic, or as separative as pontifical Gaelic. Language includes smells, and motions, and touch, and sound. So when I speak I am recording these subordinate junctures as the unification of tenses, never staging myself as contorted old litmus. In the latter regard, I am the in-derivative, the in-successive, having leapt the vis inertiae, the oppressive non-inhabitance common to failure. Therefore, the powers around me are invaded and de-invaded, so that a respiration occurs, which ignites a psychic lantern, through motion, and smell, and feeling. Text and sub-text become tonally inter-angled, its instinctive kinematic being a processive kind of grace. Within this inter-angling one cannot combine the seven rites of Christ, the anointing of the sick, baptism, the Eucharist, confirmation, followed by matrimony, ordination, and confession.

I understand none of these things to be. I understand none of their tenets, their wishes, their commandments, connected as they are to burial and salvation. None of this begrounds me, or sets me on a course as if I flew like a hatchling, from unburied belief. Such standards can never beguile me, or open in me the inducted super-ego as stabilized dependence. I do not open and close myself. I can never be the judge who assaults and rules against the less stable tendencies in myself. As for perichoresis I can never analogize it to the model of water with its aspects of liquid, ice, or steam. So the Father, the Son, and the Spirit are not as water to me. The latter exist as encoded narratives , as cultural faux pas, restricted to a levelling hermeneutics, thereby confining inner laterality.

This has been Zomaya's source of food, her evidence, her chronicle of benediction.

Superficially she seems not to tarry in spirit, nor to admonish her own persona, but this seems not to be the case. Her monologics is unnerved, uprooted, draped in imbalance. I've infected her secretive mythemes, having renounced her baleful psychotics, which always looms in my explosive self-comment. Her reality, as I've over and over extended, remains the brutes in the dungeon, with their acrimonious wails, with their various sincerities of addiction. Unprosperous contradiction begins to loom inside her soma, her pretensions sending signals from the realm of the unclean. But of course I'm repeating the obvious. As for now, I've loosened a cryptic flaw and exposed the source of the hacienda as being no longer protected by crypto-immunology. As chiropteran I feel like a force intuitively pulling needles from a stream. Grasping different sizes, and then creating from these sizes a palace which exists according to invisible integer. And within this palace a hall balanced on transfinites. This is a hall where the unforeseen is allowed to appear, where exhaustive conjuration takes on a ferment which the sighted must conclude as shapes which startle through stellar orientation. This being the hacienda as new balance, where new concerns are thought out, where electrum erupts and infuses its new atmosphere with acculturated rarity. Because each assaultive startling mode I've turned into a gainful structural chemistry, so that what now exists in my favour is a new interior stamina, which exists to Zomaya as a sinister and uneven blankness. What I've learned is that one gains tenacity by simply existing. By sitting in this curious parallel state I've withstood the protraction of an entropy which seems to close around me with an unfortunate temperature which seethes. But because I am nimble the Sun responds and begins to rotate in my system.

What I can say is that I am favoured by the Sun and it provides me with the germinates of a lightning filled aura. Again, the Sun favours me, and absorbs me, so that I am not divided against my own persona. For instance, a volcano is incapable of occluding its power through reason, being able to know its depths through apocalyptic threading. Which means return to the source of its internal timing, a timing which someone has called "special individual relations." Which remains in polar opposition to the proselytizers who dwell within the catholic restriction, calling their attempts at conversion the "Great Commission of Jesus." So what I say is not homiletic, not some topical preaching about fate as theological witness to someone like Amos or Mary Magdalene. Nor am I making as part of my exposition an exegesis so as to relate its volcanic fire to stunning excavations from a text. As for converting unknown prey to my spirit I profess to no living example. What I verbally behold is not a theology of crises, but an energy which I've grown to understand as a dis-recognition of old strictures. I'm not setting down markers as if ascribing to a populace mortal technology, or disguising my cognition as conspiratorial flux, thereby deflecting my powers to a ruthless symbolical rote. What I know of what I say offers no tangible concordance to the ire which reigns from the voice of John. Not that his voice fails to transfix the recipient, but its premise poses no possible consequence to my status. To me, it retains a certain risibility as if I were psychologically approaching a fire engulfed pond. A pond which I hear in my spirit as something reduced, understood in terms of phenomena being ad hoc as spectra. Certainly John is relying on belief in terms of his neurological foreboding. What seems to inspire his mind is a loathsome furnace combined with gangrenous extermination. It is the flame of God as nefarious affair. A void perpetually divided into stupefying symbols schizophrenic with wrath. I cannot ascribe to Zomaya such totality of reaction, but like John, she has authored a gangrenous fire, which only allows for forensic allegation.

To the likes of John I once again attempt to contrast the ghosts which I contend are Edmundo and Catalina. Take Edmundo, his final days must have been scorched with trepidous dishonour, flooded with lucre he had no higher calling than to sleep again and again with the blossoming Zomaya. Near the end of his stay on terra firma he attempted to ransack the dwindling vitals of Catalina all the while tormented by his leprous desire for Zomaya. Because he believed so strongly in judgement he was eaten alive by his own prognostics. As for Catalina she was always consumed by the salacious, always evincing in this regard less concern than Edmundo. Perhaps Edmundo always listened to the death he condemned his workers to. Combined with his wilful and prolonged engagement with Zomaya he could channel in his mind raging scenarios of horror and the dangers which accrue from descent down stations of the abyss. He had lost command of himself. His initial poverty in Santa Rita, his tainted accrual of wealth from the mines, his engorgement on the flesh of his daughter and his wife, took on a life of hellish quanta. I smell this from Zomaya. When I was instructed to lick the fumes from her privates Edmundo would aurally flicker in my nostrils. At other times Catalina would aurally engulf me the instant my tongue would increase the flow of Zomaya's saliva. Both of their ghosts would extend themselves and evince their hauntedness as if I were listening to a glyph of rotten sparrows singing. No one can accuse me of anacrusis, of being devoid of what I hear. Of course I am consumed in that what I hear has provided me with sustainable grasp which has morphed into my abilities gained as chiropteran. Because I hear the dark, and I hear inside blood. I find this essential for my body, unconcerned as it is with superficial motility. It is no secret that I sit, that I am cryptically isolate, yet always tumbling within contingency. And what do I mean by contingency? An energy en-sourced as an outpost of the hacienda, an index of blood in the service of destroying old phobias. Perhaps I have retreated 500 years and brought back to life the art of the Western courtesan, so admirably evinced in the person of Angela del Moro. She being the code for learned Venetian prostitutes who had in their power all manner of reach. Mathematics, symbols of magic, systems of state power. Perhaps in my own way I've become more exacting in this reach. Perhaps Zomaya attempts to align my energy with metrics, but a metrics which is ominous, like a nascent hurricane spinning.

So I've become this cataclysmic obsession, this tedious pressure fallen inside myself forced to process a whole history of assault and misnomer. Here I am stunned by parallel situations, psychologically arched, with my body in one dimension imperfectly parallel with its oneiric manifestation, creating a subversive liminality in the feelings. This being the source of a third or synthetic tension so that other ineffables arise and become partial fractals symbolic of that which humanity attempts to parse as sums of the unreached. So for me the latter is beauty which creates itself through audition. Certainly not the beauty which Catalina ascribed to the art of good society. But what I'm speaking of is beauty as the unexpected. The charged locution, the grammar by olfaction. Because I am transposing by smell I live by anomalous escalation through insight. Which creates a depth not unlike the mathematical theorem which abounds with the recondite. This is something that a eulogy on Edmundo could never deliver, he, who successfully occluded the death of miners on his watch. According to Edmundo none of these deaths ever existed. And because all the dead were Indians, none of them ever existed, and none of them had ever died. This remains his testament as nadir, his testament which sealed their fates, which ultimately increased the corporate coffers. He covered up death for Moneda Mines, and so Moneda Mines saw to it that he was properly rewarded. Because I am channelling these horrors from the depth of Zomaya's odours, I somehow know of the Moneda Mines, of the covering of the death plunge in the Moneda Mines, then the recording of the Indians as ciphers.

I've extended this summary from aboriginal timing. I've concluded certain traces based upon magnetic olfaction. Yet I can't procure from my olfaction the details which led to Edmundo's financial securement. I mean the papers unsigned, the dates obscurely diverted, the discussions conducted by fraud and base adjustment. But the means by which I've appeared is resultant of the death plunge, and all advantage gathered from the death plunge. It can be said that I sit and speak because of the death plunge. Of the unclaimed bodies descending as the death plunge. Yet for me, the Indians didn't die in vain. This is why I'm here to proselytize their living combustion. I am listening to them plunge inside a glacial picture mill knowing that their spirits have arisen in my voice, and that Edmundo and the Spaniards have further rotted in common memory. The question comes to mind, am I now the disfigured compost lying in wait for the future to come and eviscerate my protest? Am I that mistress in the poisoned drawing gown composing an unclean moral fiction?

Am I merely the reversal of Edmundo and Catalina captured on complex double planes?

And if this is true am I ultimately the feral mistress of Edmundo, being a ghost writhing with a ghost whose offspring has emerged, from our combining waking as Zomaya? Furthermore, has this congress preceded Catalina, and projected the outcome of say, Jesus, so exploited in spirit?

As for Oraculos and Esteban, are they now my captured sons? Are they the result of genetic offal arriving on this plane from pre-eruptive liquor sows? So am I the pre-eruptive erupting from the pre-eruptive?

I orchestrate these questions because there are elements in me concerned with perdition, with its after-effects, its lingerings. Not that I reside inside its trigonal mappings, but it exists as apparitional weather as if I were breathing as a para Catalina who welcomes her own engorement by a rapacious, inclement Edmundo. Edmundo, the liar, the stoic foreman on the witness stand. Then, of course, the interchange of phantoms, with Oraculos being the stand-in for Edmundo, and Edmundo being the ilk of the barren Esteban, as if feeling the ethers from the brio of Panamanian rum. And I mean in the paradigmatic sense of relation and counter relation between the living and the living dead. Perhaps, at another remove, it can be called genetic surplus, or eavesdropping on the primeval physical constitution, where primeval flaw surmounts primeval flaw. Maybe I'm the final outcome of this species, seemingly drained of intentional foliage, always listening for congenital harassment.

Again, I beg to differ. And I differ because the Divine is always seething as an inevitable incunabula. It is for this reason that Zomaya cannot scale me. I have surmounted the body according to one law and one instant. I have eclipsed the common hydrational pony.

If I'm asked to respond to a thinking Indian body circa 1549, could I kindle the power of its wheat from this distance? I can confirm no observable possibility in this regard. As chiropteran and psychic chiropteran I can claim no miracles as to entry into a prior or anonymous body. I am not the Goddess who regulates a literature of miracles, who stokes a pyretical empire in order to subject her law to the emparcelment of cells. Not being disposed to portions, or to the chronicle as minimum, I am spirited by a dense cosmogony which evinces life through the immoderate. Because it is the immoderate which has given rise to me, be it the fumes from Catalina, or the undesirous fondlings of the brutes, it culminates in the utterance governed in its depths by the articulatory pronoun.

So I am the fugitive in the depths of self-regard. As to mortification I am oblivious. For me there is only motion which listens to the burning inside my organs. What has issued from this motion is the notion of carnivorous opportunity, woven by states of grace from a spontaneous osmotic termed in the vernacular as in-derivative originality. The prior kinetic of the family I've defeated. In them I've plotted no stake or atmosphere. When evolving there is always the stage and the prior stage linked to thoughts of privation in the past. But this is not regression, but simply a summary of opprobrium allowing the evocation of medicinal distance, which in turn allows me survey of private samsaras. Me, I'm mediumistic as palaeontologist, being psychic chiropteran flying through threats and threats of causes. To this degree I have no tolerance for any form of modification. As I've said before and before, Esteban slurs and drinks himself to death on Panamanian rum. As for the cups of heroin that Jesus subsumes… As one can see, further comment is not needed, yet the chronicle gnaws at me, even in the midst of transcending my own persona. As I am at this hour, some would consider this to be my final mortal dance, my penultimate specificity, which allows nothing other than itself to be. So in the deepest sense I do not mobilize disaster, or promulgate pyres, or insist on general damage by pyemia. Thus the feeling arises of internal solar intensification, of appeal to the deepest forum of the invincible.

Again, not armour, or any form of civil rulership. It is a rare absorptive paradigm which permeates the various engagements which conjoin in the very marrow of being.

The Divine is not only the current through which momentum is issued, but works at levels the human can in no way assume. And when I say human, I mean the human as derided by the Western mental setting. There always exists quantification or a leaning towards quantification. A quantification which persists in saying that biology is the only persistent source of creation. I call this the paradigm of rat collectors. I think of the aspiring bourgeois of Lima circa 1952. Accoutrements from Paris and London. Ingénues frantic with Imperial aspiration. This I surmise was the mythos of Catalina. With her penchant for the sumptuous detail, for the pastiche of legendary what-nots she evinced display complexified by display. It was her sign of entry into the world of the Spaniards. To further embellish her socialization she may have empowered the myth of Edmundo as being fathered by one of the Spanish progenitors of the mine at Santa Rita. That he had sprung full blown from Empire. That he was someone grounded in the ages. That he was at one with the ilk of Vargas and Coronado.

This is what I'll call aspiration as disfiguration. The pontoon where the drowned survive as the drowned. And what is ironic is that they are so fastidious in the choreography of their drowning. That they relish point by point their respective oblivions. So they are a community which restricts themselves to mores which they equate with the canonized. The canonized being none other than the crown of what they consider to be the completed person. This is what I'll call the memoirs of an oblivious tournament, where competition reigns in terms of public appearance, of ostentatious parades, of financial donation to maintenance of the garments of the Virgin. Catalina, with the unreserved beauty of the perfect baby, with an acceptable summary of wealth, entering into the social fray of the regressive Folkloristas. Having ingested this realia from the polluted canals of Zomaya, I can register two words: substantiated wreckage. A whole legacy of scarring, active in one dimension as secret sexual tearing, and in another, a Christian impediment sprung from galling Hebrew leanings. Hear I am absorbed in meditational dungeons haunted by starvation and nothingness.

Because of this haunting I am conjoined by the clarity of anger which allows me to feel Zomaya as she sulks like a tarantula, hearing her scurry in the manner in which a carnivorous urchin retreats.

As is known, Zomaya is not unacquainted with jealousy. I remember a day when Oraculos hoarded Zomaya for many entangled hours. Because of this Esteban attempted to cast a spell of panic upon Oraculos. It did not work. He threatened flight to a local Botanica. But because he had no money, and no knowledge of direction, all of his seething failed. On that day he cackled like a vulture at nightfall. A sound unevenly applied. It was nothing more than the crazed plenitude of the surroundings. One could feel during these hours a strange emotional saliva as if Esteban had suddenly attempted to possess Zomaya in a binding contract of love. This was a sudden acme for him, a sudden maturity if you will. Because of this he felt all the more denied by Oraculos as he concretized possession of Zomaya. He didn't approach me during those hours. His full embodiment centred on Zomaya. All his breathing was imminent with rapture. He made no attempt to hide the closeness of those moments. As if the act of love could be hidden away, and at the same time brought to a summa in the feelings as if it were appearing and disappearing within the power of his neurology. He had come to love her at that moment, and I heard him whisper over and over "Yo soy enamorado, Yo soy enamorado." Yet it seemed out of place, as if he were imaginary sea fowl flying over land locked volcanoes.

This was part of my genetic Braille. Being the addition and subtraction of vertigo. These being the various hoverings of vertigo. A dalliance of feelings not unlike a matrix sprung from a suprarational index of numbers. A personal salt tornado. Yet, in my personal regalia I am merely one of an epic of a 100,000,000 species, as if I've become a strenuous powder worm straining to procure a power of curious mountain skills not unlike an Ezekial desert goat. Because as chiropteran I am a drinker of ghosts drifting through levels where I feel the desert goat rising through paroxysmal elevation, allowing alchemic visitation at the juncture of land and air. This is where a voided paradigm arises as an unfed curiosity which persists not unlike those unfounded Suns in regions akin to the local Trifid Nebula. These are telepathic Suns full of instigational transparency. An aural transparency audible with zeniths. This is a level at which my existing deficits don't measure. This is why I can tell that Ornelas and Zomaya guess between one another trying to secure an estimation concerning the assets which seem to assume themselves in my silence. Whatever faith they've experienced cannot pursue me at such height. Because I am truly outside of myself I can never be enclosed in terms of specific assignation. Not a quantification of height, or the questioning of a child concerning the official constitution of the polar caps. No methodology persists which can unseal me. So Zomaya in spite of all her powers remains proportional to the novice who orchestrates her own confusion, who frantically pursues her own bacteria. Thus she dwells in tautological schematic which morphs and further morphs into ongoing regression.

This being a regression which I've no idea how I've escaped its tendentiousness. Or how my subtle invigoration was employed. At all hours of the day there would be scratching on my door with any one of the brutes seeking to force me into congress. With Jesus it was an insistent vertical scratching. With Esteban it was horizontal in nature. The only voice came from Oraculos insisting on lewd behaviour when he thought all the others were asleep. A pack of raptors with Zomaya at its incriminating alpha summit. To me, they were and remain the source of an extinguished fossil record. It was like listening to poisoned sea fowl in the dwelling. And it is not like I've anointed myself with blizzards of forgetting in order to surmount the ingrown gist of the circumstance. Again, having surmounted the gravitational suggestion I've escaped, I speak to Ornelas as my provisional mediation, all the while my eyes seeming to peer from a pointless median tower.

I can always expect Zomaya to arrive providing me with one tape per day. Why not provide five or ten at one sitting. But as I've said, her visits are a holding pattern. When she comes with one tape per day she satisfies the minimum of my demands. And at the same time it gives her an excuse to monitor any eruption that I may have infused into the corridors of St. Catherine's. As for the content of what I say she remains severely concerned. Because of this I command a thousand Earthquakes in my power so her constant concern remains synonymous with unease. And so I'm sure that Zomaya and Oraculos seek to mine with absolute ferality any motion that they declare which moves inside the crucifix. I can assume that they pray to this motion, that they dispatch their Spanish suplicas so as to unleash a palpable code of answers. Of course answers as regards the mystery of my person. In this they respond like colonials as if I carried elements of an old Algerian guerrilla. As if I haunted the walls of an old colonial cafe. In this regard my spiritual fathers remain Osceola and Pope. In this regard I am inundated with immanence. By combining Angora goats with Aegean constellations I create sigils of sound to provide productive guesswork when Zomaya arrives and attempts to unravel my mind. It is simply sound which ceases to travel to any continent in particular, as I can easily transpose the goats to gryphon vultures, or as for stars speak of Lepus, the Hare, or Monoceros, the Unicorn, or Pictor, the Painter. These are sounds which irradiate from my thoughts, which cross into the zone of complex interregnums. That uncharted totality where no prior study can configure. I, myself can never know when such thoughts of sound increase or diminish, having no scale of exacting replication, or reformed enigma attempting to re-surface in the mind as concretized information. Nothing applies. It is simply uncharted totality which no prior study can configure. Zomaya knows that I have increased my capacity to live, and that my silence dazzles not from engrained dementia, but from power which drifts inside nefarious insomnias, which in turn spins as a summary of breathing. I know that the yogins speak of the interior of breathing, this being the energy of its mysterious happenstance. Zomaya seeks askewment of my increasing respiration seeking to disarticulate this motion by dosages of anger. When she faces me her breathing takes on a disrupted tenor, and by having me replicate this tenor it would bring me closer to her fraught electrical sensitivity. For her, this would allow my structure of energy to re-ignite from the void and concentrate my life according to a measurable status. I do not think she conspires with Ornelas at this level, but it seems to be her principle exercise to somehow ferret me out so as to fulfil her consuming investigatory mission. For neither one of us is this an inventory. It is the summation of a plight at different levels, one gravitized to consensus understanding of matter, and another, enunciatory with immersion and ascent from that immersion, being liberty as matter. And myself as the enunciatic having raised my hearing to a heightened articulate cinnabar, not promoting a greater or lesser valour, but understanding the art of primal solar audition, over and above the sound from a Lydian belfry. Synonymous with strengthened elevations I have crossed a gradation which extends above an isothermal ozone, which transmutes through gradation into sonic interiority. An interiority which understands its voice to be the Sun. So by understanding my state as the purest essences of the Sun a wave of galactic power seems to enkindle my nascence. This being both alien and of self-configured speaking. Of course distance conveying the unimaginal magnitude of the alien, and the self-configured as evidenced by the body across all the traces and possibilities of the infinite continuum. And by the latter I am not speaking of a specific space populous with unchronicled objects, but something other than the 22 nameless moons of Jupiter and Saturn. Such realia in no way approaching a final crystallization of nebulas. This, of course is not the medicinal erosion of someone like Jesus scratching for entry through my doorway, or Oraculos cajoling me for gifts of menstrual spillage. If I were a known quantity to the law I could convince the powers that be to hang a lantern and have the family face the consequence of stunning legal execution. Knowing that they would face the ramifications of chronic judgement. Yet to me, this does not qualify as revenge, as purposeful or abbreviated Lecanomancy. Because somehow I know the fates will preserve these tapes and expand their liquids to unpublicized Crimeas. Perhaps I'll set up a Federation of Vampires who live out their days fuelled by means of ingested belladonna. Yet I know the ravages of the so called practical world that continues to wreak havoc on my person, to make of my vernal body an unalleviated leper's nest, where my opprobrium is transfigured by verdicts which respire in vernacular bulletins. But being beyond such response I am no longer the bride superficially clawed in sacrificial trigamy. Because my worth cannot be gauged according to sums in an isolated bell curve. I, being low pitched with flux have no bearing on any topical issue, because my cogitations soar and reel with occulted tenacity. This is how my inner jubilation endures. This is how the tornadic instructs me. As for society and its constructs the best I can give are absurdities which accrue from diminished obligation. Even if I could converse with daily events I would be no more than an incognisant hailstone mountain strangely embraced by wordless selenologies. As to what my thoughts can configure I am no more than an index of fragments, at best, a thronged notational discipline taut with saliva and blood. By speaking night after night I face the Sunrise reeling as if vomiting imaginary Sun birds. Yet I feel immaculate in this regard in that I both ingest and vomit up beauty. I know my blindness stares and debates with itself concerning various shifts in ferocity. Because my exercise in memory remains so pure there has been growth through austerity and bitterness. I am therefore electric with desolation, knowing that Zomaya has transfixed her understanding with modes which have descended from abrasive eugenics. I can only dictate to presence letters of scorn in keeping with the traces of scorpion that I feel from her pigment. As I speak I feel I am always gambling with unwashed dice, seeking a number which causes integers to implode. I am oneiric when my voice convulses the air, and I listen to the void quake, and hear the Sun spin at the cusp of extinguished pavonian cliffs. Yet this is where doubt blazes, where energy in the cortex reverses. Because I understand these reverses as a curious narrative arc I am no longer subject to its traces as locatable dementia. For instance, I do not value each day as exhibit, this being day as enclave, as coded material warren. I posit none of my energies concerning the year or the memory of the year. Thus, I hail the strictures of the zodiac as being of no account. Thus, my credentials burn as degenerate fulgenosity, replete with no known amplitude as origin. Again, Zomaya is defeated by oneiric concentration which gives to my presence an oblique energetics. Because there is much effort combined in sleeping and speaking I've become this sensitive hybrid, as psychic Seminole and chiropteran, who casts her remarks within the direst strata of the language. A direness which I must admit is always lingering in my osmosis. Energies which always irk me and sting by their auric prickings. And in the wake of these prickings there always evolves intrinsic mental burning leaving me haunted by irregular recall. As for friendship and any extension beyond friendship I can truly say that none has ever existed.

My most dominate designation being blindness I was never wrought with accoutrements of the blind. No vision enhancement devices, no Braille, no optacon, no calculator which spawns sound from its limits. As I've stated I had congress with some of the classics through Zomaya. Early on I knew Smerdyakov, I had a summary of Beckett's speaking voice. There were immersions in Quixote and Melville, in Octavio and Joyce. Perhaps she felt in me something she could never be. She was someone who was never quite capable of magnificence. She aspired to inculcate me with a level she could never endure. I lived as her ironic legacy. During these readings the tenor of her voice was not unlike a barrister or a school marm, insistent with all the substratums of broken personal abundance. Here I was a circuitous dimension of destabilization for her.

But how can I not reek at some level from a fundamental quavering.

I know that Oraculos carried blindness in his semen. That he marked me with trachoma. I had no chance against damage, against the glossary of scarring that has entwined me in its fate. With that said the word evil ensnares me at this moment with its offspring which entails the obdurate, the flagitious, the piacular, the malignant. I call this condition inborn, error, biochemical alteration, excessive accumulation of intermediate toxins. Oraculos was autosomal recessive. He passed the blindness through my genes. The blood became mixed with Cooley's anaemia, with Galactosemia, with Phenylketonuria. And as result I am engrained with impaired fertility, my population of nerves, a broken analytical breeding. Much the way animals are born with an absence of light within the body. To this degree I was born like a treeless water newt with optical messages scrambling in the brain. There remains absence in the lateral geniculate bodies. Sight being the electro-chemical which shoots along the outer membrane of the cell with its long principle fibre, the axon with its impulse velocity at 100 meters per second. Not strength in amplitude but as frequency.

Because of personal lack in this realm I am obsessed with terminal misdirection of the synapse, of the chiasm, of the post-lateral gyrus. I mean the pure trapezium of seeing unsustained by the energy of an intervening oxygen. A suffocating umbra, a soiled acetylene foundation. Being blind is like rowing through a sea of curious lepton fibres, the atmosphere hissing, always confusing with tests. Conversely, it can be said that advantage has been gained because of this condition. Or that I've gained discipline from the chaotic spoils formed inside my body. I remember when I fiercely refused the creeping of Jesus one day. Zomaya was seemingly exhausted from a random encounter with Esteban. The afternoon to that point teemed without record, then explosion occurred. Jesus searing with rejection went tearing after Oraculos while the latter was pondering a phenomenon in chess culled from complex openings. Of course it was a mongrel study claiming no wider outcome. Yet he had attained some peak of sensitivity when Jesus invaded his region accusing him of having too a great a claim upon my body. I was crouched on all fours when I heard blows about to be struck. Then suddenly I heard a stick explode against the floor tiles. It was a shocking acceleration. Zomaya just as quickly threw away the stick and decried them both as being doubly depraved. Silence began to palpitate. House injunction was imposed. This was Zomaya at her height signalling to her world unquestioned authority. Her authority is what is now in question. I've frayed her. I've somehow managed to obliviate her system. Having fought back from nths, from the limits of dazed curricula, I've become the incalcuable heiress. Now she is isolate. No one but me knows the fundamental lightning crackling at her base, I know her devastation. I know the source of her weakening psychic crops. If an objective party were to stare at the workings of the hacienda one would see the depraved interactions between a toxic alpha being and her confused and violent underlings. My intuition tells me that there are arguments concerning my present mode of mind. So there exists this consuming bedlam, this tension which ratchets in the pores. I am missed, my absence burdens, I provoke in them wakeless mental embranglement. Jesus beyond all others must be concussively distressed. Why do I say this? Having a consciousness which no one takes into depth, he remains the pariah, the one whose visage registers consummate distrust, suffering punishment as result of the melanin which suffuses his integument. Because of the climate of ridicule a deepening has transpired within him, having gained a kind of strength from having time and again come back from the dead. Because he and I seem to occupy the strangest positioning. To Zomaya, and Oraculos, and Esteban, we've been condemned as living spleens, as fulminate devolutics, Jesus as the base deleterious who is Olmec, and myself who he's named, twice and more than twice, as being replete as Mexican and Seminole. Thus, we've formed a bond by resistance, being the excluded of the excluded, I, because of youth and blindness, and he, because of undesired integument. Having taken on cyclonic diffuseness I am the one who has escaped the empirical hull of family poison leaving Jesus to stammer in moroseness. Being separate from controlling powers I imply to Zomaya that her mind has fallen through imaginary mesas. Having eluded general social conversation I've been freed to create amniotic bibliographies, to create dislocated tracing signals, so that a covert manna spills from my paroxysms. When Zomaya sees me in trance I must exist to her as a weightless cemetery icon always scrambling visibility. And this how Ornelas treats me, as if I've scrambled visibility. Perhaps upon Zomaya's instruction Ornelas approaches me to probe my electrical instability. I am approached in this manner as if the hacienda had already fallen, and by bringing my energy back to view it would somehow restore its possibilities. I feel her seeking to secure a script to be reported to Zomaya. But I know that Ornelas is divided. On the one hand, she sees me as occult, sacred, possessing transforming power. On the other hand, I burn as a financial template fuelled by Zomaya's control. Zomaya financially overcompensates St. Catherine's in order to keep my existence a secret. So every day Ornelas is asked about the number of tapes she has retained. Zomaya then balances her retention with the number of tapes she has issued. Because she must always keep the amount in balance. Anything other than this would create a persistent panic. She rightly suspects that I tally linchpin after linchpin, that I bare teeth and announce the bones of my ordeal phoneme after phoneme so that I refute any possible argument she could invent.

Knowing what she knows, she feels her legacy precipitously linger at the cusp of explosion. For one, a damaged local hubris; two; the absence of grace in the after-dimension. But she has no choice but to let me sit and listen to myself igniting mirrors in the bramble. Her conventional thinking feels that time will somehow revert my position, and I'll relent, and fall apart in myself. That on a blank or simple Thursday afternoon I'll summon Ornelas in order for her to soldier the tapes to Zomaya. Immolation would transpire. Zomaya would breathe with new arrogance. She'd suddenly feel stronger in her congress with Oraculos, reaping new gifts from her cruelty. This would be her new conservative pastiche, her neo-ruination of truth. And over time I'd feel the gain of destructive energies within me. A plummeted appetite, wandering mental a-rhythmia. Then she could quietly boast victory to herself. Of how she had mastered and sustained through such mastery the curious plane of the unmanageable. She could then take credit for harvesting devastation. A devastation self-fructifying through argumentative substantiation. For her, a new Imperial rebus condensed within a ganglia of restive forces. This remains a lonely distractive warfare, singing to myself in expressive nightmare plazas. Always prone to celestial thirst, to tense kilometers rising in the limbs. I've come to a language roughened, and ploughed, and emitted as jaundiced remnant. A language aching with plasma and ciphers. The voice responds as concentrated glare, as burning ramification, as transmogrified syllabics. During certain registers I self-convince myself as a hieroglyphical fabulist, half salt and half magnetic as if I were during these moments a magical dromedary hydra disarraying time. At another extension I could be an imaginal Juan Cepero singing through the deftness of crystal. The latter cannot exist as a self-imposed mapping, as an argumentative wisdom which persists through self-sequestering. It is more an elemental voltage, rising up in being as an anagrammatic magma.

But at a lesser scale I have blackmailed Zomaya in order to continue living. She is without doubt off balance. Without this threat which hovers about her my future time on Earth would conspire with disappearance. I've held her in check by threats of verbal lightning strikes, by mumbled rumour in the veins. Not that I'm posturing for a flagrant moral crusade provoking stoic heavenly concern. Certainly I am not a leitmotif whose energy has been subsumed by the industrious. How could I ever expect myself to be a whole gyre perfectly divided on a yes and no basis. Instead, there exists what the sighted would respond to as a gargantuan greyness where no one tact can be eternally incited.

Without Edmundo and Moneda Mines no largesse would have been forthcoming and I would not be here condemning his ilk and his complicity in murder. Without the animal zeal which provoked Zomaya I could not partake of terra firma and its powers. At this stage I do not have to explain or to clarify to myself that I am upholding the clan with surreptitious promotion when I speak as such. I am not here to embellish or justify the indefensible. What I can say is that I know I have jarred the record having polled my own standards, breathing against dazed corruption. What I can say is that I'm surrounded by neo-Romans who regressively splinter the biosphere. Within this maze I've disappeared to such a level where even the censors can't find me. In this regard I feel I am without precedent. I know there are victims. Suicides, martyrs, soldiers impaled, limbs scattered across plazas. I know this level prevails where God retreats and envelops in hiding. When Edmundo stated that the Indian miners partook of no known existence he was simply reasoning as a selfish jealous God consumed by contorted self-bickering. It must have been like listening to a brooding lizard's digestion aroused by a noxious personal craving. As if the Indians were no more than a terse bohemia of straw, who remained for Edmundo those souls of no value condemned without let up by the negligible auspices of the Christos. As I say this no self-suppression delays me. I am not excluded from self-example, because at times I feel that what erupts from my feelings is not unalike the rhetoric of a monster. The thoughts which swim inside my blood are like the fauna implied on Eris or Makemake. I am always seething with astonishment. My thought waves concording with the fauna on Makemake, then flowing out to the open galaxy and beyond. It is a telepathic movement, not unlike Olivier Messaien, with his flow of verdet warblers responding by interior comment on eternity. In this sense I am attempting a kind of cure for contemporaneous consumption.

What of the present populace in 6000 years? What of the panic that it's sown? What of its coalescence with evil? Let me go further. What of the half-life of uranium with its billion year odyssey, with its trenchant ambit for the rest of the life of the Sun? This being the spell of the neo-Romans with their timings hurtling inside a pointless cul de sac. So am I didactically impeaching the era, impacting compounds on Eris and Makemake that I know are impossible to explore? I cannot implore such studious Arcana. But what I'm speaking of is a spirit which persists beyond hypothetical conjuration as a developmental spoor which reaches back to Greek division and sciences. I call the latter a code for the hatred of nature, and the rule of perpetual war. A nexus limited to the life and death mean.

Do I argue from the invincible? Do I see myself as its enigma of promulgation? Am I that spectral force destined to survive the artefacts of the species?

Believe me, I am not blinded by elocution, by waves of thought by one perfectly deluded. I understand my capacity, I understand the general state of de-limitation conjoined as it is to the empty flame of time. Yet there is a state more eloquent than Rosanna, more eloquent than elements I embody as chiropteran. This is a covert understanding, I agree, but covert in the sense that I reveal to myself a majority which has failed. Yet it can be said that I've merged with duplicity as loss, that I've been guided by invidious metrical fire. What I say is not compunction by austerity, by sincerity which breathes by naïveté. What I do maintain is tenacity of perch, of power invigorated by solemn phantomical wandering. At these double levels I am chiropteran, and at synthetic remove I am chiropteran. Therefore I cannot plagiarise the energy which flows from the self. I have already revealed my exposure, my riveting enunciation due in large measure to oblique discomfort. Forced to know what I know by fragment I have come to a deeper yield than anything monitored by conscripted instruction. Therefore glimpses, mirages, semi-comatose narratives. If anything I speak as uninstructed voice. Without plan, creating aural animal figures according to the depth which I hear through subjective blankness. So to analyze what I think along the lines of a cretinous secondary means can at best be defined as cultural super-imposition. Breaking with the super-imposed always places one in peril. One then emerges on the plane of the un-intended. Baffling, vociferous, magnetic, guided by the in-particular. The in-particular being erratic flight through paradigms, through human psychological migrations. Under present conditions I feel an ominous intensity. A transpersonal intensity knowing that the waves and the Sun are poised to wear away the animals that we are. And I am not speaking of the in-accelerate assumed when assessing Geomorphology, but upheavals, apocalyptic sand mires. But even under these extremes I am blessed by living as duration, as contortionistic quanta which has brought me to a pitch of critical stamina. This is a stamina which has allowed my nerves to rotate, to vibrate across an enigmatic ubiquity.

True, goodness has failed to embrace me, plummeted as I am into fumes. Therefore I live in a zone of tense suggestibility. Thus I am subject to slippage by nutation, by the barest minimums which foment new and increasing direction. Without the chronic acts of Zomaya would I have become at one with the warblers of Messaien? Would my voice empower their eyes with fires from the uncanny? I cannot answer a yes or a no. She exists as a creatural omen which pontificates. Whatever my feelings she remains my provisional ladder up which I climb coming closer and closer to some unknown reaction. What I can say is that ruination has provisionally engulfed me. By breaking this engulfment, at every moment, at every second of every moment I've united all my feeling into the dynamia of concentration. Even at my lowest ebb I always focus upon extriction. I can say that the intelligence of Oraculos and Zomaya has bred into me fuel, has allowed me to flourish by means of thaumaturgical atomics. But I cannot thank them. Irony has somehow held them so that the salt they spewed has begun spinning in another rotation partially analogous to the rotation of Iapetus. Now I am living through various modes and infinities, so in this sense they have given me the desire to reject reduction, however it bears its minimums. Even as bitter as I am I do not wish to entangle my response in a consumptive cult of victory. Not simply coping with these patterns but somehow coming to live beyond complete suspension. Being feral I've discovered the state where numbers advance into numbers and abjure themselves incapable of conducting themselves in terms of counted ordination. Thus, quality suggests its own condition and begins to live for the sake of itself, dwelling within its own advancement. Having found partial corroboration with Jesus I cannot say that it lessened me. It gave me a curious anti-blessing, it whispered offering to me. Yet there was always the fact that life burned by regression. Every act by Oraculos, every act by Zomaya, burned by regression. So there exists this natural haunting about me. Actual respite remains unclear. As I re-peruse Jesus I think again and again about his remark on my resistance. He must have sensed that I lived in my interior as Seminole, that I knew the Indian race in its Blackness. Within this state not a brutish creature, but an unrecognized savant. He's the only one I can thank. I've been summoned by the worst. So if I seem microbial, daunting, it is because I remain intensely removed from the signals wrought by the human domain and its standards.

What is ironic is that the brutes pray to the saviour daily. Their prayers go out for sustainment against sin, and yet before their breath has recovered from obtestation they begin milling around Zomaya like a pack of dogs hungry with mange, ready to pounce at the briefest suggestion. For them, this is the way that they prove movement in the limbs. This is how they prove their own kinetics, allowing them to optimize debasement. Within the threat of their unbalanced episodes Zomaya intervenes and ushers their torment into various dimensions. I remember when I managed to finally sleep the threat of their brooding would always wake me, and tangle my nerves through stark interior confusedness. During those times I seemed to drown in my own endurance.

The hacienda was the perfect opportunity for the Acts of God.

No wind arrived, no voice from a bramble of bushes. Nothing descended from the uranian, nothing spoke from the imperceptible. Instead, diseased formation rooted. Every nook, every cranny, was necrotic and imploded with phantoms. The higher power seemed to concertise with this state of constant derangement. No Gnostic congress could ensue within the circumstance. It was like listening to a choir of afflicted vicars. Always blockage, always excuse for Divine reproach or indifference. True, I sent no prayers as such, I made no inner circumstance which was apt for the original sinner. Perhaps I was suspected by angels as being committed to behavioural rampage, because of a depth of disbelief. To the angels in question I was a Jew or a witch in the European circumstance circa 1348. Amongst the aforementioned I could also have been singled out by a jealous angel as a scorned mother on the Middle Passage, or closer again, as an Apache thriving in a medicine cult, taking strange journeys to worlds in formation with uncommon rays which form outside the galaxy.

This is not a paranoia reduced to jubilation in dissonance, to psychic arch rivalry with myself. I have no possessions by which to bargain with the Gods, to carve my immaculate soliloquy so as to present it as barter paving the way for my conduction into paradise.

Zomaya has sustained me on minimums, on assets which she summed as detritus. Thus, I am never considered a material burden. Believe me, the money spent at St. Catherine's has never been the issue. She only cares about my verbal instigations, my revelations which may spark unpardonable scandal. To her I am an anti-Sun always issuing an oblique pressure, which causes her to opaquely waver. She understands that my energy always trembles on a fault-line, that eruption is always imminent. Because this type of quaking does not take place in the geological inferno one cannot rely on rabbits or squirrels to pass signals of panic. And if Zomaya looks for Ornelas to preindicate my utterance she is utterly bereft in this regard. I give no indicatives to those who thrive by foretelling. The hiddenness which coalesces within my person cannot be probed by defiled or incendiary schema. Being chiropteran I ignite in sleep at dawn, and waking has seldom claimed me when Zomaya appears for her daily appraisal. At the beginning of my stay Zomaya would always attempt Ornelas in my presence. Being semi-comatose during those episodes I would always hear her question Ornelas about the tone of my psychic whereabouts. As I've stated, no answer has been forthcoming.

As then, as now, there exists no signs, no susurrant embers giving off enigmas to be examined. How long can this last, how long can my energy continue to scald and not waver? Again, no dominant behavioural trilogy, no clearly factored unriddling. Trilogy in this instance concerning the conscious, and the subconscious, and the supramental genes of the Elysian. Because each person possesses a language when sleeping and waking Zomaya can only seek to reference as to my daily leaning. The codes or signs she seeks create no sums in the Elysian. Neither Ornelas or Devota can post no reference vis-à-vis this upper dimension. I know that I haunt her, and further that I facilitate general commotion. So again, this is power, this is the hatchery by which strategy is maintained. It is analogous to a style of chess not unlike the creations of Tal, or Botvinnik, or Capablanca. Me, I have a personality which exists without seething, without a righteousness which envies. I cannot cherish myself as despot, as she who rules by extroverted terror. None of this bespeaks me. I carry no overt quarry, no blatant or measurable growing space which even mediums fail to apprehend. This is why rapt magicians cannot approach me through quantitative inferentials. Let me say that I am shamaness as chiropteran, or chiropteran as shamaness, who peruses the Martian plains, and the Columbia Hills. I mean flight by transmutation which activates motion beyond vapour as blood. Being chiropteran on Mars is another draft of the physiology. Another draft of the proteins in the cells living through other parallel physiologies. And I, like certain shamans, know that there exists a parallel transpicuity between the Earthly spectrum and other living emissions in the cosmos. Let us take sharks, and rays, and humans, and bison. All of them tending towards one another, the sum of their vibrations emitting an evolutive chorus as if each one were listening to a nautical cosmography. Because I understand the essentials of cosmic fractals this choral plenitude rings through ghostly solar rhyming. Space is thus condensed by nautical curvature so that other planets and planes exist through concordant soliloquies which daunts the human view of a single understanding. So to breathe within the zone of transpolar revelation allows for inevitable heightening. One then feels the interval between a grain and the void. The leap, the fractional cusp which penetrates, which wakes pluperfect atmospheres, creating dawn by unbelievable dawn.

Not a vernacular gathering with its hoof marks, with its common signatures aligned by collateral tenor. My inner veering burns with inclement shifts, with rapturous veracity. Not mortal configuratives, or points from clannish morals. As chiropteran I am yet unfamiliar with gatherings, with response from habitual collectives. Always spiralling with invisible pressure I can feel the sensing of all chiropteran with their unbeholdable staring attempting to surmount me through thought and speech and code and word. A kind of alchemical tribulation surrounding me with an aurality in shards, wanting from me a return to wonted blood drinking thereby creating in me the desire for general self-renouncement. A call from the collective for telepathic remonstrance. And Zomaya, and Ornelas, and St. Catherine's are conditioned by the repressive as response, ultimately aligning themselves with thought as base consumption. As chiropteran I have left their corruptive scent smouldering with all their separate concealments. And as for vicars and their psychic apologists I can announce them as conservators of those who resist vertical intervallics. For me, these vertical intervallics, these leaps, these frequencies which embrace the unforeseen as composition. It is I who refuse the powerless habitat as gist. Not being party to myself as empire I am removed from the remedial, having implanted in my hearing herds of fleeting micro-scales which probe the depth of every phoneme, which allows me to always listen for new insight, for new ways to kindle the recondite through in-audia. Certainly not a recipe, or data revealed by laryngographs, testing the various quiverings of my voice. I could be a ghost from the quakings of the sea floor making comment on all the species that have ever existed. Certainly I do not cosy up to sepulchres to pray. Because at any moment I can respond to forces more subsuming than prayer. Zomaya, when placed beside this deeper critica becomes no more than a functional disorder. She attempts to exonerate herself by remaining a house apart, by functioning surface behaviour. But she remains overwrought by existential disorder.

I call her the single elusive gene, a damaged uterine beacon. Capable of trenchant laterality she attempts to quell and requel a deformed condition. In this sense her movement continues to absorb her own aberration. A loyalist to her own stagnant ambition. If I had to designate a verbal insignia it could be nothing other than heteromorphism. Saying this I am not concerned with the carnivorous institution which starkly emboldens itself by castigating human atomics as nothing other than original sin. Or another way to state it, the chronic failure of beasts. This is why day after day I resist, giving me resource to greater and greater depth. Unlike the actual physical locales of caverns these depths are not unlike the Einstein-Rosen bridges leading to other unknowable domains. Contrary to standard analysis I am not engaged in isolate catastrophe. I am not like Zomaya limited to one spectrum. Or to a band of doubled neural spectrums. Through my contact as chiropteran I have organically broached the parallel and have through that contact been invigorated by a proto-repleteness which is allowing my energy to develop as if biology had been exchanged for being. In this parallel state I'm sensing suns that don't exist, moons and seas which don't configurate. Yet continuums occur, universe after universe supercessional in motion, eternally empowered by the emptiness of suns. These are not aimless suns in samsara but energy which roams and is simultaneous with the penetrant condition of riddles. Space-time? No, a sudden leap to being. As a result, I've come to the broad enabling gesture which transmutes mammalian limit. As to scarification by form: cipher. Impetus by scale: unutterable.

Even as I speak as Rosanna and chiropteran I'm adapting to other scales of salt, to other genes and combinations. Between human and chiropteran there exists connecting environments. Biology then raised and invigorated by the spirit. To echolocate, to fly, to hear, to ambulate. These powers, of course, chiropteran, and again, the human as transmuted by chiropteran. By this flux at the level of the mammalian it has opened possibility giving me exercise at levels not prone to human limit. As Rosanna I am open to the unimagined, having congress with the symptoms of the unimagined, so much so that the physiology becomes rife with perpetual intimation. Thus, I've left the ordination of consensus neurology. I've tested space with its turbulence, with its irradiated voids. And from the din of the hacienda I've learned the code of compound interregnums, of how days become voids and pass back into days. Then from this knowing how voids spawn into voids and pass unnoticed into themselves. This is beyond what one would note as a crowning mystical patience. Conversely, having existed at the fringes of deep time I understand monotony and the danger which exults as monotony. With such imminence embodied I attempt a levitational rowing which gives me cosmic exercise flying to the tallest galactic mountain peaks. And like an olden Seminole mother I call these orthodiagonals Dogon adumbrations. It is extending orthogonality from the soma of the human system so that it makes contact with the interwoven essence which pervades the invisible integers of the cosmos. When I say this I am not signalling out a region of countable exoplanets, but that which accounts for the proto-numerology of atoms, this not being just simple terminology to be advanced as occluded pneuma. As Seminole and Dogon I've been a self-embodied initiate into the feeling which precedes the eons, because every moment of every moment the cells commingle and communicate beyond the Sun. Thus, I am not a body prone to sudden abstraction, prone to ideology as galactics. Therefore I am not what is commonly called a generic example. I am specific, unlapsed as regards the body as chronology in the cosmos. For me, these are not inflammatory issues, or gross or interior poaching by idea. Therefore, no artifice is siphoned, no result is enchained within former vacuums of broken identity. As chiropteran I am not accessible as analogous physical property. As spectre I cannot be physically produced in accord with the dimensions of the Egyptian rosette, or Geoffrey's tailless bat, or a Lesser mouse-tailed bat, or a Mauritian tomb bat. In spirit I am more the Vampire bat or the Mexican funnel-eared bat. Like the funnel-eared I am rapid of flight, as Vampire I seal the fate of certain humans. I've transposed the rapid flight of the funnel-eared to the instantaneous power in my thinking. As for the Vampire, I feel it manifest in the presence of Zomaya's psychic weakening. I'm empowered by psychic blood withdrawal. As of now, I've not applied these powers to the populace at large. I am isolate, sometimes famished from lack of invisible blood. Odd, illusive, singular in destruction, always possessing in my wake an uncommon secrecy. As of now I know Zomaya is creating a séance in her system, and is attempting to call on that system in order to ferret out the inscrutable which seems to imbue me. Because she can plot no day when I will weaken, I remain the sole insidious matron, the senorita who seems to console with her subconscious shroud.

She was the Queen-Princess, the Mother. She forbade, she angrily tossed aside, she created in her wake a whole rung of degradation. And I have reiterated and reiterated again and again, that the lowest rung was reserved for Jesus solely defined by his colouration. Zomaya had been trained to be self-poisoned, to think that the Whites were a separate species from the Divine. As if they were self-authored, defining for themselves the necessary minerals, the power of concussive authority. This remains for her an ingrained devolution, forcing her to strive for their illusive separation. This is why all the animals are dead. This is why all the peoples are depleted. As for the glaciers and the poles, disappearance has now become sovereign. The whites being plagued by pessimism and disorder, have passed on their panic to the rings of Saturn, to the fractals which roam beyond geometry. This remains Zomaya's paradigmatic, her toxic ritual which gestates. As I speak, I am draining her power, I am reversing the domain in her village. From my personal reconnoitring I understand corrosive colonialisation. Although Jesus was participant as rapist, as viper who cooked his veins with powder, I felt, in my heart of hearts that he was the one true leader, the unheralded potentate. Even under the pressure of pure derision, he always whispered respect for my resistance, of my gain from tempered bitterness. It was during these uncanny instants that we combined our states of difference, that we understood, under those strained conditions of delay and remoteness, an electrical rawness was allowed to live. This was the minimum voltage which spawned in me renewal, so that I was exposed to something other than singular drift, to something more than mere opinion. There existed grasp, and I understood how Jesus and I existed as fractionated savants. To the sighted we would be analogous to stars of 10th magnitude, pulled towards invisible magnitude by a star which can't be seen. These moments with Jesus have taught me the charisma of the instantaneous, the unreplicated, the in-sufflated sigil. So in the oddest way he inspired ascendance, he inspired in me an untoward activity. And it is this activity which persists within me, which provides me with honour, which burns, which weaves from my leanings an inseparable sagacity.

Being the derailed of the derailed a telepathy existed between us. And I continue to take it upon myself to be the Indian, to be the Seminole who magically listens to the hacienda. Even with the fumes of heroin in his system Jesus knows that I listen, that I decipher remoteness through sorcerous election. And I know that Zomaya remains in the role of the Spaniard, and by extension she is Belgian, and English, and Norwegian. Because she has extended such reach in this dimension, she has become part of a provisional expertise prone as it is to mechanics and brutality. But because the psychic loam has now deepened her point of view has now become possessed by an energy which writhes attempting to fend off extinction. Her whole realia concludes upon the visible. It is life production magnetized by aesthetics. By nothing other than the fuel of tangible enclave. Therefore she clings, she designs no betterment of her position. Her enclave being matter, I contend that she defends the infinitesimal as it relates to the cosmic lair. In contradistinction I am in the field of the infabricate, of the energy which issues light out of darkness, being unitarian as sound, of intaglio as energy. I will never wake as a grammatical truncheon, but extend as something more perilous, as something absolutely illusive, which gives to my breathing a centripetal implosion, being rays of sound commingled with verbal chromasia.

Zomaya represents a recent indictment of energy which destroys and infacilitates, who seeks power in her life through the threat of termination. Yet I have turned this power on her, I now give her her own ghosts to chew. Even as Jesus implodes he must garner a certain satisfaction by my liberation from the enclave. An escape from its feral glaciation, from its fraught imbroglio as tension. Even as the absence of my body must afflict him, he must admit at a certain level of his compost that I've offered a beacon to him, a dazed intensive inspiration which even in his demise will allow him to ascend. As for the other two, they remain closer in spirit to Zomaya. Not that their degradations are identical, but they stand as listed with the incarcerated emblems of Zomaya. In contrast to Jesus, they are upright as cadavers. They've done nothing except conduct themselves through invasive thought disturbance. Never have they stirred the intangible in me. Never have they staunched the flow of degradation, nor sealed from their drifting energies inspired by the inferno. Always demons, always throngs of spontaneous tension. But curiously a tension which never sponsored itself as movement. They symbolize their essence through purposeless stationary enactment. This is how intelligence stratifies, this is how the dendritic wizens. This being the irrevocable substance by which evil is invigorated. In a lesser sense I can say that Oraculos and Esteban suffer from daunting mental adhesions. This is why the knowledges explored remain in absence through antispeculation. Which means the hypnotic as derogation. The hacienda being nothing more than a structure which houses the pulse of hyenas.

Secrecy has been uppermost. It has been the catalyst at the omphalos of living. In this sense Zomaya contains eternity. As if the totalic of the family could persist beyond eons. Because she cannot think beyond the present parentheticals there exists no deeper understanding than her present historical perception. She can think of nothing other than its buildings, its crafts, its mores. For me, I think of the double ice sheets around us. The one which existed prior to history, and the other to come which is encroaching from the future. A future when the continents freeze, when the Sun will suspend itself in motion. This is not poetic inveiglement, nor psychic misnomer poised as revenge. No, these remain the stark conditions, a brazen summary vis-à-vis the human. Someone like Ornelas would argue that the narrative from Judea remains the compelling franca, the tone by which the moon is kept in balance, the tone by which the infinite Suns are subsumed by land. If anything, the human narrative is a curious signal which pulses between ages. Under this circumstance a moribund set of actions. Yet within this downward complexity there exists circumstantial quality. I'm thinking of the first kingdoms where writing commenced, where spoken forensics were alchemically exchanged. Nubia not being an idealized peak, nevertheless it gathered the spark, the first intuitional grasp of that which provokes phenomena. But in the western lands the unexplainable persists, even the science which is known is explained through samsara.

So as I persist as Rosanna, and Seminole, and chiropteran, I remain the gist of the unexplained. It is like knowing in one's being the provocation of comets, knowing the random rotation of gas and the infinite variables of cosmic climates. Which can never be the gist of Zomaya or St. Catherine's. They remain tainted by restrictive phobias. And so ironic in the case of Zomaya, being lesbian, whore, polyandrous, sinner. Corrupt to the very acid of her tissues. Living as if she were wrought and re-wrought according to the tenets of the Lateran Councillor and the precepts of Pope Gregory. Then further deluded by conclaves and pronouncements whispering in her ear that the body is bad, that the body has been stained by corrosion. This is the source of her infamous daily mass. The mass that I've mentioned where wafers and wine are submitted to the brutes. As if such daily conduct had force enough to balance their Jurassic suffocations. By critiquing this act I am not exchanging phenomena for phenomena. That is, lessening my feeling of guilt by extolling the scandalous debris left by Zomaya's actions. I do not participate in such exchange so as to come out basking in the diamonds of St. Peter's.

For believers, destroy the body, and by destroying the body ascend to the gargantua that is heaven. According to this general case the instincts are held hostage, excruciation is threatened. A vicar is invoked. Then one confesses to an evoluted persona concerning crimes evinced according to physical urges. This what's so strange about Zomaya, she accepts this contortion while distorting its mythos with her brazen self-squalor. Yet she submits to the rites. I cannot specify the rite which subtends her. Perhaps it is the Braga, or the Ambrosian, or the Mozarabic. What I suspect is that it is the standard Roman rite with its dominant liturgical Latin. Thus she feigns the eminence of the triplicate body, of the Father, and the Son, and the Holy Ghost. By mechanically adhering to a centralized rite she gained self deceptive absolution from the insult she had heaped upon reality. After such tainted blessing she would return to the hacienda to further fuel its abject baseness. She had faced the world. She had been absolved at St. Dominic's, and many times returned to Abaddon and limbo witnessing me entwined with the likes of Oraculos. Then, after a rancorous delay home mass would be conducted. And of course this garnered from me an absolute disrespect. Zomaya in this role becoming the transgendered vicar, the harlot in charge of one's heavenly faeces. It was like Livia exhorting gladiators to goodness. By having the discipline to exert this travesty day after day it was to her as a trade in indulgences which allowed an artifice of confidence to continue her perpetration of crime. The cross she would wave would fission like a hellish password which allowed her to evolve to greater and greater frenzy. It was Mass as boiling evasion, as activity which extolled carnage. To resist in such a sitting was akin to small mammals escaping the power of mountainous lizards. One cannot display ferocity, or coil with propensity towards insult. There is nothing other than the biding of time. The filing down of stone, by stone, by stone, with each filing carrying no greater motion than surreptitious nutation. I relate this condition to biogeology where the contemporaneous merges with its depth as circuitous historicity. Each moment is broken down into moments, which then occur through deeper fractionation, so much so that reality then gathers as a cavernous kinematic, swallowing up all the traces which gather at the surface. This is how I've slowly gained power by swallowing up the traces. Because I have gone so deeply into the cavernous this is how I've evolved my powers as chiropteran, as energy which echolocates the psychic in the span of each moment. Because in being moments descend and ascend ad-infinitum. Because I am beyond the concerns of feckless energetics bound by personality. As chiropteran I sense the spirit inside the body and its definitive proto-leanings. For instance, in Esteban there always exists a carnivorous indifference, in Oraculos, stylish misnomer, and Jesus, always Jesus, with his ancient and ominous burning. I can make these intuitive distinctions. But I am not like a doctor making statistical distinction between trained monsters. Yet through the echo-locative I know them, I understand their recessive imbalance within the pressure of the Quaternary. And out of all the souls in the Quaternary they nest with me as proximate bodies. It is understood by the gist of sages that there are no accidents, no mishandling of specifics. I sometimes wonder, and wonder again concerning the strictness of such specification. I know that as Rosanna I have now brought myself to another level of birthing. It is a condition which I feel no fate can know of. I know in myself that I've been released from the extrinsic as something magic, as something heightened with obscurity. A life which cannot exist as nostalgia, or as imprisoning residue from the memory. What Zomaya does is act as alchemical spur giving me a susurrant interior key which opens the door on her new found paranoia. Zomaya's advances were curious. She would creep towards me like a haunted panther, stealthily, without a trace of commotion. She was a panther with the tongue of an asp. Before I knew it I would be convulsed in writhing beneath her probings. I was nothing more than an animal doubled over by heat and regression. She always told me that that is the way that Catalina always used her. And that Edmundo approved and would then proceed to consume the both of them. She was never regular with me in this regard. Just as earlier she would randomly demand Dostoevsky of me, she would do the same when consuming my body. Because she was far too busy with regulation of the brutes, and the ruses of the outside kingdom, there was no telling when she'd consume me. On one occasion there would be Esteban, on another occasion there would be Oraculos, and Jesus at times between them. Mayhem reigned, yes, but after time a depth of orchestration seemed manifest. Which brings to mind the manoeuvring of game boards. Take certain openings in chess such as "Alekhine's Defence", or the "Alapin Opening II," or perhaps "Abrahams Variation". Or maybe endgame stratagems like the "Lucena position", or the "Philidor drawing method." Then there exists only another motion of methods such as "Flohr-Saemisch manoeuvre II," or the "Closed Ruy Lopez, Chigorin Defence" circa 1902. These are oddities in my circumstance, true, but they erupt from within, and I feel they are applicable to my status as one whose emerged from a den of chattering skua's teeth. Somehow Zomaya understood all levels of manoeuvre. Somehow she extracted from its motion a paradigm which obscured the awkward fallacy of the hacienda. It fed the general mind a fallacious subsistence. Yet to the outside world Zomaya remained a paragon of integrity. She, the immaculate heir of a curious copper inheritance, combining the seeming good will of Edmundo, with the social jocularity which was native to Catalina, continuing to commingle with the conservative Folkloristas, she possessed nothing but advantage, nothing but the cultural stipends which heightened her charisma. Being blessed with physical allurement she always dangled like carrion a dram beyond the reach of the wolves. By gracefully denying advances from suitors she further strengthened her status which in the reasoning of those less read gave her the aura of someone in contact with the immaculate. With the four of us being ciphers she was none other than the miraculous persona, a living canticle of scripture. Some called her "God's bride" which no one could possess. I understood this telepathically because at odd moments she would intone in my ear that she was the "Bride of God" and that her power was untouchable. Yet this was the "Bride" who forced snails from my gullet in order for her to gain pleasure from my torment. These were like episodes from Petronius, something ancient and vile, something sinister and private . In the wake of these unnerving episodes she would regale me about life in the age of great meteors, and when I would fail with sufficient engagement she would solemnly stroke my brow and force me to imbibe another ghastly round of snails practically reaching the pitch of vomit. As if she spoke on behalf of her own enormity. During those moments I was no more to her than a sacrificial tapir.

The latter has changed. I am no more the in-considered animal. I am now alive in a fecund neural river. I've overstepped all previous means and can say that I feel the atmospherics of the authors who created the four Egyptian books of astronomy, "On Risings", "On the Syzygies and Phases of the Sun and Moon", "On the Disposition of the Sun and Moon, and Five Planets", "On the Disposition of Fixed stars and Stellar Phenomena." I've become persistent with unbending prana feeling from all my struggles a cataclysmic exploration. I understand from the books mentioned, an initial contact with the heavens, with the poles as they project beyond the walls of a Spartan terminus. Always there being effort to reach the sum of whole causes. Not that I haven't trod upon the gravel of Einstein, or embarked with post-Cantoresque Physique into unstructured quanta, babbling with the menagerie of tinctures in my cells. Speaking by clauses of starlight as if I were sighted, and were able to reveal from my findings a mathematical marginalia giving me release from samsaric calculation. Therefore I now know what it is to utter outside one's boundaries. So am I damaged throwback? Am I a brooding calendula in insufficient soil?

I can only say that I've come to understand myself as susurrant solar mongrel whose gone beyond trial by barbarian litmus, fully able to witness the lunar apogees in my feelings. Which means that I am more than a learned wolf, and as is known have become this self-suggested chiropteran. A kindled hyper-instigation, who both crawls and flies and subsists on her own oneirics. An elliptical mass, an inordinate conjuration. I must emit the energy of an errant signalling drum. An energy concomitant with audition. All this arising from the after-effects of struggle. So I remain this open admixture, operant as pure trigonal implication. Which has led to an alphabetics which understands evil and generates blackness. What results is a language which is able to translate suffocation and tension. Yet this is a language which subsists by the instantaneous. To this degree I am always confronting my own absence, breathing by personal cryptography. Not a theatrical mesmerics to simply speak through a stark or maniacal wisdom. At best, the current New Mexicans could say that my legacy exists through embittered functionality. That I will never recover my balance even through the suddenness of death. Under the present point of view I can only be assessed as being structurally incapable.

Perhaps this remains a necessitous assessment given that I could never hold court as a mother with an infant and a daily home to balance. Because I've become this feral complexity the rumours which surround me will be abrupt, nescient, tied to a strife where the personality seems abandoned. Rosanna seems appended as depressive mortality, as energy which is prone to extinction. What will probably accrue is refutation of all my facets. A terrible assault upon the fire of my remains. Having been diminished by surrounding consensus I feel analogous to the Earth itself, which rises and ascends without the scent of any structural hubris. And I sense this so much so that any level of outward mean exists in order to de-exist never purporting to perfection, or holding in my neurology any remainder of the angelic. Perhaps I protect the amatorial realms removed from the peculiar acids of history. Perhaps to some degree I am paragon in this regard, filtering, osmotic, cleansing the cells through parallel transfunction. Of course not the lower denomination such as the Komodo Dragon, or the short faced bear, but something of greater and greater confoundment which escapes the prevailing circumstantials of the monstrous. Again, this cannot be filtered through reason, or described through the mimicry of ordinal placement. Each motion, and each motion of utterance exists through splendiferous renewal. This being the most prominent benefit of hiddenness. I, Rosanna have no numbers, have been bequeathed no assets that would rivet the beaureaucrats to spur investigation. In the deepest sense I am anti-coagulate, moving from void to void, being Rosanna as part of Enceladus, as part of the methane lakes on Titan. My spirit then sending signals through these partial diameters, through dangers magically implied by powers which roam the pandemoniacs of the Oort dimension. Perhaps Zomaya has blessed me by creating the condition of my passive neural calligraphy. Samsara is now clear to me. When Jesus grunted when passing himself into me it was like a boar relieving himself of his innards. Oraculos with his conniving descents like a corrupted male swan. Then Esteban, a slurred and indicted gryphon. And it is these animal pallors which now exist without recoverable identity. What comes to mind is no quotidian state of succession. So for me to date and spawn entry into a journal signals nothing but dearth. Because the calendar has become nothing but a commercial acrobatics in decline. It carries nothing but blocks of weight. To pit signs against themselves reveals itself to be a harried obsolescence. Thus, the zodiac is marred, and now, its tendencies seem to unravel and become random, absorbing the human tree in the insidious. It now exists as a poisoned conduit, a flow of sulphur aligned with November as drainage, the latter riven as it is by both cool and dark exposure.

So am I without origin on Earth? Have I suddenly appeared as an unscripted paradigm who battles self devourment? If Zomaya is void and has issued me as void from her void, then through diligence I am released from reversal. And I know that I have gained by this release a power accrued by nomadic sonority. A post-energetics, an anxiety called into play by prophetic prediction. So if I know my birth at one level of the mind I can contemplate myself as combustible performer, as an heiress who schools her blood by numerous exercise through human rivalry. In this sense one is scripted, and combined through blasphemous persona. When the living speak of the dead they raffle them off as monuments, as being somehow privy to re-electrical summary. This will be impossible in my case because I will simply be known to never have existed. I who have done nothing except breed phantoms in my belly, perhaps post-chiropteran, perhaps a resemblance to Ramses and Hapshepsut. And I think of the latter as ether other than ordinary blood flow. Perhaps in my oddness I am pointing towards a pure life beyond carbon, to a vicinity of life yet unreached. Perhaps, to post-transitional respiration. This being another genetics rather than the body conceived through New Mexican terms. For me, New Mexico being fumes from the galaxy, being in its own way a mannered replication of transcendence. In this odd sort of way I refute my own infamy, this more and more becoming my incipient detonation.

The parochial emblaze themselves with flags, with gestures of adoration to this or that inferno. And not just the sighted. If the war dead could speak what would they claim? Then what of the maimed and the blinded? What are their standards? I know there are causes for liberty. I know there are causes that create chaos and delimit. Inwardly I am not unlike the eschatology of Osceola. All the same I am not here to foment, to create by medicinal holocaust. Nor is anything I think implied by constitutional imperative. As nature struggles in these failing days I've became this idiosyncratic urbanite living as a millenarian hybrid in-locatable as to density. As if I were fishing for rays, or chopping up scorpions in the desert. Even as dire as it's been, I continue to eat, I continue to unfold. Nothing such as squab or exterminated hawk, but fish, and black beans, and tortillas. All that I remember from childhood is that meals were taken in hiding. And on odd occasions Zomaya would force me to rinse vegetables. Then when she had the old Apache mothers come in to cook I was hidden in a separate laundry room where all utterance was prohibited. This is why to this day I have minimum relation with cutlery and mastication.

Sin to my understanding is a senseless transitory schism. It is only that which certain cultural forces have deemed incommensurate. The body is understood to be clepsydra by salt, and geography by anger. The body born to life as arthritic stupefaction, prone in its leanings to perfect moral wreckage. In my case there exists proto-original contaminates born as I've been under ostentatious deficit. From such origination self-assault has accrued, then at times, feeling a thorough exhaustion in myself, feeling that I amount to nothing more than a soma of poached carrion. I cannot deny that I have mocked my own body, that I can accrue no reasoning for my living. I have survived the most intentional agitations. So by all accounts I should not exist. I should not be at St. Catherine's, surviving plinth by psychic plinth. In the deeper sense I'm outmanoeuvring what the prosaic mind perceives as fate. So as proxy for what the vicars consider as fount for the Almighty Zomaya has been moved by threat to her reputation. Therefore I am her ultimate disfigurement. I act as a caloric which invades her, day, after day, after day. So by imbalance I've broken through a density not normally approached. And by breaking through this density I've cleared a path of mental tundra, getting rid of the dross, and the sterile elements which distract. I will say, and I will say it alone, this is a level not even the Gnostics sought to endure. I've taken into account the haunting of universe after universe, searching in myself for the essence of causation. Looking in myself for the tremor of tremors over and beyond the blankness through fabled luminosity. Nothing other than the state which overcomes states, so that any median investigation prone to delimit can only apply to isolate numeration. God in this sense being a barren and separate eclampsia. God being a part of separate infinities which are subsuming and non-subsuming. Yet there exists no critical barrier between them. Creation then becomes eruption by charisma, by a state of affairs which precedes the atomic and the sub-atomic allowing the mind to extend and no longer know what it knows. So since Zomaya and the Spaniards seek an isolate status, they have no recourse but to condense their emotional stasis in the micro-biography of the Christos. When gathering the brutes on a daily basis, and by waving the cross within flummoxed earshot she feels she brings up powers condoned by the Adamic. To her, she is condensing first reasoning. She, who claims to restore a famished clairaudience. But what she considers to be a solemn replication remains a damaged co-authorship as she attempts to summon forces from a higher ungovernable roulette. What she does is plant dosages of anomaly into her governing ritual so as to barter her time in exchange for eternal worth.

So tomorrow when she comes I'll remain in my daylight coma, being again the partially inspected sow, carrying an interior infrangibility no longer entangled by personal criticality. I tend more and more in her thinking to take on the riddle of a neutered cadaver. But unlike the brutes I've had nascent contact with the world. I always recall those blurry visits to Mass, and the indifferent parishioners, and the warm Albuquerquean Sun. Which has given me enough evidence to speak as I speak knowing that someone's ear may be ajar. I will strengthen in them the anticipated flame, the already called for. A reality not commenced according to havoc or power, but unlike Zomaya as Sadducee, flaunting her Christian invention. As if God were gazing down on her wilful travesty, forgiving her for the quantity of her lies. As if quantity took flight through furtive modification, with the false act of blessing further mutating the voice of final judgement. But having those two Sundays at Mass has given me a necessitous edge, and left a difference at the hacienda. Unlike Oraculos I do not dwell on stunted superiority, or drown like Esteban on the whisky of agave roots. All that they've known are various forms of defeat. Pertaining to this condition I am without them, having nothing to do with their struggles, with the triggering points of their gnawing ulcerations.

When Zomaya conducts her travesty of Low Mass she embraces a bevy of unsubstantiated insult. Because she conducts it in private she hopes for maximum tolerance from the God of Leviticus and Deuteronomy having confused the dialectic of the Bible. She seeks to please him by routine, invade his worries, fool him, master his weakness for an unforetold lasciviousness. This is how she preaches with a gnawing electrical taint, making the gastric juices surge, making the colon tremble with panic. Because she prays to a God of whims she succumbs to chronic waywardness, to an energy not unlike the drunkenness of Lot. This is Zomaya. This is how she immolates. Therefore, she does not consider the source of the Pueblo Lakes, or the energies imbibed in an Anastasi kitchen. Therefore she is peripheral, unsteady.

Because of the money that's been accrued Zomaya can sustain me at St. Catherine's. The same could be said if I lived in Reykjavik, or Caracas, the krona or the bolivar would support me. In Zomaya's case she feeds them dollars. She sustains my liminal status. Objectively, I live as abbreviation, without answer, without subjective hope as treatise. I am no more than an object, no more than a monad condensed by marginalia. To her, I am the glass always filled up with poison. Therefore she talks to Ornelas by coaxing catastrophics. She seeks the precise degree of my bodily information. When I bathe, when I eat, if I'm about to die. At one point she inquired about suicide as a corridor, about my insomnia as presignifying insanity. Of course I've mined her verbal concerns, and kept her codes surrounded by my spontaneous mental pawns. Thus, I keep her energy exhausted by unregulated curfew. What, with trying to monitor my utterings, weaving at home political polyandry, then abruptly adapting so as to fuse with society, I understand the angularity of her torment, so I ignite chess, and intensify the pressure by creating in Ornelas a hypnotic camaraderie. A camaraderie based on vibration. A vibrational psychology where we commune through damaged singularity, as persons who've survived the most savage of manipulations. Just by Zomaya's approach to me she knows I've lived through trying times. Not unlike St. Rita she knows the poison of domestic endangerment. She knows how my blood responds in circles, how the scroll of my intelligence burns by in-dominate sonority. She can sense that I smell like malarial philodendron, or leprous oleander, stark, riveted, absolute in my demeanour of oddness. Therefore, she understands my response to situational humiliation. To this extent she is a halo which surrounds me, quite unlike something one could conceive as the temperature of connivance. Hers is a response which feels, which associates with the general threat surrounding my fate. All of this keeps Zomaya stymied, short of breath, without source within the ambit of navigable recrimination.

As victim, must I take nails from my ark and turn them against her? Or must I scorch her foundations with a random flambeau?

Because she protects Oraculos she excuses the rhyming points of their evil. At the out-start of my stay at St. Catherine's I would confront Zomaya concerning the whereabouts of Oraculos. Had he left the hacienda? Had he wandered into some other seismic kingdom? She always averted and turned my infernal queries to ash. Now he lies hidden in a maze of vertiginous hissing. And so my queries have morphed to imploded seizures, and turned my waking to retro-causal silence. Therefore I no longer converse with her lurid combustion, placing its tension at a cortical remove electrically prone to a type of legal seasoning. A state of litigation which my mind has no calling for. I feel I have broken beyond what I know of known conceptions. I want not a single episode of struggle to sully in my voice the power which imparadises. Because there is fire in my nothingness, a flickering of Suns which fuels my accentual squinting needles. Always I am gnawing at sodden release points, moving to a plane which escapes all jurisdiction. I know that St. Catherine's is provisional, as well as the being that I know is Rosanna. As far as the hellish under omens I am chiropteran. As for the upward journey, I trespassed the angelic enlivening the mystical components of the self. What has amazed Ornelas and Zomaya is that I sometimes glow green in the daylight. I know this, because at times I hear comment while in coma about the utter light which seems to escape from my pores. From what I gather my apparition has strengthened over time.

What must be remembered is that this is not light which has appeared from a sudden climacteric. It does appear from the strictly physical as ordeal. It is not strictly the substance of the Sun as it rains down on Bogota or the Congo. It is something which cannot be explained according to containment. Poetically it could be akin to suggestion which mystically emanates from intra-circularity. In Sanskrit it is known as dvanhi, as that which casts fumes, as that which envelopes beyond the thought which seeks proof by describing alembics. Not a secondary phase which seeks transposition within the gates of God. As this Rosanna, I am another plane of terra firma, another biological occurrence which speaks through other saturations of being. Therefore, deliberation does not exist. My exposed and wayward biography is only a partial indication of these other saturations of activity. When she sees me Zomaya has less and less certainty concerning her unequalled actions. Her former outlook is obscured. Near the beginning of my stay she attempted to vindicate herself, asking me on occasion, was I really assaulted, was I forced to vomit up detritus. I know she wanted to test my febricity to see if my memory was kindled. I would never reply. My response to her began to lurk as occlusion, as imminence enshrouded by apocalyptic concern. Because I condense no kinetic paper I remain beyond reach. My interior subsistence always concludes upon an irritant which no one can decide. At the deepest level I condense as the suggestible as disjuncture. The perplexity I emit has tended to swarm the very roots of St. Catherine's creating an ambiguous emotional mood. There is nothing they can offer by which to contrast my presence . To Devota and her ilk I am an unsettling corpse who feeds on burning apples. I hail from serpents, to them I reek as a fetid stellar omen. These remain my suggestibilities, my fraught trans-functional complexity where no sums can persist. Thus, I am a citizen of emptiness, an apparition that has yet to be born. Therefore, I confuse the blood in all who witness me. The birth mother. The overseeing nuns. My body has voltage and it survives through the in-possessive. Because the profound has no limit I've come to understand partial infinities through the active gaze of meteors. Because in this partial sense I inhalate the Sun. I then understand its respiration through darkening. Because of this I am now beholden to seclusion.

When I speak there are moments when liberty erupts from my mind as if I were one with Nilotic arrow construction, or held in my hands a naturopathic treatise on proto-Etruscan medusae. It is something mendaciously perfect about extending such a synthetic over and beyond medicine and war. The latter being such a wayward undertaking that the hurt which I've experienced feels truly resolved. This being exercise by circuitous alter extension. Thus, I am in a second or third state released from venereal estuation. In this sense I do not resemble Goya fighting off syphilis, or Storni inverting her works under lamps of despair. Because I am filled with such fibre the ptomaine in me has not so far come to the level of final negation. Since I cannot regulate my bravery, or compel my instincts to avert dislocated ardour I am at random times morose, my lumbar region brackish, my feelings marred by corrupted telepathy. Yet I am poised to take into account these findings, at times, scattered across the diaphragm as unstable mappings. But I maintain that whatever lessening has occurred within me has been balanced by my incendiary skills as they erupt from within. Having had no other example than myself I have no need to consult extrinsic social forces concerning the pain I've had to swallow as my pabulum. Yet for all this dissonance I have not arrived at dearth, I've only spoken to myself in a language which I'll describe as unspoiled tornado. A language which never arrives at itself by continuing to spin by seeming in-direction. It opens me, it allows me to arrive at destinies no conscious experience could illuminate. On the surface of things I've been force fed parts of canons, and strangled on waves of written emotional data. Verbal nebulas, phonemes enriched by the tenor of infinite gathering. According to this methodology language condenses with pointed specification, and then suspends itself, and quite suddenly burns and freezes, and shifts, and turns towards its origins in keeping with the presenter's mental tectonics. Which is my experience of inner breaking and renewal, being an inward state not unlike the mysteries kindled in Laurasia, or the Laurentian Mountains, or the Laurentian Plateau. Yet if I spoke Creek, or uttered names in spotted Huron, other sparks and withdrawals would arise. Again, what I'm referring to is the endopsychic respirator's prism, which produces a joy, a risibility in the spirit. Thus, a depuration, a cleansing via psychic sudariums, so that in comparison, the lavabo in Catholic ritual remains stunted, a gross miscarriage through abbreviated symbol. I understand these contrasts not by quantity of intellectual ballast, but by fissure which dwells inside me which explodes at times within a sudden thesis. Amongst those who advance through scholarship I advance as the vicarious looming, as the idiot-savant, peculiar, striking, rising through bodiless combustion. Because energies do combust within me as if I've become concomitant with the Earth during its beginning primal exchanges. Living at such depth I am not to be confused with elements which concur through destructive observation. Nor do I want to make of my experience energies equitable to a nauseous secondary hamlet. This is not equitable to archaeology in the sense that each layering or supercessional realia is not of simultaneous binding. A leap issues a response which soars from prior cognitive limit. A different level is absorbed. The mind then escapes the pall of the gloomy resurrectionist. Having reported all level of personal horror it is because it lives in me and is alive and remains alchemically active. I am organic, and because I am organic I do not live as an out of body monster. This is the only way that new disruption exists. It thrives in my system as an intensive generosity, as a poise which seems to saturate in the core of an older myopia. Thus, I've become an essence which lives beyond a theoretical osmosis, not unlike omens ascending from occulted puzzling warrens.

Traces of sadness remain a seasoning for me. It is now a legacy which allows me teleportation back and forth between the anguish of memory and the restless integers which trace sums across the galaxies. Within this ambit there is no precedent, there is not one iota to be plagiarized; I can be mistaken for no other inspiration. As Rosanna I am inviolate. Having escaped the trap of carnal psychology I can now question previous dimensions of enactment. Put another way, the standing social body; with its axioms and its victims poised as it is across strenuous episodes of confinement. This is why Zomaya has to trouble me daily, she has to mine from me some spillage of secrets, But by remaining in this unbearable balance I've stolen accusations from her, I've tossed her secretions into invisible ambrosia. So who's become this hellish non-entity, this leper whispering into her isolate mental gnats. This is Zomaya. And now I've become her galling vampire daughter.

Amphibology?

Heteromorphic instability?

The mystico-anagogic as manna?

Clairaudient water riots?

Life flows, the character of detour does not delay me. After Esteban, after the damaging aristocracy of Oraculos, after Jesus tinged by ferality and sadness, I am in-diminished by human contraband. This is not to say I've completely been absolved of damage. Should I leave St. Catherine's eternally comatose, I will be an unfledged citizen of a curious proto-necropolis. It will be naturally understood that I will never return to the hacienda, and that its negative array will evince a prior motion as I ascend from visibility and comment. Am I saying that Zomaya is now arranging my unconditional extermination, having me gainlessly ejected to the invisible? It is a question which I seamlessly contemplate on certain given days. At any moment Zomaya could make her own self-arrangement with poison and have me mellifluously stilled right here on St. Catherine's terrain. Yet at some level she knows that I am more strategic than she. My poisoned body would return to her over and over until some strange inscrutability would pull her into the grave. She would be captured and she knows this. I remain an obstacle to her schemes, because I've gained prominence with Ornelas and have established a solemn routine. I am more believable than she. Being blinded and quasi muted I've instigated presence in this chair. I simply sit here, withdrawn, requiring a minimum of sustenance. It seems I'm most active at twilight when I wake from seeming coma. Then I relieve myself, feed, and then relieve myself again for good measure. I maintain a routine which any hysteric would envy. These are actions I've not once sought to revise. I am sitting here in this one escalation of the body seemingly stranded in targeted sand. All the time I am advancing a covert dimension, my sigil being the stranded parent body as it simulates long term besetment. Yet I am not like a Buddhist falling away from samsara only to be whisked away whole soul and body to Nirvana. Let me explain myself. Rosanna the chiropteran is not a tragically stilled approach, nor am I an error simply darting through hostility. No. I am committed to Rosanna as Rosanna not stilled in a passageway through contested obstruction. Passing signals from Rosanna to chiropteran to Rosanna is exercise restored to a first flexible criterion. It establishes contact with an introductory mode imbued with self-reliance. In this sense chiropteran is both descent and expansion in constant expression of fabulous imponderables. Thus, it is an opening to a fabulous glossolalia. Fear is thus inverted into light. To common thinking it remains a despicable incentive. Not just the swallowed Sun and guano, but puzzles, squakings, a living code as incendiary rebus. So I am mining this level as biosis, as cryptic soaring in grandeur. A motion which finds itself in itself. And when it finds itself in itself inexplicable verticality transpires. This occurs by mining darkness to spark crystal through audition. Which then generates explosives. And these explosives rise, and surmount their potentia, and begin to resonate at a level that I can only describe as universal singularity. Or better put, an enriched condition. If anything, as chiropteran, I've opened up powers which understand as their strength the height and depth of what I'll call the decarnated lightning signal. As I sit, I've become this decarnated lightning signal, flotational, teeming with in-numerous adventure. So that each breath that I take within coma takes on a divinising pattern, always expressing itself as solar adoration which in turns filters its rays through the cells. A quintessence, a magical fire, a photological solvent.

In these latter day the rays have poured from my pores with stunning evolvement. I know that from my depths that it has suspended Zomaya, and whatever mayhem she may seek to ignite is further compounded by confusion. During coma I sometimes feel her swimming towards me like a dog in a deafened boundary. Recently, Ornelas has implied that she feels from me ascensional mirages, being differing strata from other psychological momentums. So have I overcome the contagion combined within the civic mental state? Have I breached its contending traversals? What I know is that I thrive more than banished dust, as more than a body threaded by insufferable rashes. Even in watching over my corpus Ornelas contends that I've risen from the mouth of a serpent always replying to myself through unintended data. In this I've become the perfect chart of the countersign, rising to its zenith with the gradual occlusion of its setting. In this sense, I am Mexico, I am Peru, I am Japan. I am Varuna in India, Ahura Mazda in Iran. I am Horus, Ra, Nephthys. Thus I carry volatile diamonds in my breathing. This is the element which now so intrigues Ornelas when she relates to Zomaya that there are diamonds in my breathing, that she sees flames condense, that suns spiral forth from my palate.

It could be said that I am nothing other than a piercing fabulist, a mythological garuda only suggestive of flame. This is something other than what was posited for me at birth. Perhaps a combination of sins. Perhaps lust, pride, and avarice. Or perhaps, ruse by gluttony and anger. Born into life according to complex circumfusion perhaps all of my subsequent moments have taken on a menacing dictation. It is a part of me. A lingering oscillation, an approach, a new energy for alien planes and distance. Because as I've said on previous occasion I will never walk this Earth as a heiress or a mother. I will always live by unknown breathing. Knowing that rocks and forests and beasts are all woven from superior priority. Because I've fused with this level of kinship I am simultaneously beset by interior friction. It is a friction which ignites and electrically conveys the stirrings of an upward vapour. If I know things by depth or cross reference it is by this vaporous eruption. The body then embroiled in defenceless flickering. There is never the settled maze. So I am not thinking of life with all its cellular forces combined according to structured ordination. In contradistinction Zomaya's aim is to keep the mind bound, curiously bound by lack. Here I am naked with my cylindrical grasping emitting diamonds from my stare. And these diamonds unlike the reddish apparitions Ornelas describes take on an iconoclastic heightening which I've heard Zomaya equate with the ripening of the afterlife. In this sense she senses something closer to what the Chinese consider as absence, vis-à-vis the Earthly realm. Therefore, she always wants to test my breathing, she always wants to know if my partial entry into the unsettled remains this side of the afterlife. This proves to me that she is no more than a student seeking to come to terms with my inordinate nuclear density, with its unknown principle of motion.

Let me say that I believe in the dormant, and not only do I believe in the dormant, I've experienced the dormant. This is how the cells lay fallow and take on properties over and beyond the obvious. They remain suspended like proto-Suns in an unbalanced rebus. This remains the deeper condition of my coma. It is a subconscious voltage, unhindered, undetectable as to present electrical conditioning. One is neither dead nor alive. The unapproachable subsists.

During this coma or interregnum I understand the cells as governed by a form of suspiration, by implemational action. Because I am always considering the species, with extending the like of the body over and beyond the activity of time. Perhaps I can exist in this state for 500 years, and within such span other crystallizations can occur. I mean other criticalities no longer contained by the atomic. An elixir if you will, which escapes the dialectic and becomes through such enrichment incapable of dying. There exists in me no defeatist instigation, no in-mineral fibres eclipsed by their doubting. So what lives in this state are modes of energy which shape the body towards ungraspable plasticities, to what certain astrologers would call the fate of ascent. Within this state all motion is studied, the tone of voice, the proclivity to accident through doubting. Believe me, Zomaya remains no candidate for such flight, She of conservation, she who obtains as revisionist tactician. Let me say, if some other being feels the depth of my unvoided tendencies, there will form a constellation between us, unimpacted by matter as present paradigm, so much so that a new morphemics will riot much like a nascent star formation. I'm not speaking of imperious model, wanting to extend my body in being forever and ever, but simply to say that I am stirring a new impulse which I feel has begun to writhe in the species. I'm preparing consciousness to react without gravity, to react to other planes of spatial firma. Under present proportion the human somus cannot at present respond to a climate as partially feral as Mars. Within such circumstance of being all the consequence of status is dissolved. The doors of historicity are exploded. This is something Zomaya is unable to include in her thinking. At some level she barters her notion of heaven by means of her tainted copper largesse. To her whose cynically grounded she may seek to relieve her anxiety by claiming my coma as linked to epochal psychosis. Neither bounded by adolescence or menopause I am entering no half hewn phase in development. I am not tending towards sight, or any large leap in terms of horizontal velocity. Because I am not ordinal I seem to be evolving a transparent density which contributes to my transitional dismay. My upset, my burning array of discomfort. As I speak I'm purging corpses from my psyche, thereby cleansing my interior physicality. I feel I am a specimen in the making, evolving my attempts from water, to land, to sky. So is my condition of chiropteran provisional useful as conditional criteria? I can say that it is an organic given, a trance, a power through affirmative issue. This affirmative being trans-physical in demeanour, opening for me the uncanny, combing both the proto and the forward leaning over and beyond the timing of fate. This being an energy other than Rosanna, other than the captivated person emerging on Earth from a cold November Sun. I've now merged with a realia which has subsumed the restive nomos of the zodiac, becoming in no uncertain measure a light which evaporates its incessant streaming.

Now I realize this is why I never conceived. My transitional realia neutralized the sperm. Because I was transitionally absent the sperm always contacted an unequal tenor so no true conjoining could be made.

As far as I'm concerned this requires no exceptional or constant study, say, like an unskilled monarch poring over ancestral battle fragments. To procreate, to entwine body with body remains the forceful magnet in human coupling. I don't deny this. It is the single foundation for human renewal. But because of maturational advancement I presently live in a dimension where dialectics have morphed. Where the previous stratagems of the race no longer combine. I feel I am a singularity in this regard, an example of someone unclaimed by present human habituation. Which has brought me to an unfigurable zenith, to an atmosphere flooded with an enthralling uranian elevation. I am other. The constellations erupt and send strength into my pneuma. Which brings again to mind my thought concerning offspring. What would I have produced? A facsimile of Oraculos, or the exacting chaos which functions as Jesus? Perhaps a damaged girl would have issued from the thoughts of Esteban. Or maybe a son embittered, scattered amongst all three. Maybe such a being would be entering a fifth year of time genetically swarming in the crimes which have converged within Zomaya. So pregnancy and birth for me are not good. It exhausts me. It raises in my mind the thought of tubercular narrative, as if my mental body were stung by a swarm of constant insect bodies.

Only the inferior can fault me. As if they are flat worms who seek to co-exist with regression. Passing values back and forth as beasts embittered by reason. It is behaviour compounded by no obvious gain. Since they are the replica of themselves as majority, it is as if I were listening to the rhetoric from an unhappy monster. One chained to ingrown deliberations filled with spite and error. I know in my depths that this is a spirit littered with the odour of fallible conniving. It is the further decay of bad civic magic. As an isolate monographer I've never been prone to reckless judgement. Nevertheless it is an acuity fuelled by insurrection. To Zomaya I cast an unnerving glimmer, as a homonym which contradicts her crippled cellular kinesia. Since the risible has never been a part of my formation, there has never been an iota of respite within my system. If Zomaya had had me governed in schools for the blind I may have conversed with another soul who had points in common with my torment. But nothing, nothing. There's been no sustained contact with any group of beings beyond the hacienda. If she were more tactical in her approach she would have honed another setting for me, and let me find my way as a pioneer in this body. Instead she was greedy, she carried no purposeful clauses in her stomach. Instead, everything condensed upon the regressive, of life engendered by denial. With any basic approach to learning I would have taken up the cello and dazzled the sonic world with new apparitional infinities. I would have taken up the populous chronology of Bartok or Kodaly, or the early orchestrations of Xenakis. Perhaps I could have imagined the music of turbulent warblers, or created sound from an infinity of morays. Being blind I could have imagined clouds as partaking in a wholly other infinite, maybe in a manner that a crow could feel the Sun. Of course I've been hobbled. Repartee has beckoned, but I've been hobbled, always forced to mingle with acidic unrest. I am something other than epiphenomena, something other than believing the body as vehicular separation. Being in the midst of an evolving integral body my mind trans-exists and takes on other properties of presence. Being Rosanna and chiropteran magically transmutes as synthetic other, being a riddle which floats beyond the tendency of known dissection. I can say nothing other than it is a trans-nucleic kindling. So in this sense I've dispossessed any prior expectation of what the genetic is capable of inscribing. This being the endurance which carries back and forth across the barrier of life and death. This capacity being other than the institutional body drafted by consensus limit. Having absorbed this endurance my energy persists by means of the uncanny. I've become a trace which marks itself by signals. For me, expiration no longer exists. The dates which bracket a corpse expire through evanescence; which means the body transmutes beyond its previous argument with existing. There no longer exists the old suggestion of death. The marred remains, then the corpse's eating utensils left branded in a closet. For me the state of death is now perfectly osmotic. It has lost its mean as barrier, as ongoing revetment. At an opposing level the hacienda trembles when death seems to breach its occulted limits. Under the polyandrous as spell the hacienda quakes and has become a conservation which continues summoning itself through regression. Because Zomaya owns the hacienda and all the bodies therein she consecrates what is known of economies and religions. Life is thus mired in the quantitative portion, in obscuring bodily evacuations which functions in rhythm as progenitor to mass collapse. This can be written off by those who claim to have balanced thinking, weighing my remarks as coming from someone embittered due to peculiarity and isolation. I am she who seems to stumble through morass after grating morass possessed at heart by an erratic grandeur. Believe me, I have no desire to surmount Zomaya and become the haunted concubine who dwells in sclerosis. As for her outer life, it is synonymous with the failure of fallen institutions. If I take the population of the Earth I can only winnow it down to those who resist its coming omegas. Its massive and downfallen terror, its commitment to moribund dispensation. In contradistinction I feel I am a shamaness now preparing powers on Titan. I feel I am intuitively listening for the expansion of the coming Sun, because I understand existing as partaking of provisional hospice. This being my response to the brokenness of the human form. There is no way for its struggle to simply continue as base production. Yet this is the template which condenses in Zomaya, which remains the awkward canon condensed as Catholic sin. I need not sit here and dwell on its unique and unalterable etceteras. As if

I were a chef burning down its kitchens with mockery, spilling fire on its floors simply to waste atoms. What I will say is that St. Peter's is a larger, more extended, besotted hacienda. I've survived on Earth in the land of the comets, now I can begin soaring inside the mystery of the multiverse. The story of old karmas and freedoms are tied to the Earth and its colonial tropopause. Therefore I feel magically divested of this era, which means the Holocene no longer acts as a primary factor. I am a wraith who generates the nonsubsistent, the vanished ejecta as scattered corpus. This is not decree according to accentual burden. I am not attached to discovery which promulgates limit, which breathes according to damaged mud. This being the unseen plot through the mystical field, where the galaxies multiply and go dead, and re-ascend through their highest tendencies. This is what I'll call the confutable as atomic, osmotically soaring through clotted tremendums. Commingled quanta, sound which issues through electrical eruptives. Because I am not riveted by termination all sovereign projection partakes of its absence, commingling as two separate signs simultaneously imploded. Which means there is no preparation, no translated optimum. One is thrust into zones without lateral replication. Thus, the spectacular property which ignites by foreshowing the principles which roam through magnetic exotica.

Such exotica is by no means contiguous to depraved incentive. This is not an atmosphere in which one absolves one's human response by attempting to gain from the nightmare vacuums which haunt the very distance. For me, it's become a microscopic serum, thereby, acclimating being to the rigours of alien purity. It is to assemble one's psycho-biology through transitional substrata, the fire of the nerves then invaded by simultaneous spectra. As if one's self-intuitives were flooded with autosomal Suns. I mean Suns which flow as immortal animations falling during certain states of the cortex as ironic alien snow. So by bringing such impossible animations to bear, they are made relative by the chiropteran that I am, to the Sapiens Sapiens that I am, so that all flows are linked by telepathic aurality.

So am I solipsistic, panpsychist?

Am I the figmental animist?

True, I've not spoken of the interstellar with its deadly burst of rays, or of the complex turbulence which riddles the organic. Never have I once stated the dangers or geriatrics of the void. These are turbulent assignations of chaos. But perhaps I'm ascending to some other theatric, to a condition where gravity ceases its advance as molecular demise. Just as I do not desire to dwell around coffins and discuss the merits and demerits of the deceased, I do not wish to mine from my thinking the explosive burial of stars, with their true transformation hidden from the mind by untold deduction. Again, there is something in life higher in life than the electricity which combines itself in physical forces. Yet, now, I cannot be seduced by deities, by totalitarian comment which sends the mind on a rampage of tedium and torment, always spurred at their essence by ruthless political incentives. By seeking to grasp the beyond, my only experience remains unction as flash, as sign through Jupiter Fulgur. This is where my mind scatters and begins to sporulate gaining access to the sigil of stillness. Not surcease, but the power which Rosanna continues to emit itself as something other than what transpires from the bilious notions of the majority. They who imparadise suffering, they who obfuscate remorse. Again, they who conjugate guilt in terms of omission and commission.

Ornelas and Zomaya both live under the spell which seeks to resurrect old bodies. Good Friday takes on meaning as special triumph, as unrepeatable bedazzlement. No other consideration can respond at this pitch. To me they are still Romans who remain transfixed by the goods and services of death. The soul to them remains a coveted entity, a source of value where sesterces are exchanged. Christ becomes paraded as a concussive symbol which self-investigates itself, which then falls to the rhetoric of thought, which further translates to the priest as God's quotidian representative.

How can this represent the true electrics of mystery?

How can this ascend through the particles of binomial depravation?

As I go deeper into anagogics I know why Zomaya more and more hesitates to plumb my action and reaction. She being the catalyst farming debacle from her spirit can no longer derive from her heart an energy which accrues from what she considers to be a satisfactory status. She prefers an ozone which responds to self-limit, as power within a tolerance which unites her control. When she sees me daily in coma I trap her between planes. She somehow feels herself mixed with excessive reversion. Her code of terra firma, added to samsaric sexual chaotics, and you have someone who suddenly exhausts her previous stores, taking on microbial debility. A lessening of life, becoming a frenzy which ingests secondary solace in the form of words gathered through blankness. But now she has realized a force which has no use for her frenzy. Objectively the force is Rosanna the chiropteran, Rosanna the in-gathered fragment, who repeats and repeats a plane gathered from itself through nervous devastation. By repeating myself through coma I've eroded the current of her temperament to such a degree that all ownership which she self-announces fails in its attempt to cauterize her experience. When she sees me what does Esteban mean at that moment, how does the lessening of the lowly Jesus bolster any self-suggestiveness? There exist no answers. What I've done is to agitate a furious moral banter which has failed to subside. She is more and more ensconced in the dialectic of molten listening to herself drift further and further into personal cacophony so that she can less and less relate to any previous entitlement. I'm eroding her addiction to containment. Her mind is now rowing through insolvent momentums, uselessly flowing backwards. She is beginning to feel the ominous ocean of herself relentless with its overextension through nothingness. This is replacing the locality which she sought to protect her. For her, the Sun is now teeming with cosmic disturbance. And now I've taken on an emptied form around the Sun. I am the crucial insinuendo who has vomited up snails, who has physically indulged both her mother and her father. And I say that it is all nothing. It is nothing who speaks to nothing. Being the gainless embodied in the gainless. Because I am not proclaiming any effort, or attempting to harvest finality by delimiting flaws which poach from the interactive streaks in my spirit. I've splintered my own trajectory from a fissioning of threats which have issued from my great monomial leprosy. Which has created in me a raw ascensional vastitude, allowing me further millennia although the bodies about me will all have been destroyed. Because I speak out of blindness I am able to respond to spiritual extremity, which has transmuted dearth and soulless nightmare relations. Of course I am speaking from auto-causality, from an enriched alkaline insurrection, altricial, haunted, partaking cacophony from the cinders of nauseous aeronautics. Because I am Mexican and Seminole I breed schisms, I breed eloquent ransacking laws.

I've heard the Sun of the Sun in my schisms taking on the character of vertical ratios and polyphony. Being scorched by the irreducible I am able to interpret the flaws in my thinking so that they never take on a stunted exposure which beckon as aural sirens. Because I can hear through them I begin to hear the invisible bells, the lithographic sparks rising from waste. Perhaps Zomaya and Ornelas see me as an eclipsed glycerine food, as an ample minority who wizens. Yet my oppositional totality revels at the height in incommensurate unity. My boat of glass, my response to the infinite. Because I am a perpetual party there is no time, or place, or level, by which I can be traced according to almanacs, according to horology, or to date marks, or to any Republic which fosters itself according to Gregorian fixation. I do not speak through a daybook, or through a time sheet, thicketed with horometrical elements. Instead there is the coeval, the concomitant, exhausting and re-exhausting through living intensification. Me, I am the lava who rotates, who hears through constant instigation the lawless heightened through withdrawal, existent by the energies which roam through self-contention. Because now I have broken off in mazes, I have insisted on insidious cross flinching, I ...

www.ingramcontent.com/pod-product-compliance
Lightning Source LLC
Chambersburg PA
CBHW031147160426
43193CB00008B/279